M000121769

The *Big* Book of
Snacks
and
Appetizers

Bristol Publishing Enterprises, Inc.
San Leandro, California
www.bristolcookbooks.com

Printed in the United States of America
ISBN 1-55867-239-7

Cover design: Shanti Nelson

This collection is a compilation of the following books:

APPETIZERS
Joanna White
©1996 Bristol Publishing Enterprises, Inc.
ISBN 1-55867-138-2

TAPAS FANTASTICAS
Bob and Coleen Simmons
©1999 Bristol Publishing Enterprises, Inc.
ISBN 1-55867-233-8

THE NEW INTERNATIONAL FONDUE COOKBOOK
ed Coleen and Bob Simmons
©1990 Bristol Publishing Enterprises, Inc.
ISBN 1-55867-008-4

THE BEST 50 DIPS
Joanna White
©1995 Bristol Publishing Enterprises, Inc.
ISBN 1-55867-110-2

THE BEST 50 SALSAS
Christie and Thomas Katona
©1995 Bristol Publishing Enterprises, Inc.
ISBN 1-55867-112-9

THE BEST 50 BRUSCHETTA RECIPES
Dona Z. Meilach
©1999 Bristol Publishing Enterprises, Inc.
ISBN 1-55867-112-9

THE BEST 50 SUSHI ROLLS
Carol M. Newman
©1999 Bristol Publishing Enterprises, Inc.
ISBN 1-55867-211-7

Table of Contents

1 Appetizers

1 Tips
6 Superfast Appetizers
15 Appetizers That Travel
30 Appetizers From the Oven
41 International Appetizers
56 Low-Fat Appetizers
67 Dips and Spreads

77 Tapas Fantasticas

79 The Tapas Pantry
84 Parties and Menus
90 Nibbles
96 Cheese and Egg Tapas
105 Vegetable-Based Tapas
123 Seafood Tapas
138 Poultry Tapas
145 Meat Tapas
155 Basic Sauces and Pastry
162 Drinks

167 The New International Fondue Cookbook

168 Introduction
169 Cheese Fondues and Hot Dips
181 Hot Oil and Hot Broth Fondues
195 Baked Fondues
205 Rarebits
212 Dessert Fondues

216 *The Best 50 Dips*

217   Tips
220   Savory and Cold Dips
234   Sweet and Cold Dips
237   Savory and Hot Dips
247   Sweet and Hot Dips

250 *The Best 50 Salsas*

251   Tips for Making and Serving Salsas
254   Vegetable Salsas
264   Fruit Salsas

279 *The Best 50 Bruschetta Recipes*

280   A Study of Bruschetta
282   Bruschetta with Tomatoes
290   Bruschetta with Cheese
294   Bruschetta with Vegetables
299   Bruschetta with Poultry and Meat
303   Bruschetta with Seafood
306   On the Sweet Side

309 *The Best 50 Sushi Rolls*

310   The Basics
315   The Old School
322   The New School

Appetizers

Joanna White

Appetizer Tips

An appetizer is not the main course, but a tempting nibble that should excite rather than satiate the appetite. If serving predinner appetizers, the cardinal rule should be: keep it light. If serving a cocktail party or appetizer buffet, a variety of appetizers in a substantial amount is the ruling guide.

Be certain the appetizers complement one another. It is important to balance flavors and textures, hot and cold, raw and cooked, simple and elegant. "Starters" are appetizers that are usually eaten at the table before dinner is served. They often precede a more formal or elegant dinner party.

Overall, one of the most important rules is try to design the menu so the hostess or host can enjoy time with the guests and not be tied to the kitchen. Planning is the key to making a party successful!

Appetizer Guidelines

- Serve a contrast of hot and cold appetizers.
- Offer different textures for food served together, such as crisp vegetables or crackers with a creamy dip.
- Avoid being monotonous with flavor — for example, using onions in every recipe.
- For variety, plan on serving at least one appetizer from each of the following categories: vegetables or fruits, meat or poultry, fish or seafood, and something with cheese.
- A general rule for quantity at cocktail parties is to consider at least 6 appetizers per person per hour. When serving appetizers on trays, always try to supplement with self-help foods like spreads and dips.
- If possible, spread foods around on several tables to encourage socializing.
- When serving a buffet, try to have serving dishes that add height to the presentation. Make sure hot foods are more accessible.
- If appetizers are replacing dinner, count on 10 to 12 "bites" per person, and offer at least 5 to 6 choices.
- Coordinate appetizers with the type of cuisine being served for dinner, such as dim sum before a Chinese meal, or tapas before Spanish cuisine.

- If guests are standing and holding a glass in one hand, consider serving only finger foods so guests won't have to do a balancing act.
- To prevent soggy breads and canapés, spread softened butter or cream cheese over bread before applying the filling. Calculate about ¼ pound for every loaf of bread.

The Appetizer Pantry

Prepared foods in jars, bottles, cans and packages provide instant, delicious appetizers for drop-in guests.

anchovies: mash and mix with oil, butter or cream cheese for spreads

artichokes: marinated or plain; serve as is or mix with cream cheese for spreads

barbecue sauce: pour over meats, poultry or cream cheese

breads: crusty breads to dip and spread; dense-textured breads, such as bagels, for sandwiches; flavored breads to dip and spread; pita bread to dip, or to butter, sprinkle with herbs and bake

capers: sprinkle on top of creamy spreads for piquant flavor

caviar: serve to those who appreciate it

cheeses: hard cheeses to shred and sprinkle over fillings on toasted bread; soft cheeses to serve with crackers or to make spreads

chips: variety of potato chips, corn chips and bagel chips

chutneys: add flavor to dips and spreads

corn tortillas: fry or bake into chips or make small filled tortillas from leftovers

crackers: an assortment to serve with dips and cheeses

deviled spreads: ham, chicken or beef; spread on bread rounds or crackers

fish: smoked or not, canned or frozen; serve as is or mix into spreads

green chiles: diced; mix into spreads or sprinkle on cheese dishes

ham: canned; cut into chunks or add to spreads

hard-cooked eggs: chop and add to mayonnaise for spreads

horseradish: add heat to sauces, dips and spreads

marinated vegetables: serve as is

mayonnaise: an essential base for quick-fixes such as spreads

mustards: variety to make sauce, dips, and to serve on breads

nuts: variety to serve as is or to caramelize with butter, sugar and/or spices

oils: variety of flavors for frying, creating dips or spreading on bread; mix with flavored vinegars to use as a dip for hearty breads

olives: a variety for serving as is; or chop and add to spreads

onions: cocktail varieties; serve as is

patés: canned or from the deli case to spread on crusty bread, toast or crackers

pepper jellies: serve over cream cheese with crackers

peppers: bottled pickled peppers to serve as is

pesto: mix with cream cheese for spreads

pickles: serve whole or chop and add to spreads and dips

sauces: variety of bottled sauces like teriyaki, garlic sauce, Worcestershire, soy sauce, A-1 and dressings to make dips; Tabasco or other chile sauces add "spike" to all types of recipes

spices: variety for quick recipes

sun-dried tomatoes: serve on top of or mix into bread spreads

vegetables: fresh or bottled, marinated; dip or eat as is

vinegars: variety of flavored vinegars for sauces and dips

water chestnuts: add crunch to dips and spreads

Preparing and Storing Appetizers
Handy Equipment for Preparation

set of good knives
mixer
food processor
blender
deep fryer
graters
toaster oven
baking sheets
cookie cutters
miniature muffin tins

rolling pin
colander
whisk
melon baller
lemon stripper ("zester")
rubber spatulas
butter curler
brushes
baking pans
piping bags and tips

Helpful Serving Equipment

chafing dish
electric heating tray
slow cooker
fondue pots
napkins
silverware
serving tableware (including
  spreaders and ladles)

wooden skewers
variety of glasses
platters
ovenware dishes
plates
toothpicks

Storage

- Store all appetizers in tightly covered containers or freezer bags.

- Use airtight containers if planning on freezing the appetizers.

- Freeze appetizers in a single layer on a baking sheet. Then stack frozen appetizers with layers of waxed paper between them.

- Party sandwiches can be frozen as long as the filling ingredients can be frozen. Fillings made with butter or cream cheese are ideal for freezing.

- Do not freeze lettuce, fresh vegetables, tomatoes, eggs, mayonnaise, salad dressings, aspics or gelatins.

- Freeze baked pastry shells and toast cups separate from their filling in airtight containers. Bake in a 350° oven for 10 to 15 minutes before adding filling.

To make pastry shells: Use dough of choice, and line miniature or regular muffin tins or tart tins. Bake at 350° until brown. Fill immediately or freeze.

To make toast cups: Trim crust from bread, brush both sides with melted butter and press carefully into muffin tins to form cups with 4 uniform points. Toast in a 350° oven until crisp and golden brown. Fill immediately or freeze.

Crab-Stuffed Mushrooms

This elegant appetizer is delicately flavored and rich. Remember that the purpose of an appetizer is not to fill up the guests, so limit the quantity to 2 per person if you want them to enjoy the meal.

8 oz. cream cheese, softened
½ lb. crabmeat
½ cup finely crushed seasoned breadcrumbs
1 clove garlic, finely minced
16 large mushrooms
2 tbs. grated Parmesan cheese
paprika

With a mixer, beat cream cheese until soft. Gently stir in crabmeat, breadcrumbs and garlic. Cut stems off mushrooms at base of cap and mound mushrooms with filling. Sprinkle with Parmesan and paprika. Broil until piping hot, about 5 minutes.

Pesto Mushrooms

These whip together in minutes. For another variation, try using chive-flavored cream cheese and crumbled bacon.

2 tbs. butter
1 clove garlic, minced
16 large mushrooms
salt and pepper to taste
4 oz. cream cheese, softened
⅓ cup commercially prepared pesto

Melt butter in a saucepan and sauté garlic until soft but not browned. Slice off mushroom stems at base of cap. Brush mushrooms with garlic butter mixture and place in an ovenproof dish. Sprinkle with salt and pepper. Mix cream cheese and pesto together and mound in center of each cap. Refrigerate for several hours or overnight. When ready to serve, bake in a 400° oven for 5 to 6 minutes or until filling is soft and mushrooms are warm.

Paté Mushrooms

Makes 60

Many grocery stores have wonderful delis that offer an assortment of patés. Experiment with paté flavors and pick a favorite for this simple and fast recipe.

60 medium mushrooms
1/4 lb. paté of choice
finely chopped fresh parsley for garnish

Wash and dry mushrooms and cut off stems at base of cap. Mash paté with a fork and fill each cap with a small mound of paté. Broil for 2 to 3 minutes until piping hot. Garnish with a sprinkling of finely chopped parsley.

Marinated Blue Onions

Makes 2 1/2 cups

This one is fast to make, but you need to start a couple of days before you plan to serve it. Serve with small rounds of rye or pumpernickel bread. Flat-shaped onions have a tendency to be sweeter than round ones.

1/2 cup olive oil
2 tbs. lemon juice
1 tsp. salt
1 tsp. sugar
1/4 cup crumbled blue cheese
dash pepper
dash paprika
2 cups finely sliced red onions
whole sprigs or chopped fresh parsley for garnish

With a food processor or blender, thoroughly mix all ingredients, except onions. Place onions in an attractive serving dish and cover with processed mixture. Cover and chill for 2 days before serving. Garnish with parsley sprigs or a sprinkling of chopped parsley.

Holiday Brie

Serve this easy-to-fix appetizer with apple wedges and mild crackers. If desired, garnish with unpeeled apple slices (dipped in lemon juice to prevent browning) and walnut halves.

1 large wheel Brie cheese, 6 lb.
2 medium apples, peeled, cored and chopped
1 1/4 cups brown sugar
1/4-1/2 cup crumbled blue cheese
1 cup chopped toasted walnuts

Slice Brie in half horizontally. In a bowl, combine apples, brown sugar, blue cheese and walnuts. Spread mixture over Brie half and cover with remaining half. Place on an ovenproof platter and bake at 325° for 20 minutes.

Brie in Puff Pastry

This recipe makes a beautiful presentation, made easy by using prepackaged puff pastry. The French name for this is Brie en Croute, and it should ideally be served with either fruit or crackers. If you don't buy your Brie in a container, just use the cheese round as a guide.

2 small wheels Brie cheese, 2.2 lb. each
1 pkg. (17 1/4 oz.) frozen puff pastry, thawed
1 egg yolk
1 tbs. cold water
dash salt

Using the empty Brie container, cut 4 circles out of puff pastry and place a circle on top and bottom of each cheese round. Cut 1-inch strips of remaining pastry and use to encircle cheese sides. Crimp edges together. Beat egg yolk, water and salt together and brush over top and sides of pastry shell. Be creative: cut pastry strips and make a lattice on top of rounds, or cut decorative shapes like leaves and grapes, placing them artfully on top. Brush again with yolk mixture. Chill until ready to bake. Heat oven to 450° and bake for 10 minutes. Reduce heat to 350° and continue baking for 20 minutes. Crust should be puffed, light and brown.

Cheesy Crab Toast

Makes 32

It's very simple, but it tastes elegant. If your budget is a consideration, the "fake" crabmeat can be substituted in a pinch!

4 French rolls
½ cup butter, melted
6-8 tsp. Dijon mustard
12 oz. crabmeat
8 oz. sharp cheddar cheese, shredded
2 tbs. minced fresh parsley
paprika

Cut rolls in half lengthwise and brush with melted butter. Place buttered rolls on a baking sheet and toast under the broiler until golden brown. Remove from oven and spread with mustard. Evenly distribute crabmeat among rolls and sprinkle with cheese. Return baking sheets to oven and broil until cheese melts. Remove from oven and sprinkle with parsley and paprika. Cut rolls into 1-inch diagonal slices and serve immediately.

Anchovy Butter Rounds

Makes 24

Anchovies create a unique flavor of saltiness, pungency and a bit of the exotic that is appreciated by those with discerning taste buds. Capers are the small buds of plants that grow along the Mediterranean and are packed in a brine. The smaller bud variety is preferred for cooking.

10 anchovies
½ cup butter
24 small toasted bread rounds
2-3 tbs. capers

Mash anchovies and mix thoroughly with butter. Chill for at least 1 hour. Spread toasted bread rounds with anchovy butter and sprinkle with capers.

Sardines and Pepper Spread

This is a typical Spanish tapa which should be served with a crusty bread or crackers.

2 tins (3.75 oz. each) sardines
½ cup olive oil
2 medium onions, chopped
1 can (4 oz.) roasted red peppers
salt to taste

Rinse sardines in warm water and drain. Pour ¼ cup olive oil in a small baking dish and layer with onions. Top with sardines. Cut red pepper into strips and place over sardines. Sprinkle with remaining olive oil and salt. Bake in a 350° oven for 30 minutes. Serve warm with bread or crackers for dipping.

Grilled Marinated Prawns

This very simple but elegant appetizer wows your guests. If a barbecue is not available, the prawns can also be quickly sautéed in the same marinade mixture.

1 lb. prawns (18-24 per lb.)
1 cup olive oil
2 cloves garlic, minced
1 tsp. salt
½ tsp. chili powder
1 tbs. chopped fresh parsley

Peel prawns, but leave tails on. Mix remaining ingredients together and pour over prawns. Marinate for 1 hour. Grill prawns on a barbecue grill or under the broiler, basting with marinade.

Bacon Scallops with Béarnaise

Makes 36-48

These crispy tidbits are dipped in a Béarnaise sauce that can be made in minutes in the food processor or blender.

1 lb. bacon
1 lb. scallops
3 egg yolks
6 oz. butter, melted
salt and pepper to taste
1 tbs. lemon juice
1 tbs. vinegar
1 shallot, minced
1 tsp. mixed tarragon, chervil and parsley herbs

Cut bacon slices into thirds and boil for about 5 minutes to remove excess fat and impurities; allow to cool. Wrap each scallop with a piece of bacon and secure with a toothpick. Place on a broiler pan. Broil until nicely browned.

Beat yolks in a food processor until light yellow in color, and add hot melted butter slowly in a stream. Add salt, pepper, lemon juice, vinegar, shallots and herbs. Taste and adjust seasonings and lemon juice.

Smoked Turkey Roll

Makes 48-60

This is fast and easy to fix. Serve with honey mustard dressing as a dipping sauce.

1 lb. sliced smoked turkey
½ lb. cotto salami, thinly sliced
8 oz. cream cheese, softened
½ red bell pepper, thinly sliced
½ yellow bell pepper, thinly sliced
½ green bell pepper, thinly sliced

Place a slice of smoked turkey on a piece of plastic wrap. Cover with salami, spread with cream cheese and place 1 strip pepper of each color in center. Roll tightly and chill. To serve, cut into ½-inch slices.

Teriyaki Chicken Wings

Makes about 30

This popular recipe will disappear fast when serving a crowd, so be sure to make plenty. Keep it warm in a chafing dish and serve with lots of napkins!

2 lb. chicken wings
1 small onion, chopped
½ cup soy sauce
½ cup brown sugar, packed
1 tsp. minced fresh ginger
2 cloves garlic, minced
2 tbs. dry sherry
sesame seeds for garnish, optional

Disjoint chicken wings and discard tips. Place wing parts in a baking dish. In a food processor or blender, combine remaining ingredients. Pour over chicken, and if time permits, marinate for at least 1 hour. Bake in a 350° oven for 1 hour. Keep warm in a chafing dish and sprinkle with sesame seeds if desired.

Pesto Parmesan Swirls

Makes 96

Because you use commercially prepared pesto and premade puff pastry, these delicious appetizers take just minutes to prepare and are kept frozen until ready to use.

12 oz. cream cheese, softened
½ cup grated Parmesan cheese
2 green onions, finely minced
¼ cup commercially prepared pesto sauce
1 pkg. (17¼ oz.) puff pastry sheets

In a food processor or blender, combine cream cheese, Parmesan, minced green onions and pesto together. Lay pastry sheets out and spread with filling. Roll up tightly in jelly-roll fashion. Wrap in plastic and freeze. When ready to bake, thaw rolls for 15 minutes and slice into ¼-inch rounds. Place on ungreased baking sheets. Bake in a 375° oven for 10 to 15 minutes or until nicely browned.

Smoked Salmon Rolls

Viking bread can be found in most grocery stores, usually in the cracker section. If canned salmon is all that is available, add a few drops of liquid smoke to the recipe. Viking bread is a large, round cracker bread that is usually rye-flavored. If you can't find cracker bread, then thinly slice a round loaf of bread horizontally and remove the crust. It is not necessary to run this under water.

8 oz. cream cheese, softened
½ cup butter, softened
4 oz. smoked salmon
2 green onions, chopped
1 pkg. Viking bread

Mix softened cream cheese with butter until smooth. Add smoked salmon and green onions and mix to combine. Run each slice of Viking bread quickly under water until lightly moistened. Spread with salmon mixture and roll up. Wrap tightly in plastic wrap and refrigerate for several hours or overnight. Just before serving, cut into 1-inch pieces.

Quesadillas

A quesadilla is a cheesy Mexican delight that is ideally served with a side of guacamole and sour cream for dipping. This is a favorite of every group and should be served with a lot of napkins!

vegetable oil for frying
12 flour tortillas, 8-inch
4 oz. sharp cheddar cheese, grated
4 oz. Monterey Jack cheese, grated
4 green onions, diced
1 can (4 oz.) diced green chiles

Heat a small amount of oil in a medium skillet and place 1 tortilla in pan. Sprinkle with a handful of both types of cheese. Sprinkle with green onions and diced chiles. Cover with another tortilla. When cheese is melted, flip quesadilla over and toast other side. Remove from pan onto a paper towel to absorb oil, cut into 6 wedges and serve immediately. Repeat this technique each time.

Spiced Melon Balls

This makes a cool, refreshing appetizer that takes minutes to prepare and won't fill up your guests before dinner.

1 medium honeydew or Crenshaw melon
1 large cantaloupe
2 tbs. lime juice
2 tbs. honey
1/2 tsp. ground coriander
1/2 tsp. nutmeg
fresh mint sprigs or lime slices for garnish

Cut melons in half and remove seeds. Using a melon baller, form fruit into balls and place in a bowl with remaining ingredients. Stir to coat and allow mixture to chill for several hours before serving. Garnish with mint sprigs or lime slices and serve with toothpicks.

Stuffed Strawberries

Refresh your guests with this sweet appetizer, or use this recipe as a light dessert. If desired, surround fruit with attractive greenery such as mint, watercress or well-cleaned greens from the garden.

1 pt. strawberries
8 oz. cream cheese, softened
confectioners' sugar to taste
orange-flavored liqueur to taste: Grand Marnier, Orange Curacao or Triple Sec

Cut stems off berries to create a flat surface that will allow berries to stand upright. Then cut a crisscross slice 3/4 of the way down the opposite (pointed) end of each berry and place on an attractive serving dish. With a mixer or food processor, beat cream cheese and flavor with confectioners' sugar and liqueur of choice. Taste and adjust flavor. Place ingredients in a piping bag with a star tip. Pipe cream cheese mixture into the center of each berry.

Brie in Aspic

Brie decorated in this fashion makes a really pretty, very impressive appetizer that will wow your friends. It requires few ingredients. Aspic is a savory jelly made with flavored liquid and unflavored gelatin. Serve with special crackers or rounds of French bread.

2 pkg. (1/4 oz. each) unflavored gelatin
1/2 cup cold water
2 cups Chablis wine
1 large wheel Brie cheese, 6 lb.
pansy flowers (or any edible flowers) for garnish

Soften gelatin in water and heat in a small saucepan until gelatin is dissolved. Remove from heat and add wine, creating aspic. Allow mixture to cool slightly. Brush a layer of aspic on top and along sides of Brie. Artfully arrange flowers on top and gently brush on more aspic. Chill for 5 minutes in the refrigerator and spread on another layer of aspic (only on the top, not on the sides). Repeat this step several times until flowers are completely immersed in aspic. Chill until ready to serve.

Festive Brie with Savory Stuffing

Here is another treatment for the always popular Brie, which makes a beautiful, elegant appetizer that can be made ahead of time. Serve with rounds of crispy French bread, or crackers.

1 large wheel Brie cheese, 6 lb.
1 tbs. butter
2 cloves garlic, minced
1 small onion, chopped
8 large mushrooms, finely chopped
1/2 jar (4 oz.) roasted red peppers, chopped
1 can (4 oz.) sliced black olives
1 tbs. dry sherry
salt and pepper to taste
chopped parsley or chopped red and green bell pepper for garnish, optional

Slice Brie wheel in half horizontally and keep chilled until ready to use. In a skillet, heat butter and sauté garlic and onion until tender. Add mushrooms, peppers and olives and cook for 3 minutes. Add sherry and season to taste with salt and pepper. One hour before serving, spread warm filling over bottom of sliced Brie and cover with remaining half. If desired, sprinkle top of Brie with chopped parsley or peppers.

Date Bread with Pineapple Cream Cheese   Makes 40

Make this sweet appetizer ahead and freeze. Then simply defrost, cut into small rectangular shapes and spread with cream cheese mixture. Garnish the serving platter with colorful flowers.

2 cups boiling water
1 lb. dates, chopped
2 tbs. butter
2 tsp. baking soda
2 cups sugar
3½ cups flour
2 tsp. vanilla extract
1 cup chopped walnuts
Pineapple Cream Cheese Spread, follows

Line 2 bread pans with brown paper and grease well. In a bowl, mix water, dates and butter together and allow to cool. Add baking soda, sugar, flour, vanilla and nuts, stirring until just mixed. Pour into pans and bake in a 325° oven for 1 hour or until a knife inserted in center comes out clean. Slice bread; cut each slice in half. Spread each slice with *Pineapple Cream Cheese Spread* and arrange on a serving platter.

Pineapple Cream Cheese Spread

8 oz. cream cheese, softened
1 can (10½ oz.) crushed pineapple, drained
sugar to taste, optional

In a bowl, beat cream cheese and pineapple together. Add sugar if desired. Makes 1½ cups.

Pumpkin Tea Sandwiches

This sweet appetizer is ideal during the fall season. Serve with either orange butter or mango spread. This recipe is great for tea parties.

1 cup butter
2 tbs. molasses
3 cups sugar
6 large eggs
1 cup orange juice
1 tbs. grated orange zest
1 can (30 oz.) pumpkin
5 cups flour
1 tsp. baking powder
1 tbs. baking soda
¾ tsp. salt
1½ tsp. cinnamon
1½ tsp. ground cloves
1½ cups raisins or dried currants
Orange Butter or *Mango Spread*, follows

Line 3 loaf pans with either parchment or brown paper and butter the sides of the pan. With a mixer, cream butter, molasses and sugar until light and fluffy. Beat in eggs until mixture is lemon-colored. Add orange juice, orange peel and pumpkin and mix well. Combine dry ingredients and add to pumpkin mixture, mixing well. Stir in raisins or currants. Spoon mixture into pans and bake at 350° for 1 hour or until a knife inserted in the center comes out clean. Cool in pans for 10 minutes before turning out onto racks. Cut bread into slices and then slices in half. Spread with *Orange Butter* or *Mango Spread.*

Orange Butter

½ cup (1 stick) unsalted butter, softened
¼ cup orange marmalade

With a food processor or electric mixer, mix butter and marmalade until well blended. Makes ¾ cup.

Mango Spread

8 oz. cream cheese
½ cup mango chutney

Soften cream cheese and stir in chutney. Makes 1½ cups.

Marbleized Tea Eggs

This is an elegant alternative to the standard deviled eggs. Using vegetables as natural dyes, the hard-cooked eggs are cracked in the shells and allowed to steep in colored water to create a beautiful marbleized affect. If desired, garnish each egg with a small piece of parsley and a tiny sliver of red pepper.

18 eggs
1 tbs. salt

Add:
2 cups beet juice for **pink color**
    or
3 pkg. (10 oz. each) frozen spinach and 1½ cups water for **green color**
    or
4 whole onion skins and 2½ cups water for **yellow color**

Filling

½ cup mayonnaise
3 oz. cream cheese
¼ lb. butter

dash Worcestershire sauce
1 tsp. Dijon mustard
salt and white pepper to taste

In a large saucepan, place eggs, 1 tbs. salt and enough cold water to cover eggs by 1 inch. Bring to a boil. Cover and reduce heat to low. Cook for 20 minutes. Drain at once and chill in ice water for 5 minutes. Crackle egg shells by tapping lightly with back of spoon, rolling gently on surface, or between hands. Leave shells on and dye 6 eggs at a time.

Pink Color: Pour beet juice over eggs in a small bowl, deep enough to cover cracked eggs. Steep overnight.

Green Color: In a saucepan, combine spinach and 1½ cups water and bring to a boil. Reduce heat, cover and simmer for 30 minutes. Strain juice and cool to room temperature. Pour juice over eggs and steep overnight.

Yellow Color: In a saucepan, boil onion skins and 2½ cups water for 20 minutes. Strain juice and cool to room temperature. Pour juice over eggs and steep overnight.

Remove eggs from dye and peel. Split in half in the center horizontally (not lengthwise) and cut a little piece off the bottom so the eggs will stand up. Scoop out yolks and combine, using a food processor or mixer, with mayonnaise, cream cheese, butter, Worcestershire, mustard, salt and pepper. Process until smooth; taste and adjust seasonings. Place mixture in a piping bag and pipe into egg halves.

Shrimp- and Vegetable-Filled Pasta Shells

Makes 12

Stuffed pasta shells are a quick, unusual and substantial appetizer that can be made ahead of time. Serve on a bed of lettuce. If desired, several of these can be an entrée for a luncheon.

½ cup chopped water chestnuts
2 cups chopped celery
2 cups grated carrots
¼-½ cup chopped green onions
2 cups fresh baby shrimp
2 cups shredded sharp cheddar cheese (can use low-fat variety)
1 cup mayonnaise (prefer low-fat or nonfat)
1 tbs. lemon juice (or to taste)
1 tsp. sugar
1 lb. jumbo pasta shells, cooked and drained

In a bowl, combine water chestnuts, celery, carrots, green onions, shrimp and cheddar cheese. In a separate bowl, blend mayonnaise, lemon juice and sugar. Combine both mixtures and fill shells. Refrigerate until ready to serve.

Mango Chutney Mold

Servings: 10-12

Cover crackers or plain bagel chips with this creamy, sweet, exotic spread.

12 oz. cream cheese, softened
3 tbs. mayonnaise
3 tbs. chopped peanuts
3-4 tbs. chopped raisins
4 slices bacon, fried crisp and crumbled
1 tbs. chopped green onions
2 tsp. curry powder
1 cup chopped mango chutney
½ cup shredded coconut

Combine cream cheese and mayonnaise in a food processor or with a mixer until smooth. Add remaining ingredients, except chutney and coconut. Lightly oil a 3-cup mold and fill with creamed mixture. Chill for several hours or overnight. To serve, remove from mold, pour chutney on top and sprinkle with coconut.

Blue Cheesecake

A delicious spread always makes a winning appetizer. Serve with rye bread rounds or crackers. Garnish with colorful fresh flowers or carved vegetable flowers, or consider a sprinkling of minced red bell peppers and green onions.

16 oz. cream cheese, softened
8 oz. blue cheese
1/4 tsp. white pepper
2 1/2 cups sour cream
3 eggs
1/2 cup chopped toasted pecans
1/4 cup minced green onions

In a food processor or blender, process cream cheese, blue cheese and white pepper until well blended. Stir in 1 cup of the sour cream, and eggs. Stir in nuts and green onions. Pour mixture into a buttered 9-inch springform pan and bake in a 300° oven for 65 minutes. Remove from oven and let stand for 5 minutes. Spread remaining 1 1/2 cups sour cream over top and return to oven for 10 minutes. Cool completely and refrigerate overnight.

Cheese Terrine with Pesto and Sun-Dried Tomatoes

Servings: 12

This is a great recipe that can be thrown together in minutes. Both pesto and sun-dried tomatoes are popular flavors, and this recipe has beautiful eye appeal. Serve with crackers or sliced baguettes.

2 lb. cream cheese, softened
8 oz. goat cheese
1 jar (8.5 oz.) sun-dried tomatoes packed in oil
1 bottle (10 oz.) pesto

Combine cream cheese with goat cheese. Line a terrine, mold or loaf pan with a wet cheesecloth. Place 1/5 of the cheese mixture in bottom and spread with 1/2 of the tomatoes. Cover with 1/5 of cheese mixture and spread with 1/2 of the pesto. Repeat layers, ending with cheese mixture. Chill for several hours or overnight. Unmold, remove cheesecloth and serve on a platter.

Roquefort Mousse

Another tantalizing spread is delicious with an assortment of crackers and fruit. This goes especially well with pears.

1 cup cream
2 eggs, separated
1 lb. Roquefort cheese, room temperature
8 oz. cream cheese
1/2 cup butter, softened
2 tbs. unflavored gelatin
1/4 cup cold water
1 tsp. Dijon mustard

Whip cream and set aside. Beat egg white until stiff and set aside. In a separate bowl, beat egg yolks, add Roquefort and beat until smooth. Add cream cheese and butter and beat until smooth. In a small saucepan, dissolve gelatin in cold water; gently heat and stir until completely dissolved. Add to cream cheese mixture with Dijon mustard. Fold in egg whites. Fold in whipped cream. Pour mixture into a greased 7-cup mold and chill until firm. Unmold to serve.

Note: If you are concerned about using raw eggs, increase cream to 1 1/2 cups, and substitute 1/4 cup pasteurized eggs, such as Egg Beaters, for egg yolks.

Molded Herbed Cheese

Shape this standard spread into molds to fit the theme of the party. Consider using this mixture to stuff celery sticks or to use as a spread on small, shaped bread slices.

16 oz. cream cheese, softened
6 green onions, chopped
4 cloves garlic, minced
1/2 cup chopped fresh parsley
1/2 cup chopped fresh basil
1 tsp. dry mustard
1 tsp. Worcestershire sauce
1/4 cup lemon juice
1/2 cup chopped black olives
salt and pepper to taste

With a food processor or mixer, blend ingredients together. Taste and adjust seasonings. Spoon into a 3-cup mold, cover and refrigerate until mixture sets. Unmold onto a platter.

Lattice Cream Cheese Mold

A favorite spread is a fancy one to take to a party. For a change, try different combinations of cheese and alternative meats in place of the ham. Serve with an assortment of crispy crackers.

First Layer

8 oz. cream cheese, softened
2 tbs. butter, softened
6 oz. smoked ham, minced
2 dashes Tabasco Sauce

Second Layer

8 oz. cream cheese, softened
2 tbs. butter, softened
1/3 lb. grated sharp cheddar cheese
2 tbs. milk or cream
few drops orange food coloring,
   optional

Third Layer

8 oz. cream cheese, softened
2 tbs. butter, softened
4 green onions, tops only, finely
   minced
few drops green food coloring,
   optional

Garnish

4 oz. cream cheese, softened
sliced black olives
sliced pimiento

Line a 9-inch springform pan with plastic wrap. With a food processor or blender, process first layer ingredients until creamy. Spread on the bottom of lined springform. Place pan in freezer.

Process second layer ingredients; add food coloring if desired. When first layer is chilled enough so it won't mix with this layer, spread second layer and return to freezer.

Process third layer ingredients and spread this on top of chilled second layer. Cover with plastic and allow to chill in the refrigerator until well set, at least 1 hour. When ready to serve, remove mixture from pan (green layer should be on top) and place on a serving platter.

Whip 4 oz. cream cheese until soft and place in a piping bag. Pipe a thin lattice of cream cheese across the top of the mold and alternate black olives and pimiento slices at each crisscross section.

Salmon Log

This creamy smoked salmon spread can be made far in advance. If you are going to serve this the next day, roll it in the nut mixture about 1 hour before serving. Serve with a variety of crackers or bread rounds.

8 oz. cream cheese, softened
1 can (1 lb.) salmon
2 tsp. minced onion
¼ tsp. liquid smoke
1 tbs. lemon juice
1 tbs. horseradish
¼ tsp. salt
1 cup chopped toasted pecans
2 tbs. chopped fresh parsley

With a mixer, beat cream cheese, salmon, minced onion, liquid smoke, lemon juice, horseradish and salt until well mixed. Shape mixture into a log roll. (If mixture is too soft to form, chill in refrigerator until firm). Mix pecans and parsley together. Roll log in pecan-parsley coating. Cover with plastic wrap and refrigerate until ready to serve.

Chicken Relish Swirls

A good way to use leftover chicken! Make sure the rolls are well chilled before slicing so you can make clean slices. Place these in a single layer on platters and garnish.

8 oz. cooked chicken meat
4 tsp. mango chutney
2 tbs. mayonnaise
¼ cup chopped green bell pepper
4 green onions, chopped
4 gherkin pickles, chopped
¼-½ tsp. curry
salt and pepper to taste
6 slices bread, crusts removed
½ cup butter, softened
1 cup whole stuffed green olives
chopped fresh cilantro for garnish

With a food processor, chop chicken meat into a fine mince. Add chutney, mayonnaise, peppers, green onion, pickles, curry, salt and pepper. Process just enough to combine. Taste and adjust seasonings. Using a rolling pin, flatten bread slices and spread with butter. Spread with chicken mixture and arrange a row of olives along the edge of each slice. Tightly roll up, jelly-roll style, and wrap in plastic wrap. Chill for at least 2 hours. Cut each roll into 4 slices at an angle and garnish with a sprinkling of cilantro.

Smoked Salmon Treats

Salmon is a popular flavor and these are relatively quick to fix. Of course, true smoked salmon can be substituted for the salmon and liquid smoke.

8 oz. cream cheese, softened
1 can (7¾ oz.) salmon, skin and bones removed, flaked with fork
4 drops liquid smoke
3 tbs. minced green onion
½ loaf sliced bread
½ cup butter, softened
paprika for garnish

Mix cream cheese, salmon, liquid smoke and green onion together. Remove crusts from bread slices and flatten bread with a rolling pin. Butter ½ of the slices on 1 side and butter remaining slices on both sides. Cut all bread with a small round 2-inch fluted cutter. Spread salmon mixture on bread rounds buttered on 1 side only. Cover each with a round that is buttered on both sides. Sprinkle each buttered top with paprika. Press lightly together and chill until ready to serve.

Cucumber Mint Coolers

Cucumber tea sandwiches make a light and refreshing appetizer. Consider serving this at your next tea party.

1 large cucumber, peeled
1½ tsp. salt
8 tsp. chopped fresh mint
½ tsp. sugar
1 tsp. lemon juice
12 tbs. butter, softened
16 slices bread, crust removed
pepper to taste
mint sprigs for garnish

Slice cucumber very thin and sprinkle with salt. Place in a colander and drain for 30 minutes. Pat dry on towels and set aside. With a food processor or blender, process mint and sugar together until finely minced. Add lemon juice and butter; blend until smooth. Spread mixture on bread slices, place cucumbers on ½ of the bread slices, sprinkle with pepper and cover with buttered bread. Cut each sandwich into 3 long fingers and serve garnished with mint.

Bacon-Stuffed Cherry Tomatoes

Makes 24

This extremely popular appetizer is reminiscent of a BLT. Be aware that they will go fast, so make plenty!

2 lb. bacon
⅓ cup chopped green onions
½ cup mayonnaise
24 large cherry tomatoes
lettuce leaves

Finely dice bacon and fry in a skillet until crisp. Drain and cool on paper towels. In a bowl, mix fried bacon pieces, green onions and mayonnaise together. Refrigerate while preparing tomatoes. Cut the bottom (opposite the stem end) from each tomato and scoop out pulp with a melon baller or small spoon. Allow hollowed tomatoes to drain on paper towels. Make sure stems are removed. Fill cavity with bacon mixture and set stem-side down on a serving platter. Surround tomatoes with greens and refrigerate until ready to serve.

Cucumbers with Herbed Cream Cheese

Makes 36

This is a delicate and refreshing appetizer. The cucumbers can be cut into shapes to follow a theme, such as hearts for Valentine's Day.

2 large cucumbers (prefer English variety)
1 clove garlic, minced
¼ cup chopped fresh parsley
2 green onions, chopped
8 oz. cream cheese
dash Tabasco Sauce
1 tbs. white wine
white pepper to taste
finely minced red bell pepper or fresh parsley sprig for garnish

Peel, slice and, if desired, use a cookie cutter to cut cucumbers into shapes. Using a food processor or blender, blend garlic, parsley and onions until finely minced. Add remaining ingredients and process until well mixed. Taste and adjust seasonings. Transfer ingredients to a piping bag and pipe mixture onto cucumber slices. Garnish and chill until ready to serve.

Marinated Vegetables

Instead of the standard vegetable tray, consider an artful display of marinated vegetables. For additional color, add a variety of black and green olives to the tray. The marinade can be used over again.

1 head broccoli
1 head cauliflower
4-5 carrots
2 cloves garlic, minced
1 ½ cups vinegar (prefer balsamic)
2 ½ cups olive oil
1 ½ tbs. dried dill weed
1 ½ tbs. sugar
1 ½ tsp. salt
1 ½ tsp. pepper

Cut florets from broccoli and cauliflower and cut into bite-sized pieces. Peel broccoli stems and cut into thin slices on the diagonal. Peel carrots and cut into diagonal slices. Place remaining ingredients in a food processor or blender and process until well combined. Taste and adjust seasonings to personal taste. Pour mixture over vegetables, cover and refrigerate overnight.

Barbecued Chicken Wings

Makes about 60 pieces

This is a great recipe for traveling, because you simply unplug the slow cooker and transport it to the party. To help your hostess, bring an extension cord so it can be easily placed. Serve directly from the pot with lots of napkins!

4 lb. chicken wings
2 large onions, chopped
2 cans (6 oz. each) tomato paste
2 large cloves garlic, minced
¼ cup Worcestershire sauce
¼ cup vinegar
½ cup brown sugar, packed
½ cup sweet pickle relish
½ cup red or white wine
2 tsp. salt
2 tsp. dry mustard

Cut off wing tips and discard. Cut wings at the joint and place in a Crock-pot (or other slow cooker). Add remaining ingredients and stir. Set slow cooker on low and cook for 5 to 6 hours.

Honey Chicken Wings

A nice alternative to teriyaki chicken wings. Be sure to make a large quantity — this one is very popular.

3 lb. chicken wings
salt and pepper to taste
1 cup honey
3 tbs. ketchup
½ cup soy sauce
2 tbs. vegetable oil
1 clove garlic, minced
sesame seeds for garnish, optional

Disjoint chicken wings, remove tips and discard. Place chicken pieces in a shallow baking dish and sprinkle with salt and pepper. Mix together remaining ingredients, except sesame seeds, and pour mixture over chicken. Bake in a 350° oven for 50 minutes. Sprinkle with sesame seeds, if desired, and serve warm.

Sausage in Brioche

Makes 12

Great for picnics or boating. Traditionally, this is served on Bibb lettuce and accompanied by gherkin pickles and Dijon mustard. It goes well with soups and salads.

1 pkg. active dry yeast
3 tbs. warm milk
2 tsp. sugar
½ cup butter, cut into pieces
2 cups flour
1 tsp. salt
2 eggs
1 sausage, 6-7 inches long, about 2-inches diameter
1 egg yolk mixed with 1 tsp. water and dash salt

Mix yeast, milk and sugar together and let stand for 5 minutes. Add butter, flour, salt and eggs and mix in a food processor for 3 minutes. Transfer mixture to an oiled bowl, and slash top with an X. Cover and let rise until double in bulk. Heat oven to 400°. Punch dough down and form into a 10-inch rectangle. Trim ends of sausage and encase with dough. Transfer to an oiled baking pan and glaze with egg mixture. Bake for 35 minutes. Cool for 10 minutes before cutting. Cut into 12 slices, about ½-inch each.

Turkey Meatballs

Makes 36

Serve either plain or in any sauce that goes well with beef meatballs. A delicate sour cream sauce is especially nice. Be sure to provide toothpicks.

1 lb. ground turkey
2 tbs. mayonnaise
2 tbs. minced onion
salt and pepper to taste
seasoned flour for dipping

In a bowl, mix turkey meat, mayonnaise, onion, salt and pepper together. Roll into small balls, roll in seasoned flour and place on a baking sheet. Bake in a 350° oven for 20 minutes or until no longer pink.

Sweet and Sour Meatballs

Makes 32

Instead of barbecued meatballs, consider serving sweet and sour meatballs. You can make this into a meal by serving this recipe over rice.

½ cup breadcrumbs
½ cup milk
1 lb. lean ground beef
¼ cup chopped onion
2 tsp. salt
¼ tsp. pepper
2 eggs, beaten
½ cup flour
2 tbs. butter
1¼ cups cold water
1 tbs. cornstarch
¼ cup sugar
¼ cup vinegar
1 tbs. soy sauce
⅓ cup sliced green and/or red bell peppers

In a bowl, combine breadcrumbs and milk and let stand for 5 minutes. Add beef, onion, 1½ tsp. of the salt, and pepper; combine well. Roll meat mixture into small balls, dip in beaten egg and roll in flour. Heat butter in a skillet and brown meatballs on all sides. In a saucepan, combine water and cornstarch and stir until dissolved. Add sugar, vinegar, soy sauce and remaining ½ tsp. salt. Add meatballs and cook over medium heat until mixture thickens. Add peppers, cover and simmer for 10 minutes. Serve in a chafing dish with toothpicks.

Caramelized Nuts

The secret to great nuts is soaking them in boiling water and drying them in the oven before you begin the caramelizing process.

1 lb. whole walnuts or pecans
boiling water to cover
2 tbs. vegetable oil
1 tsp. coarse salt
¼-½ cup sugar

Place nuts in a bowl and cover with boiling water. Allow to sit for 30 minutes. Drain and rinse nuts well. Pat dry with a towel and place nuts on a baking sheet. Bake at 300° for 30 minutes and stir. Reduce heat to 250° and check every 10 minutes, stirring each time until nuts no longer have moisture in the center. Remove from oven.

Heat oil over medium heat in a large skillet or wok and add nuts. Toss to distribute oil, toss in salt and stir to mix. Add sugar a little at a time and stir until sugar begins to caramelize, stirring constantly. This should take 3 to 4 minutes. Taste, being careful to avoid burning yourself, and determine if you wish to add more salt or sugar. When caramelized, remove from heat and spread out on buttered waxed paper to cool.

Cheese Straws

What makes this special is the ginger, which adds a little heat and spice at the same time. This is a great appetizer at a wine party.

2 cups flour
1 tsp. ground ginger
1 tsp. salt
2/3 cup cold butter, cut into small cubes
2 cups shredded sharp cheddar cheese
1/2 cup sesame seeds, toasted
1 tsp. Worcestershire sauce
4-5 tbs. cold water

With a food processor or mixer, mix together flour, ginger and salt. Add butter and cheese and process to blend. Add remaining ingredients, using enough water to form a stiff dough, and blend until dough forms a ball. Roll dough out on a flour surface and cut into 1/2-inch strips or "straws." Bake in a 400° oven for 10 to 12 minutes or until golden brown.

Phyllo with Three Cheeses and Walnuts

Wine tasting? Choose this delicate appetizer for a perfect accompaniment.

2 tbs. butter
1 clove garlic, minced
1 onion, finely chopped
1/2 cup crumbled Gorgonzola cheese
2 cups ricotta cheese
1/2 cup shredded Parmesan cheese

1 tbs. dried basil
1 tsp. ground fennel
1 tsp. nutmeg
1 cup chopped toasted walnuts
1 cup butter, melted
1 pkg. (1 lb.) phyllo sheets

In a skillet, melt 2 tbs. butter and sauté garlic and onion until tender. Remove from heat and mix with cheeses, seasonings and walnuts. Skim top milky layer from melted butter and discard.

Brush 1 sheet of phyllo with butter, cut into 3 strips lengthwise, fold each strip in half and brush with butter. Place a spoonful of cheese mixture in top corner and fold in a triangle, like a flag, until a triangular bundle is formed. Brush outside with butter and place on a cookie sheet. Repeat with remaining ingredients. Bake in a 375° oven for 15 to 20 minutes or until golden brown. Serve hot.

Red Onion Foccacia

This popular Italian bread has a delicious caramelized onion topping. Make it on a pizza pan and cut it into small squares. This recipe can also be made on the dough cycle of a bread machine.

2 tsp. yeast
1 cup warm water
1 pinch sugar
2½ cups flour
½ tsp. salt
1 tbs. olive oil
1¾ lb. red onions, sliced
⅓ cup olive oil
1 tsp. anchovy paste
1 tbs. white vinegar
olive oil for brushing
salt and pepper to taste

Dissolve yeast in warm water with a pinch of sugar. Add about 1 cup flour to dissolved yeast and beat vigorously for 1 minute. Let rise on a warm oven door until double in bulk, about 30 minutes. Beat mixture down and add salt, remaining flour little by little and 1 tbs. oil. Knead dough well, about 10 minutes. Let rest for 15 minutes.

While dough is resting, cook onions and ⅓ cup olive oil in a skillet over low heat until softened. Dissolve anchovy paste in vinegar and add to onions. Cook over medium heat until onions are soft and liquid has evaporated. Let cool.

Punch down dough and spread in a 12-inch pizza pan. Let rise for 30 minutes in a warm place. Brush dough lightly with olive oil. Sprinkle with salt and pepper. Adjust seasoning of onions and spread gently on dough within ½-inch of edge. Bake in a 400° oven for 30 to 35 minutes until lightly browned. Using a pizza cutter or large knife, cut into small squares.

Brie Wafers

For a change, you can substitute sharp cheddar cheese for the Brie. This is a great recipe to keep frozen and ready to bake when drop-in guests come a-calling.

½ cup butter
½ lb. Brie cheese, rind removed and cubed
1 cup flour
¼ tsp. seasoning salt
½ tsp. Tabasco Sauce
¼ cup sesame seeds

With a food processor or mixer, process butter and Brie until well blended. Add flour, seasoning salt and Tabasco; mix until smooth. Divide dough into 4 parts and shape into logs 1 inch in diameter. Wrap in waxed paper and refrigerate or freeze.

Before serving, slice chilled logs ¼-inch thick. Place slices 1 inch apart on ungreased baking sheets and sprinkle with sesame seeds. Bake in a 400° oven for 8 to 10 minutes or until edges are golden brown. Serve warm.

Spanakopitas

Creamy spinach-filled flaky pastries are a Greek specialty. This recipe can be used as a luncheon entrée by making the pastries considerably larger.

1 pkg. (10 oz.) frozen chopped spinach
2 tbs. butter
½ medium onion, chopped
½ tsp. nutmeg
salt and pepper to taste
½ lb. ricotta cheese
2 eggs, beaten
½ lb. butter, melted
½ pkg. (1 lb.) phyllo sheets

Defrost spinach and squeeze out excess moisture. Melt butter in a skillet and sauté onion until tender. Add spinach to skillet with nutmeg, salt, pepper, ricotta and eggs. Mix to combine; allow to cool to room temperature. Skim top milky layer from melted butter and discard. Cut phyllo sheets into thirds crosswise. Brush a sheet with butter, place a heaping teaspoon of filling at the corner and fold in half. Brush with butter again and fold in a triangular shape, like a folded flag. Brush outside with butter and place on a baking sheet. Repeat with remaining ingredients. Bake in a 425° oven for about 15 minutes or until golden.

Spinach and Walnut Triangles

Makes about 50

Spinach, Swiss cheese and walnuts make a delightful filling that is encased in flaky pastry. There are about 30 sheets of phyllo in a package; refreeze the sheets remaining.

1 pkg. (10 oz.) chopped frozen spinach
1 cup grated Swiss cheese
1 cup chopped toasted walnuts
2 tsp. mustard
1/4 tsp. salt
dash pepper
1/2 cup butter, melted
18 sheets phyllo

Defrost spinach and squeeze out all excess water. Place in a bowl with cheese, walnuts, mustard, salt and pepper and stir to combine. Skim top milky layer from melted butter and discard.

Brush 1 sheet of phyllo dough with butter. Divide into thirds, fold each third in half and brush with butter again. Place 1 heaping teaspoon of spinach mixture at end and fold into a triangle. Continue to fold, flag-fashion, back and forth until at end of sheet, brush with butter and place on a baking sheet with sides. Repeat with remaining ingredients. Bake in a 375° oven for 15 to 20 minutes or until golden brown. Serve warm.

Olive Swirls

Makes 24

A cheese pastry surrounds olives with a slight hint of heat.

1/2 cup flour
4 oz. cheddar cheese, shredded
3 tbs. butter
dash Tabasco Sauce
1/2 cup chopped pimiento-stuffed green olives

With a food processor, blend flour, cheese, butter and Tabasco. Form a ball and chill for 30 minutes. Roll dough out to a 6-x-10-inch rectangle between 2 sheets of waxed paper. Sprinkle entire surface with olives and roll up jelly-roll fashion. Wrap rolled dough in waxed paper and allow to chill for 1 hour. Cut roll into 1/4-inch slices and place on an ungreased baking sheet. Bake in a 400° oven for about 15 minutes or until golden brown. Serve hot.

Olive Puffs

Green olives are encased in cheese pastry and served warm. Keep a large quantity of these in the freezer so you won't run out.

2 cups sharp cheddar cheese
½ cup butter
1 cup flour
1 jar (24 oz.) pimiento-stuffed green olives

With a mixer, beat cheese, butter and flour together until well mixed. Roll dough into small balls, press olives in center and cover completely with dough. These can be frozen until ready to bake (thaw before baking). Bake in a 400° oven for 20 minutes or until golden brown.

Mushroom Strudel Tarts

Phyllo dough pastry lines little muffin cups and is filled with a mushroom and onion mixture. Try this recipe with different varieties of mushrooms for a delightful change.

4 sheets phyllo
6 tbs. butter, melted, top milky layer
  skimmed off and discarded
1 lb. mushrooms, chopped
½ cup chopped onion
¼ cup chopped fresh parsley
½ cup dry white wine
dash Tabasco Sauce
4 oz. Monterey Jack cheese, shredded

Brush 1 phyllo sheet with butter, cover with another sheet, brush with butter and repeat twice more. Cut phyllo stack into 2-inch squares and place in miniature muffin tins. In a skillet, sauté mushrooms, onion, parsley, wine and Tabasco until liquid is almost evaporated. Cool. Fill muffin cups with mushroom mixture and top with cheese. Bake in a 400° oven for 15 to 18 minutes. Serve warm.

Sweet and Hot Date Walnut Wafers

A popular treat is both sweet and hot! This can be frozen and brought out at a moment's notice.

8 oz. sharp cheddar cheese
1 1/2 cups flour
1/2 cup butter
1/4 tsp. cayenne pepper, or to taste
1/2 tsp. salt
1/4 cup white wine
6 oz. pitted dates, chopped
1 cup chopped walnuts
1 beaten egg for glaze
ground walnuts, sesame seeds or grated Parmesan cheese for topping,
   optional

With a food processor or by hand using a pastry blender, combine cheese, flour, butter, cayenne and salt. Process until mixture resembles cornmeal. Add white wine and mix until moistened. Cut dates and walnuts into mixture and form into 2 logs. Roll in waxed paper and chill. To bake, cut into thin slices and brush with egg glaze. Either bake as is or sprinkle top with walnuts, sesame seeds or grated Parmesan cheese. Bake in a 375° oven for 10 to 12 minutes or until golden brown.

Black-Eyed Susans

Sweet dates encased in a cheese pastry are a Southern specialty.

1 cup cold butter, cut into small cubes
1 lb. sharp cheddar cheese, shredded
2 cups flour
1 pinch salt
1 pinch cayenne pepper, or more to taste
1 lb. pitted dates
1/2 cup sugar

With a food processor or by hand using a pastry blender, quickly mix butter, cheese, flour, salt and cayenne together. Taste dough and determine if you wish to add more cayenne. Roll dough into balls and press a date into the center of each, covering it entirely with dough. Roll in sugar and place on a baking sheet. Bake in a 300° oven for 30 minutes. Remove and cool on rack.

Shrimp Puffs

Little cream puffs are filled with a subtle shrimp mixture. Be careful not to fill the puffs until just before serving, so they won't get soggy.

½ cup butter
1 pinch salt
1 cup water
1 cup flour
4 eggs
3 oz. cream cheese
1 jar (4 oz.) olive pimiento cheese
½ cup blue cheese dressing
½ cup mayonnaise
2 tbs. ketchup
¼ tsp. Worcestershire sauce
¼ tsp. horseradish
1 tbs. lemon juice, or to taste
1 clove garlic, minced
1 can (6 oz.) shrimp

In a saucepan, bring butter, salt and water to a boil; remove from heat. Immediately add all flour and stir until dough forms a ball and leaves the sides of the pan. Allow dough to cool slightly. Add eggs, one at a time, and beat very vigorously until a smooth batter is formed. (The beating develops the gluten which makes the puffs rise, so beat very well.)

Drop batter by teaspoonfuls onto a greased baking sheet. Bake in a 400° oven for 10 minutes, reduce heat to 350° and bake for another 20 minutes. Remove from oven and cool on wire racks.

Place remaining ingredients in a food processor workbowl or blender container and process until well mixed. If you prefer, shrimp can be left out of mixture until after blending, and be stirred in by hand to allow them to be seen. To serve, split cooled puffs in half and fill with shrimp mixture.

Miniature Shrimp Quiches

Makes 18

This is a simple, creamy version of quiche with the subtle taste of shrimp.

1 cup plus 2 tbs. flour
½ cup butter
1 tbs. grated Parmesan cheese
1 egg, slightly beaten
dash salt
8 oz. cream cheese, softened

1 tbs. milk
1 tsp. Worcestershire sauce
1 green onion, minced
¼ cup bottled chili sauce
½ lb. shrimp
chopped fresh parsley for garnish

Place flour, butter, Parmesan, egg and salt in a food processor workbowl or blender container and process until mixed. Wrap dough in plastic and chill. Divide dough into small balls and press each ball into a miniature muffin cup or small tart cup. With a food processor or blender, mix cream cheese, milk, Worcestershire sauce and green onion until smooth. Pour mixture into pastry shells. Top each quiche with a small bit of chili sauce and a few shrimp, and sprinkle with parsley. Bake in a 425° oven for 10 minutes. Cool immediately on a rack.

Crab in Phyllo

Makes 48

The expense of crab makes this a special treat. These appetizers go especially well with plum sauce, found in the international section of your grocery store. This recipe can be made ahead of time and frozen until ready to bake.

8 oz. cream cheese, softened
4 oz. fresh crabmeat
2 green onions, tops only, finely minced
½ tsp. minced garlic
salt and pepper to taste
few drops Tabasco Sauce
½ pkg. (1 lb.) phyllo sheets
1 cup butter, melted

In a small bowl, gently mix cream cheese, crabmeat, green onions, garlic, salt, pepper and Tabasco to taste. Unroll phyllo. Place a slightly damp cloth over phyllo while working, to keep it from drying out. Skim top milky layer from melted butter and discard. Lightly brush 1 phyllo sheet with butter; cut into 4 strips. Place 1 teaspoon filling in one corner, fold sheet in half and brush with butter. Fold into a triangular shape (flag-fashion), brush triangular bundle with butter and place on an ungreased baking sheet with sides. Repeat with remaining ingredients. Bake in a 350° oven for 15 to 20 minutes or until browned.

Crispy Crab Rolls

Makes 72

This crab-filled flaky pastry has a touch of heat. Make these far ahead of time and bake at the last minute.

4 shallots, minced
¼ cup butter
2 cloves garlic, minced
½ cup chopped fresh parsley
1 tsp. dried dill weed, or more to taste

2 tbs. horseradish
12 oz. crabmeat
1 pkg. (1 lb.) phyllo sheets, or at least 24 sheets
½ lb. butter, melted

In a skillet, sauté shallots in butter until limp; add garlic, parsley, dill and horseradish. Remove from heat and stir in crabmeat. Taste and adjust seasonings. Skim top milky layer from butter and discard. Butter 1 sheet of phyllo (cover remaining phyllo with a slightly damp towel). Cut buttered phyllo into thirds. Place 1 tbs. of filling at bottom of sheet in the center, roll 1 turn and fold outside edges towards the center, enclosing filling. Brush butter over folded edges and roll up into a long cigar shape. Brush outside with butter and place on a rimmed baking sheet. Repeat for remaining phyllo and filling. Bake in a 350° oven for 15 minutes or until golden. Serve warm.

Crab Turnovers

Makes 24

A creamy crab mixture is flavored with dill and encased in pastry.

1 pkg. (10 oz.) frozen chopped spinach
12 oz. fresh mushrooms, chopped
½ cup chopped green onions
¼ cup butter
1 tsp. salt
½ tsp. pepper
1 heaping tbs. flour

12 oz. crabmeat
¼ cup sour cream
¼ cup chopped fresh parsley
1 tsp. dried dill weed
1 pkg. (17¼ oz.) puff pastry
1 egg, slightly beaten with 1 pinch salt
2-3 tbs. grated Parmesan cheese

Defrost spinach and squeeze out excess moisture. In a skillet, sauté mushroom and onions in butter until soft. Add salt, pepper and flour and cook for about 30 seconds. Gently stir in crabmeat, sour cream, parsley and dill weed. Add spinach to crabmeat mixture. Taste and adjust seasonings. On a floured board, cut pastry dough into 2½- or 3-inch rounds. Brush pastry with beaten egg and place 1 tbs. filling in center. Sprinkle with Parmesan, fold in half and crimp edges with a fork. Brush top of each turnover with more beaten egg and prick with a fork. Place on a baking sheet and bake in a 425° oven for 30 minutes or until golden brown.

Sausage Roll

This recipe is perfect for a crowd. It is important to choose a very tasty Italian sausage, since it is the main ingredient. If you prefer a little heat, choose a hot sausage variety.

1 lb. ground Italian sausage
1/2 medium onion, chopped
1/2 tsp. salt
1/4 tsp. pepper
1 1/2 tbs. basil
1 pkg. (17 1/4 oz.) frozen puff pastry, thawed
1/4 lb. provolone cheese, shredded

In a skillet, cook sausage with onion, salt, pepper and basil until pink color is just gone. Roll each puff pastry sheet into a 15-inch square and cut in half lengthwise. Divide filling into 4 parts and spread over each pastry sheet. Sprinkle with cheese and roll tightly. Chill rolls for at least 30 minutes. Cut into 1/2-inch rounds. Place on an ungreased baking sheet. Bake in a 375° oven until golden brown, about 15 to 20 minutes. Serve warm.

Puff Pastry Pork Swirls

Make this very tasty, easy-to-make recipe far in advance and freeze it. This is a great recipe that can be made in bulk for large parties.

1 pkg. (1 lb.) frozen puff pastry
1 lb. ground pork
2 tsp. ground cumin
1 tsp. dried thyme
1 tbs. minced garlic
1/4 cup finely chopped green onions
1/4 cup finely chopped red bell peppers or pimiento
salt and pepper to taste
1 egg, slightly beaten with 1 pinch salt

Allow pastry to defrost on counter for several minutes until just pliable. Roll pasty to 1/8-inch thick. Cut into strips about 3 inches wide. Place on cookie sheets sprayed with cold water and refrigerate while making filling. In a bowl, mix pork with remaining ingredients, except egg. Divide filling among pastry strips, spreading filling over top of pastry. Brush edges with water and roll up. Refrigerate or freeze. Just before serving, cut rolls into 1/2-inch sections. Paint with egg wash and bake in a 375° oven until golden, about 15 minutes. Serve warm.

Honey Lamb Puffs

A Middle Eastern delight has a very satisfying, piquant quality.

1/4 cup raisins
enough hot water to cover raisins
1/4 cup olive oil
1 3/4 cups finely chopped onions
1 tbs. minced garlic
1 lb. ground lamb
2 tsp. salt
1 1/2 tsp. pepper
1 tsp. cinnamon
1/8 tsp. cayenne pepper
1/4 cup tomato paste
1 cup chopped fresh tomatoes
1/3 cup honey
1 pkg. (17 1/4 oz.) frozen puff pastry, thawed

Cover raisins with hot water to plump. Heat olive oil in a skillet, add onions and garlic and sauté until tender. Add lamb, salt, pepper, cinnamon and cayenne; cook until meat is no longer pink. Add tomato paste, tomatoes, raisins (which have been drained) and honey. Allow mixture to simmer for several minutes, taste and adjust seasonings. Allow filling to cool.

Cut each puff pastry sheet into 16 squares and line miniature muffin cups with pastry squares. Place about 2 tsp. filling in each shell. Bake in a 375° oven for about 20 minutes or until golden. Serve warm or at room temperature.

Pork Satay with Plum Sauce

Satays have become very popular. Plum sauce is a perfect accompaniment to pork, but can also work as well with beef or chicken. If time is limited, plum sauce is now available in most grocery stores in the international section. Presoak bamboo skewers so they won't burn. Included is a fast recipe for Plum Sauce.

6 cloves garlic, minced
1 tbs. ground coriander
1 tbs. turmeric
1 tbs. brown sugar
1 tbs. ground cumin
1 tsp. white pepper
1 tsp. salt
½ cup coconut milk
2 lb. pork tenderloin, thinly sliced
fresh pineapple, cut into ½-inch wedges
Plum Sauce, follows

Combine garlic, coriander, turmeric, brown sugar, cumin, white pepper, salt and coconut milk in bowl. Marinate pork slices in this mixture for several hours or, ideally, overnight. Thread pork onto presoaked wooden skewers and top each with a pineapple slice. Grill or broil until done, about 3 to 6 minutes. Serve with *Plum Sauce*.

Plum Sauce

2 cups plum preserves
¼ cup rice vinegar
2 tsp. Chinese 5-spice powder
1 tbs. instant chicken bouillon granules
1 tbs. soy sauce

Combine all ingredients and microwave on HIGH for 3 minutes. Stir well and cook for an additional minute. Store in refrigerator until ready to use. Makes 12 servings.

Chicken Empanadas

A delicious Mexican treat is now made easier with the advantage of buying frozen puff pastry. If you prefer a spicier mixture, increase the pepper flakes.

1/3 cup raisins
1 cup hot water
3 tbs. vegetable oil
2/3 cup minced onion
1 lb. diced uncooked chicken
3/4 tsp. red pepper flakes
1 1/2 tsp. salt
1/4 tsp. cinnamon
1 tsp. ground cumin
2 tbs. butter
2 tbs. flour
1 cup chicken stock
3 tbs. chopped green olives
1 pkg. (17 1/4 oz.) puff pastry
1 egg, beaten
3 tbs. toasted slivered almonds

Soak raisins in hot water until plump. Drain. In a skillet, heat oil and sauté onion until soft. Add chicken, pepper flakes, salt, cinnamon and cumin. Cook for 5 minutes. In a small saucepan, heat butter until melted, stir in flour until smooth, add chicken stock and cook until thick. Stir in chicken mixture with raisins and green olives and allow mixture to cool to room temperature.

Roll puff pastry to 1/8-inch thick and cut into 3-inch rounds. Divide filling among rounds and brush edges with water. Fold rounds in half, shape into crescents and crimp edges with a fork. Lay crescents on a lightly buttered baking sheet, brush with lightly beaten egg and sprinkle with toasted almonds. Bake in a 375° oven for 20 to 30 minutes or until golden.

Pot Stickers

An Oriental dim sum pastry is gobbled up by the guests! An important ingredient is sesame oil, which gives it the special, unique flavor.

2 tsp. minced fresh ginger
2 green onions, finely minced
6 tbs. cream sherry
1 lb. ground pork
2 tbs. soy sauce
1 tsp. salt
1/4 tsp. pepper
1 tsp. sugar
3 tbs. sesame oil
1/2 cup chopped water chestnuts
1 tbs. chopped fresh cilantro
1 pkg. round won ton wrappers
3 tbs. vegetable oil
1 tbs. white vinegar
1 cup water

Mix together ginger, green onions and 4 tbs. of the cream sherry. Let stand for 10 minutes; drain. Add pork, soy sauce, salt, pepper, sugar, 1 tbs. sesame oil, water chestnuts and cilantro, mixing to combine. Place 2 tsp. of this filling in center of each wrapper. Dampen edges with water and fold in half. Pleat or crimp edges together.

Heat 3 tbs. oil in a large skillet, arrange dumplings in circles in skillet, cover and fry over medium heat for 3 minutes. Combine remaining cream sherry and sesame oil with vinegar and water. Add to fried dumplings and cook uncovered until water is absorbed. An average skillet can hold about 15 dumplings, so split vinegar mixture between 2 pans if desired.

Sweet and Sour Pupus

This Hawaiian favorite can be made ahead of time and baked just before the guests arrive. Scallops or cooked chicken livers can be substituted for the water chestnuts.

1 lb. bacon, cut into thirds
2 cans (8 oz.) whole water chestnuts
¾ cup pineapple juice
1½ tbs. cornstarch
½ cup brown sugar, packed
½ cup cider vinegar
1 tsp. salt
4 tsp. ketchup
1 cup crushed pineapple, drained
few drops red food coloring, optional

Blanch bacon in boiling water for several minutes to remove excess fat. Remove bacon from water and allow to cool. Wrap bacon around water chestnuts and fasten with a toothpick. Place in an ovenproof dish. In a saucepan, mix pineapple juice with cornstarch and bring to a boil. Add remaining ingredients, adding food coloring for eye appeal, if desired. Allow mixture to thicken slightly. Pour sauce over bacon-wrapped water chestnuts. Bake in a 350° oven for 30 minutes and serve immediately.

Hawaiian Mushrooms

This is an elegant "sit-down" appetizer (or starter) that is rich and creamy. Serve with crusty rolls. To set the ambiance, use a centerpiece with exotic Hawaiian flowers to dress the table.

¼ cup butter
3 large sweet onions, thinly sliced
16 very large mushrooms
4 oz. fresh crabmeat
1 green onion, finely chopped

3 oz. cream cheese
salt and pepper to taste
¼ lb. Monterey Jack cheese, shredded

Melt butter in a skillet and sauté onions until golden brown. Place mixture in bottom of a casserole dish or in 8 individual ramekins. Cut stems from mushrooms just at cap level. Place mushrooms in casserole or ramekins. Mix together crabmeat, green onion, cream cheese, salt and pepper. Fill center of mushrooms with crabmeat mixture. Bake in a 350° oven for 5 to 8 minutes or until mushrooms are softened. Sprinkle with cheese and continue to bake until cheese melts. Serve immediately.

Taco Snacks

This simple appetizer can be made ahead of time and kept frozen until ready to bake. This one is especially appreciated by children.

1 lb. ground beef
1/3 cup chopped onion
1 pkg. (1.25 oz.) taco seasoning mix
1 tsp. Tabasco Sauce
1/4 tsp. cayenne pepper
1 cup shredded cheddar cheese
3 pkg. refrigerated crescent rolls

In a skillet, brown beef and onion together until no longer pink; drain off excess fat. Add taco mix, Tabasco and cayenne pepper. Taste and add more seasonings if desired. Add cheese and stir until melted. Allow mixture to cool before filling dough.

Roll each package of dough into a large square and cut into 24 squares. Place 2 tsp. filling in center of each square. Pinch 4 corners together and 4 seams. Bake in a 375° oven for 20 minutes or until golden brown.

Italian-Style Meatballs

The Italian name for meatballs is "polpette." This particular recipe is from Northern Italy and can be served with your favorite Italian meat sauce, sour cream sauce or, if desired, barbecue sauce.

1 slice bread soaked in milk
1 lb. ground chuck
1/4 cup grated Parmesan cheese
1/4 cup minced onion
2 cloves garlic, minced
1 tbs. grated lemon zest
1/4 cup minced fresh parsley
1 egg, beaten
salt and pepper to taste
sauce of choice: tomato sauce, meat sauce, sour cream sauce, barbecue sauce

Squeeze milk from bread and place in a bowl. Add remaining ingredients and mix together thoroughly. Fry a small amount of mixture and taste; adjust seasoning to personal preference. Roll mixture into balls and place under the broiler or fry in a skillet until brown on all sides. Put meatballs in sauce of choice and simmer for 1 hour. Serve warm with toothpicks.

Crostini Olive Spread

This recipe makes an Italian favorite that is piquant and can be quite filling. Serve it on toasted bread rounds and, if desired, sprinkle with a little shredded Parmesan and broil until cheese is melted.

1 can (6 oz.) pitted black olives
1 tbs. minced onion
2 tbs. minced fresh parsley
2 tbs. lemon juice
2 cloves garlic, minced
4 anchovies
¼ cup olive oil
salt and pepper to taste
shredded Parmesan cheese, optional

Place all ingredients in a blender container or food processor workbowl, except Parmesan, and chop until barely mixed. Adjust seasoning to personal taste. Chill until ready to serve. If desired, spread filling on toasted bread rounds and sprinkle with Parmesan. Place under the broiler until cheese melts.

Caponata (Eggplant Antipasti)

Makes 6 cups

A healthy Italian and French appetizer is made from fresh vegetables. Serve with rounds of crusty French bread. This can be served either hot or cold. It also can be used as a vegetable side dish.

1 medium eggplant
salt
¼ cup olive oil
1 medium zucchini
1 large onion, diced
3 cloves garlic, minced
½ cup diced celery
1 large carrot, diced
1 green bell pepper, seeded and
    diced

1½ cups chopped tomatoes, drained
3 tbs. tomato paste
¼ cup chopped fresh parsley
1½ tsp. dried basil
¼ cup red wine vinegar
2 tsp. sugar
¼ cup chopped stuffed green olives
¼ cup chopped pitted black olives
2 tbs. coarsely chopped capers
salt and pepper to taste

Remove peel from eggplant and dice. Sprinkle with salt and place in a colander to drain for 30 minutes. Heat oil in large pan, add eggplant and zucchini and cook until lightly browned. Stir in onion, garlic, celery and carrot and cook for another 10 minutes. Add remaining ingredients and simmer gently for 1 hour. Correct seasonings if necessary.

Middle Eastern Delights

Makes 24

A vegetarian appetizer is surrounded by flaky pastry. This can be made ahead of time and kept frozen until ready to bake.

½ medium onion, diced
⅓ lb. mushrooms, diced
2 tbs. butter
1 tbs. chopped fresh cilantro
1 tbs. chopped fresh parsley
1 tsp. ground cumin
½ tsp. salt
¼ tsp. pepper
1 cup butter, melted
16 sheets phyllo (about ½ pkg.)

In a skillet, sauté onions and mushroom in butter until limp. Remove from heat and let cool. Add cilantro, parsley, cumin, salt and pepper. Taste and adjust seasonings. Skim top milky layer from butter and discard. Brush 1 sheet of phyllo with butter, place a second sheet on top and brush again with butter. Cut dough into 3 pieces and place about 1 tbs. filling in the center on one end. Fold sides over filling and roll cigar fashion. Brush outside with butter and place on a rimmed baking sheet. Repeat for remaining ingredients. Bake in a 375° oven for 20 minutes or until golden brown. Serve warm.

French Caviar Potatoes

Makes 60

A simple and elegant presentation — arrange the potatoes in a bed of shredded lettuce or parsley and, if desired, use two colors of caviar for eye appeal and variety.

60 tiny new potatoes, cooked until tender
oil for deep frying
8 oz. sour cream
1 jar (2 oz.) caviar, rinsed and drained

Slice off a small piece of each potato so that it will sit flat. Scoop center out using a melon baller. Heat oil in a deep fryer to 375°, drop in prepared potatoes and fry until crispy. Drain on paper towels and keep warm on a cookie sheet in a low oven until ready to serve. Just before serving, fill with sour cream and top with a small amount of caviar.

Teriyaki Chicken Skewers

Make this great recipe ahead of time, and it takes just minutes to broil before the guests arrive. Brandied Mayonnaise makes a delightful change from the ordinary.

3½ lb. boneless chicken breast
¼ cup soy sauce
1 tbs. molasses
1½ cups dry white wine
1 cup water
2 tsp. salt
2 tsp. pepper
2 tsp. minced garlic
1 medium onion, minced
Brandied Mayonnaise, follows

Cut chicken breast meat into thin strips and thread onto wooden skewers. Place in a shallow pan. In a bowl, combine remaining ingredients and pour over chicken strips. Marinate overnight.

Broil chicken pieces for about 3 minutes on each side and serve on a bed of shredded lettuce either alone or with a bowl of *Brandied Mayonnaise*.

Brandied Mayonnaise

¾ cup mayonnaise
1 tbs. brandy
3 tbs. ketchup
1 tbs. Worcestershire sauce
1 tbs. honey
1 tbs. lemon juice
salt and pepper to taste

Combine all ingredients. Taste and adjust seasonings. Chill before serving. Makes 1 cup.

Greek Cheese Puffs

Makes about 72

This delightfully unique cheese combination has a slight sweetness. These can be made ahead of time and frozen until ready to bake. If you cannot find these delicious cheeses at your grocery, try a Greek deli, or use all feta or add some cream cheese and Parmesan.

½ lb. feta cheese
½ lb. Mizithra cheese
½ lb. kasseri cheese
½ cup honey
¼ tsp. cinnamon
2 eggs
about 1 pkg. (1 lb.) phyllo dough, or 24 sheets
1 ½ cups butter, melted

In a bowl, mix cheeses, honey, cinnamon and eggs together. Brush 1 sheet of phyllo with melted butter and cut into 3 parts. Fold each part in half and brush with more butter. Place 1 tsp. filling at one end and fold into triangles, flag-fashion, back and forth to end of strip. Butter outside of dough bundle and place on a rimmed baking sheet. Bake in a 375° oven for 12 to 15 minutes or until golden brown and puffed.

Hoisin Spareribs

Servings: 8-12

These are a delightful change from the common teriyaki chicken wings. You may have to find an Oriental grocery for a few of the ingredients in this recipe.

3 lb. pork spareribs
2 cloves garlic, minced
½ tsp. minced fresh ginger
2 tbs. hoisin sauce
1 tbs. ground bean sauce
2 tbs. sugar
¼ cup soy sauce
¼ cup dry sherry
¼ tsp. Chinese 5-spice powder
½ cup water

Have the butcher cut the ribs crosswise into 1 ½-inch strips. Place ribs in a foil-lined shallow baking pan. Mix remaining ingredients together, except water, and pour over ribs. Marinate for 1 hour. Add water to pan and cover with foil. Bake in a 300° oven for 2 ½ to 3 hours. Serve warm.

Oriental Shrimp Toast

Makes 32

This popular appetizer should be fried just before the guests arrive. Another possibility is to have a fondue pot with hot oil and allow the guests to cook their own.

8 slices white bread, square loaf
1 lb. cooked shrimp, shelled and deveined
1½ cups finely minced onions
½ tsp. minced fresh ginger
1 tsp. salt
2 tsp. cornstarch
1 egg
sesame seeds for dipping, optional
oil for deep frying

Trim crusts from bread and cut into 4 triangles. Allow bread to dry for 1 to 2 hours. Mash or finely chop shrimp. In a bowl, mix shrimp, onions, ginger, salt, cornstarch and egg into a smooth paste. Spread shrimp paste on toast. If desired, dip triangle in sesame seeds. Heat oil to 350° and fry bread until both sides are golden brown. Drain on paper towels and keep warm in oven until ready to serve.

Marinated Olives

Makes 1½ quarts

This recipe gives American olives a Greek flavor. This makes a great gift to give friends for the holidays.

1 lb. large black olives
3 stalks celery, finely chopped
3-4 cloves garlic, minced
juice of 2 lemons
1 whole lemon, cut into small pieces
1 cup olive oil
1½ cups balsamic vinegar or red wine vinegar
2 tbs. dried oregano

Drain olives and, if they are not pitted, slit one side with a knife to allow marinade to penetrate olive. Mix remaining ingredients together and stir into olives. Pack entire mixture into jars, making sure liquid completely covers olives. Add a little water if necessary. Cover and allow to marinate for 2 to 3 weeks, shaking jars every few days.

Paté with Asparagus Mayonnaise

A pork-and-beef-based paté has asparagus dotted throughout. Serve this with crusty French bread and a side dish of Asparagus Mayonnaise.

1 lb. ground pork
1 lb. lean ground chuck
1 cup fresh breadcrumbs
1 pkg. (10 oz.) frozen chopped spinach,
  thawed and squeezed dry
1 tsp. dried sage
1 tsp. dried thyme
2 tsp. salt
1 tsp. pepper
1 tsp. ground dried rosemary
2 cloves garlic, minced
1 tbs. chopped fresh parsley
a few spears fresh asparagus, barely cooked
lettuce leaves
Asparagus Mayonnaise follows
chopped parsley for garnish

With the exception of asparagus, lettuce leaves, mayonnaise and parsley, mix all ingredients together thoroughly. Press part of the meat mixture into a loaf pan and place whole spears of asparagus throughout meat mixture for color. Bake on a 350° oven for 45 to 55 minutes. Test with a meat thermometer: it should read 170° if done. Remove from oven, place a weight on meat mixture and chill overnight. To serve, remove weight, unmold paté, slice off several pieces and place on a serving dish lined with lettuce. Spoon a line of Asparagus Mayonnaise down the center and sprinkle with chopped parsley. Serve with remaining mayonnaise in a dish.

Asparagus Mayonnaise

This mayonnaise can also be used as a dressing for pasta salads, sandwich spreads or mixed with filling for deviled eggs.

1/4 lb. asparagus, cooked
1 1/2 cups mayonnaise
1/4 tsp. dry mustard

Place asparagus in a blender container or food processor workbowl, puree until smooth and set aside. In a blender or food processor, place mayonnaise and mustard. Add asparagus puree and process briefly to blend. Taste and adjust seasonings. Chill until ready to use. Makes 2 cups.

Sesame Walnut Chicken Strips

The traditional way of seasoning the chicken is with ground roasted Szechuan peppercorns, which creates a unique, fragrant taste sensation. If desired, serve with a homemade sweet and sour sauce.

4 whole chicken breasts, boned and skinned
2 cups walnuts
2 cups sesame seeds
oil for deep frying
salt and pepper (ideally roasted Szechuan pepper) to taste
Sweet and Sour Sauce, follows, optional

Split chicken breasts in half and cut each half into 5 long slivers. In a food processor or blender, process walnuts and sesame seeds together until finely ground.

Heat oil to 350°. Dip chicken pieces into nut mixture and drop into hot oil. Fry for several minutes, turning once until golden brown. Remove from oil, drain on paper towels and sprinkle with salt and pepper. Cut strips into small diagonal pieces. Serve with *Sweet and Sour Sauce* if desired.

Sweet and Sour Sauce

¾ cup pineapple juice
1½ tbs. cornstarch
½ cup brown sugar, packed
1 tsp. salt
½ cup cider vinegar
¼ cup ketchup
1 cup crushed pineapple, drained
few drops red food coloring, optional

In a saucepan, mix pineapple juice with cornstarch. Add remaining ingredients and bring to a boil over medium-high heat, stirring constantly until mixture thickens. Remove from heat and serve. Makes 2½ cups.

Piroshki

This Russian traditional favorite can be made ahead and frozen. This is a hearty appetizer that is really appreciated by male guests. Consider using this recipe as a great picnic entrée in place of sandwiches by cutting larger rounds out of the pastry.

1 cup butter, softened
1 cup sour cream
2½ cups flour
1 tsp. salt
3 tbs. butter
2 onions, finely chopped
1 lb. lean ground beef
2 tbs. sour cream
¼ cup cooked rice
1 tbs. dried dill weed
¼ cup chopped fresh parsley
1 tsp. salt
½ tsp. pepper
2 hard-cooked eggs, chopped
1 egg beaten with 1 tsp. water

Blend 1 cup butter with sour cream; stir in flour and salt. Form dough into a ball, wrap and chill for 2 hours. In a skillet, heat 3 tbs. butter and sauté onion until golden brown. Add beef and cook until meat is no longer pink. Remove from heat and drain off excess fat. Add all other ingredients, except beaten egg, stir to combine and cool to room temperature.

Roll dough to ⅛-inch thickness. Cut into 3-inch rounds and place a small amount of filling in center of each, fold over and seal edges. Brush filled pastry with beaten egg and place on a greased baking sheet. Bake in a 400° oven for 15 to 20 minutes or until golden brown. Best served warm.

Fried Cheese Squares

This Greek appetizer is typically served with retsina wine and crusty bread.

1 ½ lb. Kefalotyri cheese (or kasseri, Asiago or Romano)
¼ cup olive oil
¼ cup butter
3 large eggs, beaten with a little water

1 cup flour for dredging
2 tbs. brandy
2 tbs. lemon juice
oregano (prefer Greek)
chopped fresh parsley
lemon wedges for garnish

Put an ovenproof dish in a 400° oven to heat thoroughly while preparing cheese. Cut cheese into 12 squares or triangles ¼-inch thick. In a skillet, heat oil and butter. Dip cheese in beaten eggs, roll in flour and place in heated oil. Fry over medium heat until golden brown on both sides. Remove to heated ovenproof dish. Heat brandy in a small saucepan and pour over cheese; immediately ignite. When flames have died, sprinkle with lemon juice, oregano and parsley and serve garnished with lemon wedges.

French Quiche Tartlets

How could men ever say they don't eat quiche! These are best served warm.

2 cups flour
1 pinch salt
6 oz. butter
⅓ cup cold water
8 slices bacon
1 medium onion, diced
¼ cup chopped green chiles, optional

¼ cup shredded Swiss cheese
¼ cup shredded cheddar cheese
4 large eggs, beaten
1 cup milk
1 cup cream
¼ tsp. nutmeg
½ tsp. salt
¼ tsp. pepper

Place flour, salt, and butter in a food processor workbowl and process until crumbly. Add water and process until dough just holds together. Wrap in plastic and refrigerate for 30 minutes.

Roll pastry dough to ⅛-inch thick, cut with a 1 ½-inch round cookie cutter with fluted edges and line miniature muffin cups with pastry dough. Chill while making filling.

Cut bacon into a fine dice, cook in a skillet until crisp and drain on paper towels. Sauté onion in bacon fat until wilted. Distribute bacon, onion, chiles and cheeses among pastry shells. In a bowl, combine eggs, milk, cream, nutmeg, salt and pepper. Pour mixture into pastry shells. Bake in a 450° oven for 10 minutes. Reduce heat to 350° and bake 8 minutes longer.

Taramasalata

A Greek fish roe dip has recently become popular. The tarama can usually be found in a Greek deli. Serve with hot pita bread or toasted bread.

1/3 jar (8 oz.) tarama (fish roe)
1 small onion, finely grated
1 1/2 cups olive oil, or more if desired
5 slices white bread, crusts removed
1/3 cup fresh lemon juice, or to taste
fresh oregano for garnish

Place tarama and onion in a bowl and mash together. Add a small amount of olive oil very slowly, creating a paste. Moisten bread with a little water, squeeze out excess and beat into tarama mixture alternately with remaining olive oil and lemon juice until a cream-colored mixture is obtained. The quantity of olive oil is determined by how thin or thick you prefer the dip to be. Taste and adjust seasonings. Serve garnished with fresh oregano.

Grecian Artichokes

Serve with crackers or bread rounds. This dish can also be used as a vegetable side dish; simply leave the artichoke hearts whole after thawing.

3/4 cup white wine
3/4 cup water
1/4 cup lemon juice
1/4 cup olive oil
2 bay leaves
1/4 tsp. dried thyme
salt and pepper to taste
2 pkg. (10 oz. each) frozen artichoke hearts, thawed
1 1/2 tbs. anchovy paste

In a bowl, mix wine, water, lemon juice, olive oil, bay leaves, thyme, salt and pepper together. Cut artichokes into quarters and cook in wine marinade until tender. Remove from heat, cover and marinate overnight in the refrigerator. Remove artichokes from marinade and set aside. In a saucepan, stir anchovy paste into marinade and reduce over medium heat until mixture thickens. Spoon mixture over artichokes and serve either at room temperature or chilled.

Low-Fat Appetizers

It is wise to serve at least one healthy, low-fat dish at a party because someone is always dieting, and so many people are conscious of their health. There are many new ingredients available, such as low-fat and fat-free mayonnaise, cream cheese, yogurt, etc., that it is easy to transform your old fat-laden recipes into healthy alternatives. Keep in mind that many of these new products do not work well in recipes that require long cooking or baking times.

Antipasto Giardineria

Makes 5-6 pints

This is a favorite antipasto vegetable recipe. Make a large batch when the vegetables are at their peak and keep the jars in the refrigerator year-round. Serve this on a platter with a few fresh vegetables like green onion stalks and maybe slices of a good salami.

8 carrots, peeled
8 stalks celery
2 small zucchini
2 red bell peppers
2 green bell peppers
1 small cauliflower
18 small pearl onions (or 2 medium onions, quartered)
5-6 cloves garlic
5-6 small hot dried red chile peppers
½ can (6 oz.) pitted black olives
½ cup pimiento-stuffed green olives
6 cups water
1½ cups white vinegar
2 tbs. salt
2 tbs. mustard seed
1 tsp. celery seed
⅔ cup sugar

Cut carrots, celery and zucchini into uniform 3-inch sticks. Cut peppers in half, remove seeds and cut into ½-inch strips. Break cauliflower into small florets. Fill pint canning jars with a mixture of assorted vegetables. Place 1 clove garlic and 1 hot dried pepper in each jar with both kinds of olives. Pack jar tightly and in an attractive arrangement. Place remaining ingredients in a large pot and boil for 3 minutes. Pour brine mixture into each jar to cover vegetables, clean jar tops well and seal with lids that have been boiled for 3 minutes. Allow jars to "mellow" in the refrigerator for at least 2 weeks before serving.

Herbed Mushrooms

If desired, once you have added all the ingredients to the pan, remove from heat and refrigerate for up to 2 days before continuing the cooking process.

3 lb. mushrooms
½ cup chicken broth
1 large onion, finely chopped
2 tsp. dried basil
2 tsp. dried oregano
½ tsp. dried thyme
2 cloves garlic, minced
dash Tabasco Sauce
½ cup dry sherry
¼ cup lemon juice
salt to taste

Cut stems from mushrooms at base of cap; use only caps for this recipe. In a skillet, heat chicken broth, add onion and mushrooms and cook until limp. Add remaining ingredients and cook uncovered until liquid is reduced to ½ cup, stirring occasionally. Serve hot in a chafing dish; provide toothpicks.

Marinated Broccoli

If desired, this same brine can be used with cauliflower or asparagus.

3 lb. fresh broccoli
¾ cup vinegar (cider or balsamic)
1 tbs. dried dill weed
1 tbs. sugar
1 tbs. salt
1 tsp. pepper
2 cloves garlic, minced
1½ cups chicken broth or vegetable broth

Peel broccoli stems, cut into slender stalks and place in a shallow pan. Mix remaining ingredients together and pour over broccoli. Cover and refrigerate for 24 hours, turning occasionally. Drain vegetables to serve.

Peperonata

Makes 1 quart

A healthy Italian appetizer has wonderful eye-appeal. Serve it with bread rounds.

2-3 green bell peppers
2 yellow bell peppers
2 red bell peppers
3 fresh tomatoes, diced
1 tsp. salt
1 tbs. minced fresh parsley
½ cup black olives
2 tbs. capers or chopped anchovies, optional
2 cloves garlic

Cut peppers in half, remove seeds and place peppers under the broiler. Allow skin to turn black; remove from oven and peel off charred skin. Cut peppers into a dice and add to a bowl with tomatoes, salt, parsley, olives and capers. Mash garlic and add to pepper mixture. Chill until ready to serve.

Spinach-Stuffed Mushrooms

Servings: 8-12

The trick in dealing with spinach is to squeeze it very dry; otherwise the filling leaches too much liquid and makes the appetizer too messy to handle.

2 tbs. butter
¼ cup minced onion
1 cup chopped frozen spinach, defrosted and squeezed dry
½ cup low-fat ricotta cheese
¼ cup grated Parmesan cheese
salt and pepper to taste
nutmeg to taste
1 lb. mushrooms

Heat butter in a skillet and sauté onion until limp. Add well-squeezed spinach, ricotta cheese, Parmesan cheese, salt, pepper and nutmeg. Taste and adjust flavor to personal taste. Cut stems from mushrooms just at the cap instead of breaking whole stem off (this helps mushrooms retain shape). Mound filling in centers and bake in a 350° oven for about 20 minutes. Serve warm.

Stuffed Grape Leaves

A Greek favorite is otherwise known as "dolmadakia."

1 jar (1 lb.) grape leaves
1 cup minced onion
1/4 cup chicken broth
2 tsp. salt
1 cup uncooked rice
1/2 cup pine nuts
1/2 cup raisins
1 tsp. chopped fresh parsley
1/2 tsp. dill seed
3 cloves garlic, minced
1 tsp. dried oregano
1 tsp. ground cumin
1/2 tsp. ground allspice
1 tsp. crushed fresh mint
1 cup hot chicken stock
1/3 cup lemon juice
4 cups warm chicken stock
2 tbs. olive oil
sliced lemon wedges for garnish

Wash grape leaves 3 times in cold water to remove brine. Cover leaves with boiling water and soak for 1 hour to make pliable for handling. In a skillet, cook onions for 1 minute to remove excess moisture. Add chicken broth and simmer for 5 minutes. Add 1 tsp. of the salt, rice, pine nuts, raisins, parsley, dill, garlic, oregano, cumin, allspice, mint and chicken stock. Cover and simmer for 10 minutes. Stir in 1/2 of the lemon juice and cool.

Remove thick stem from each grape leaf. Use from 1 tsp. to 1 tbs. filling depending on size of leaves. Place filling at base of leaf on dull side, fold sides of leaf in over filling and roll tightly. (The shiny side of the leaf should be on the outside. If stem end is on the outside, roll the leaf tighter.)

Place a layer of grape leaves on the bottom of a heavy kettle and place rolled dolmadakia in layers in kettle. Pour chicken stock, remaining lemon juice, oil and remaining salt over rolls. Place a heavy plate over rolls to keep them from unrolling and cover with lid. Cook over low heat for 25 minutes (water should be totally absorbed by this time). Place on a platter to cool; garnish. This recipe can actually be frozen if desired.

Eggplant Caviar

Hollow out an eggplant or colorful long squashes and fill with this healthy mixture. Serve with an assortment of crackers or bread.

2 eggplants
1 tbs. olive oil
2 cloves garlic
1 small onion
1 red bell pepper, seeded
1 green bell pepper, seeded
1 tomato, peeled and seeded
1 tbs. capers
1 tbs. fresh lemon juice
1/8 tsp. Tabasco Sauce
1 tsp. salt
1/4 tsp. pepper
3 tbs. vinegar (prefer balsamic)
1 tsp. basil
1/4 cup olive oil or vegetable broth
1/2 cup chopped black olives
1/2 cup chopped green olives

Brush eggplants with olive oil and bake in a 350° oven for 30 minutes (or until they begin to soften). Remove from oven, cut in half and scoop out flesh. Save eggplant shell if you wish to serve the dip in it. With a food processor or blender, chop garlic; add onion and bell peppers. Pulse on and off to coarsely chop vegetables. Remove chopped vegetables and set aside. Add tomato, eggplant pulp, capers, lemon juice, Tabasco, salt, pepper, vinegar, basil and oil to processor workbowl or blender container and process until well mixed.

Add coarsely chopped vegetables and process just until mixed. Transfer vegetables to a heavy saucepan and cook over medium heat for 20 minutes. Add chopped olives, taste and adjust seasonings, and chill. Serve in a hollowed-out eggplant shell or squash or colorful dish.

Baba Ghanoush

Makes 1 quart

An eggplant puree specialty that is very healthy and tasty originated in the Middle East. The trick to this dish is in the smoky flavor obtained from scraping the charred skins. If you prefer a little heat, add a dash of cayenne for variety. This is good as a dip or spread for pita or Middle Eastern flatbread.

2 large eggplants
salt to taste
2 cloves garlic, finely minced
¼ cup chopped onion
lime or lemon juice to taste
1½ tbs. tahini (sesame seed paste)
2 tbs. chopped fresh parsley

Wash and dry eggplants and split in half. Place cut-side down on a baking sheet. Broil eggplants for 15 to 20 minutes, allowing skin to blacken considerably and flesh to soften. Remove from oven, sprinkle cut side with salt and put eggplant in a colander to drain for about 15 minutes to remove excess moisture. Scrap pulp from eggplant rind, being sure to scrap some of the charred bits into mixture for flavor. Place pulp and remaining ingredients in a food processor or blender and puree until smooth. Taste and adjust seasonings. Refrigerate until ready to serve.

Sweet Potato and Carrot Dip

Makes 1 quart

Dip into this piquant, yet sweet, vegetable dip with vegetables or pita bread. For a healthy alternative, rather than boiling the vegetables, steam them until tender and add a sprinkling of salt for flavor.

1 lb. sweet potatoes or yams
1 lb. carrots
water to cover
1 tsp. salt
3 cloves garlic
1 tsp. ground cumin

1 tsp. cinnamon
3-4 tbs. olive oil or vegetable broth
3 tbs. vinegar (prefer balsamic)
1 pinch cayenne pepper, or more to taste

Peel sweet potatoes and carrots and cut into pieces. Place in a saucepan, cover with water, add salt and boil until vegetables are soft. Drain. Puree cooked vegetables in a food processor or blender until smooth. Add remaining ingredients and puree until blended. Taste and adjust seasonings to your personal preference.

Salsa

It's a must to serve salsa with tortilla chips (freshly made if you've got the time). It's also good with bean dishes, vegetable salads and chicken. For a low-fat dipper, cut corn tortillas into wedges and bake in a 350° oven for 10 minutes or until crisp.

1 medium sweet onion, chopped (prefer Bermuda variety)
3 cloves garlic, minced
½ green bell pepper, chopped
½ red bell pepper, chopped
½ cup chopped fresh cilantro
2 tbs. lemon juice
2 tsp. sugar
2 cups fresh seeded tomatoes, or 1 can (15 oz.) Mexican-style stewed
    tomatoes
salt and pepper to taste
chopped fresh jalapeño chiles to taste, optional

Place all ingredients in a food processor workbowl or blender container. Process with pulsing action until just blended. Do not puree mixture; texture should be chunky. Taste and adjust seasonings.

Dilled Broccoli and Carrots

This simple, colorful appetizer could be used as a vegetable side dish. To make it even leaner, use 2 tbs. chicken broth instead of the butter and vegetable oil.

1 tbs. butter
1 tbs. vegetable oil
3-4 medium carrots, peeled and sliced
2 tbs. dry white wine
½ medium onion, sliced
1 cup fresh broccoli florets
½ tsp. dried dill weed
pepper to taste

In a large skillet, heat butter and oil and sauté carrots for 1 minute. Add wine, cover and cook over medium heat for 5 minutes. Add remaining ingredients, cover and simmer for 5 minutes or until vegetables are tender-crisp. Serve warm with toothpicks.

Low-Fat Cucumber Dip

This refreshing dip goes well with vegetables or crackers.

1 medium cucumber, peeled
salt
1/3 cup low-fat or nonfat cottage cheese
1 cup plain low-fat or nonfat yogurt
1 tbs. chopped fresh parsley
1/2 tsp. dried dill weed
1/4 tsp. white pepper

Cut cucumber in half, discard seeds and shred. Sprinkle cucumber with salt and drain in a colander for 30 minutes. Place cucumber shreds in a paper towel and squeeze dry. Place remaining ingredients in a food processor or blender and process until smooth. Stir in cucumber, taste and adjust seasonings. Cover and refrigerate until ready to serve.

Chutney-Stuffed Celery

A delightful change for stuffed celery has a spicy, sweet flavor.

1 bunch celery
8 oz. low-fat or nonfat cream cheese, softened
1 tsp. white vinegar
1 tsp. curry powder
6 tbs. mango chutney, finely chopped
1-2 tbs. milk

Separate celery ribs, strip off any tough strands and chill until about 1 hour before serving. With a mixer, blend remaining ingredients together, using milk to thin to a thick but spreadable consistency. Taste and adjust seasonings. Stuff mixture into celery stalks, chill for a short while, cut into 2-inch pieces and serve.

Baked Vegetable and Chicken Won Tons
Makes 24

Won ton wrappers are fat-free and serve as a good alternative to flaky pastry recipes. Turkey can be substituted for the chicken if desired.

8 oz. ground raw chicken
1/4 cup chopped celery
1/2 cup shredded carrots
1 tbs. sherry
2 tsp. grated fresh ginger
1 tbs. soy sauce

2 tsp. cornstarch
1/3 cup bottled plum or sweet and
   sour sauce
24 square won ton wrappers
nonstick cooking spray

In a skillet, sauté chicken with celery and carrots for several minutes. Stir in sherry, ginger, soy sauce, cornstarch and plum sauce. Remove from heat and allow to cool to room temperature. Moisten edges of won ton wrapper, place a rounded teaspoon of filling in the center and pinch opposite ends together to seal. Spray baking sheet with nonstick cooking spray. Place filled won tons on sheet and spray lightly with nonstick cooking spray. Bake in a 375° oven for 10 minutes or until brown and crisp.

Salmon Mousse
Servings: 12

It's fun to use a mold in the shape of a fish or shell with this recipe. Surround the molded mousse with greens and lemon slices.

2 pkg. (1/4 oz. each) unflavored gelatin
1/2 cup cold water
1 cup boiling water
3/4 cup low-fat or nonfat mayonnaise
2 cans (1 lb. each) salmon, drained
1 tsp. lemon juice
1 tbs. grated onion
1 tbs. Worcestershire sauce
1 tsp. salt
1/4 tsp. pepper
8 oz. low-fat or nonfat sour cream
fresh parsley sprigs and lemon slices for garnish

Soak gelatin in cold water until dissolved. Add boiling water, stir and let cool until thickened. Beat mayonnaise into gelatin mixture until frothy. Break up salmon and remove skin and bones. Add to gelatin mixture with lemon juice, onion, Worcestershire sauce, salt and pepper. Fold in sour cream. Pour into a lightly oiled 6- to 8-cup mold and chill until firm. Unmold onto a platter and garnish with parsley sprigs and lemon slices.

Baked Clams

To create a dramatic presentation, arrange the clams on the half-shell on an ovenproof serving platter that is covered with rock salt.

40 clams
1/4 cup water
1/2 cup finely chopped fresh parsley
4 cloves garlic, minced
1/2 cup breadcrumbs
1/4 cup olive oil or chicken broth
1/2 tsp. dried oregano
salt and pepper to taste

Place clams in a pan with water, cover and steam for 2 minutes. Snap off each top shell and discard. Arrange clams on the half-shell on an ovenproof serving platter (on bed of rock salt if desired). Mix remaining ingredients together, taste and adjust seasonings. Place a small amount of mixture over each clam and place under the broiler until heated through and browned. Serve immediately.

Creamy Stuffed Dates

This recipe is quick and easy. Garnish with twisted slices of orange and a few mint sprigs.

40 whole pitted dates
8 oz. low-fat or nonfat cream cheese, softened
1/3 cup orange liqueur
sugar to taste, optional
2 tbs. grated fresh orange zest

Cut dates in half lengthwise and place on a serving platter. Mix cream cheese with orange liqueur, taste and adjust flavor. If desired, a little sugar can be added to taste. Place cream cheese mixture into a piping bag and pipe into date halves. Sprinkle with grated orange peel.

Fruit Kabobs

Fruit makes a refreshing appetizer that is ideal served in the summer months. Kids especially love this one. Be inventive about the possible dipping sauces.

3 bananas
3 apples
2 tbs. lemon juice in 1 cup cold water
3 kiwis
2 oranges
1 cantaloupe, honeydew, watermelon or other melon
1 cup fresh or canned pineapple chunks

Dipping Sauce Alternatives

- nonfat sour cream mixed with orange juice and honey
- low-fat or nonfat flavored yogurt
- plain yogurt flavored with extracts

granola for rolling kabobs, optional

Peel and cut bananas into chunks. Core apples, peel if desired, and cut into large chunks. Dip bananas and apples in lemon juice mixture to prevent darkening. Remove peelings from kiwis and cut into chunks. Peel oranges and divide into segments. Cut melon into cubes.

Place prepared fruits on wooden skewers, alternating variety. Refrigerate until ready to serve. Serve with dipping sauce and granola if desired.

Dips and Spreads

Dips and spreads should be nutritious, interesting and flavorful. The advantage of dips and spreads is that they can be made ahead of time and can serve large numbers. Serve them in attractive dishes or in hollowed out containers made of pumpkins, melons, round bread loaves or squash shells. Surround your dips or spreads with one or several of the following: bread slices, breadsticks, pita, toast, crackers, chips, pretzels, fresh fruits, cooked meat cubes, marinated vegetables, or fresh vegetables that have been sliced or cut into sticks.

Creamy Avocado Veggie Dip

Makes 2 ½ cups

Create a gorgeous array of colorful vegetables to serve beside this delicious dip. It also goes well with tortilla chips or crisp bagel chips.

1 ½ tbs. red wine vinegar (prefer balsamic)
1 ½ tbs. lemon juice
½ cup olive oil
1 tbs. Dijon mustard
¼ cup minced green onions
1 tsp. salt
½ tsp. sugar
freshly ground pepper to taste
8 oz. cream cheese, softened
2 cloves garlic, minced
1 large ripe avocado, pit removed
2 tbs. chopped fresh parsley

With a food processor or blender, combine vinegar, lemon juice, olive oil, mustard, 2 tbs. of the green onions, salt, sugar and pepper. Process until smooth. Remove mixture and set aside. Place cream cheese, garlic and avocado in food processor workbowl and process until smooth and creamy. Very slowly drip vinegar mixture into cream cheese mixture while machine is running. Blend or process until smooth. Transfer to a serving bowl and stir in remaining 2 tbs. green onions and parsley for color and texture.

Bagna Cauda

Say BON yuh COW duh. This is a creamy variation of a traditional Italian garlic dip that goes well with vegetables or bread rounds for dipping.

¼ cup butter
6-8 anchovy fillets, finely chopped
4 cloves garlic, minced
2 cups heavy cream
1 tbs. cornstarch
2 tbs. water

Melt butter in a saucepan and add chopped anchovies and garlic. Sauté for a few minutes. Add cream and heat to almost a boil. Mix cornstarch with water and add to cream mixture, stirring until thickened. Remove from heat and serve immediately.

Guacamole

Save the avocado pit and imbed it in the center of the mixture until ready to serve — this will help to keep the dip from becoming dark. Serve with tortilla chips, corn chips, vegetables or plain tortillas.

4 large ripe avocados, peeled and pitted
juice of 2 limes
½ cup shredded cheddar cheese
½ cup chopped Bermuda onion
dash salt
1 jalapeño pepper, chopped, optional
1 tbs. chopped fresh cilantro
1-2 tomatoes, seeded and chopped
chopped fresh cilantro for garnish

With a food processor or blender, blend 3 of the avocados until smooth. Add juice, cheese, onion, salt, jalapeño and 1 tbs. cilantro. Taste and adjust seasonings. Chop remaining avocado. Stir in chopped tomatoes and remaining chopped avocado, which will add a chunky texture to mixture. Sprinkle with cilantro.

Clam Dip

Makes 2 cups

Because of the uncomplicated recipe, the clam flavor can be fully appreciated. This one is quick and simple. Serve with chips, crackers or bread rounds.

1 can (6 oz.) minced clams
8 oz. cream cheese, softened
1 tbs. Worcestershire sauce
1 tsp. lemon juice

Drain clams and reserve juice. Mix together clams, cream cheese, Worcestershire sauce and lemon juice. Taste and add more lemon juice if desired. If you wish a thinner dip, add a small amount of clam juice until desired consistency is reached.

Crab Fondue

Makes 3 cups

This delicious creamy dip is best served with French bread rounds or plain crackers. Serve warm in a chafing dish.

2 tbs. butter
½ cup chopped mushrooms
¼ cup cream sherry
salt and pepper to taste
dash cayenne pepper
enough paprika to color
3 egg yolks
1 cup cream
1 lb. crabmeat

Melt butter in a skillet and sauté mushrooms until tender. Add sherry, salt, pepper, cayenne and paprika and stir to combine. Stir in egg yolks and cream and stir over medium heat until mixture thickens. Stir in crabmeat and serve warm.

Olive Spread

Otherwise known as "tapenade." This is a perfect dish to take to a party. Cut little baguettes into small rounds or serve with freshly made breadsticks.

2 cans (6 oz. each) pitted black olives
3 tbs. capers
1/2 cup minced onion
1 tsp. minced garlic
2 tbs. chopped fresh parsley
1/4 cup grated Parmesan cheese
2 tbs. olive oil
2 tbs. vinegar (prefer balsamic)
1/2 tsp. salt
1/2 tsp. pepper
1/4 cup chopped red bell pepper

With a food processor or blender, just barely chop olives; remove and set aside. Place remaining ingredients in processor, except 2 tbs. of the red bell pepper. Chop into a fine blend; stir mixture into olives. Taste and adjust seasonings. Sprinkle remaining chopped red pepper on top for garnish.

Avocado Olive Spread

This spread can be served hot, spread on toasted bread rounds with Swiss cheese melted on top, or cold, served with raw vegetables.

12 oz. cream cheese, softened
1 ripe avocado (prefer Hass variety)
1 tsp. lemon juice
1 cup finely chopped black olives
1 tbs. chopped fresh parsley
1/3 cup chopped tomatoes
1/4 cup finely chopped celery

With a food processor or mixer, blend cream cheese until smooth. Peel avocado, remove pit and mash with lemon juice. Add to cream cheese and puree until smooth. Add remaining ingredients and barely mix to combine. Chill until ready to use.

Three Pepper Spread

A quick, colorful, hot dip goes well with crackers, pita crisps or bagel chips.

8 oz. cream cheese, softened
1/2 cup shredded Parmesan cheese
1 small onion, diced
1 tbs. chopped fresh basil
1 red bell pepper
1 green bell pepper
1 yellow bell pepper

With a food processor or blender, process cream cheese and Parmesan until fluffy. Add onion and basil and mix to combine. Seed and cut peppers into chunks. Add to cream cheese mixture and process until well combined. Place in a shallow baking dish and bake in a 350° oven for 15 minutes.

Chutney and Cheese Spread

Chutney creates a spicy, savory taste sensation. Curry is an acquired taste, so be conservative unless you know your guests appreciate it. Serve with crisp crackers.

8 oz. cream cheese, softened
4 oz. cheddar cheese, shredded
2 tbs. brandy
1 tsp. curry powder, or to taste
1 jar (8 oz.) mango chutney
1/2 cup chopped toasted almonds
2 chopped green onions

With a food processor or mixer, beat cream cheese, cheddar cheese, brandy and curry until light and fluffy. Taste and adjust seasonings. Pack into a pretty serving dish and cover with chutney. Chill until ready to serve. Sprinkle with chopped almonds and green onions.

Gelatin Cheese Spread

Serve this in the center of a large platter surrounded by fresh vegetables and/or crackers.

6 oz. cheese crackers or Ritz crackers, crushed
1 pkg. (¼ oz.) unflavored gelatin
¼ cup cold water
2 cups sour cream
1 pkg. (6 oz.) Italian dry salad dressing mix
¼ cup crumbled blue cheese
2 cups small curd cottage cheese

Butter a 9-inch springform pan. Press cracker crumbs in bottom and set aside. Mix gelatin with cold water and warm gently in a small saucepan until dissolved. Blend remaining ingredients in a food processor or blender until smooth and add dissolved gelatin. Pour into prepared springform pan, cover and chill for several hours to set. To serve, invert on a platter and remove pan sides and bottom.

Crab and Avocado Molded Spread

This is a delicious chilled dish that can be molded for a beautiful presentation. If feeling extravagant, use extra crabmeat to garnish center and edges. Serve with crackers or crispy toast rounds.

1 cup water
2 pkg. (¼ oz. each) unflavored gelatin
4 ripe avocados
1 cup mayonnaise
1 cup sour cream
2-3 tbs. finely minced onion
¼ cup lemon juice
1 tsp. salt
dash cayenne pepper
½ tsp. Dijon mustard
18 oz. crabmeat
additional crabmeat for garnish, optional

Mix water and gelatin together, stirring to dissolve. Gently bring to a boil and set aside to cool. Mash avocados and stir into cooled gelatin with remaining ingredients, except crabmeat. Gently fold in crabmeat and pour mixture into an oiled 4-cup mold. Cover and refrigerate for 8 hours. Unmold and garnish as desired.

Crunchy Ham and Cheese Ball

Makes 3 ½ cups

Ham dominates the flavor of this cheese ball instead of cheddar cheese. Always wait until the last hour before rolling cheese balls in nuts, so the nuts will maintain their crunchy quality and full flavor. Serve with an assortment of crackers.

8 oz. cream cheese, softened
¼ cup mayonnaise
1 green onion, finely diced
2 tbs. chopped fresh parsley
¼ tsp. dry mustard
¼ tsp. Tabasco Sauce
2 cups grated cooked ham
1 cup chopped toasted walnuts

With a food processor or mixer, mix all ingredients together, except nuts. Form into a ball and chill until ready to serve. Just before serving, roll in nuts.

Crab Paté

Servings: 12

This fresh-tasting, elegant appetizer should be served with plain crackers or bread rounds so the delicate flavor of the crab can be fully appreciated.

3 hard-cooked egg yolks
½ cup butter
½ cup mayonnaise
1 clove garlic, minced
1 tsp. Dijon mustard
dash horseradish sauce
¼ cup minced green onion
¼ cup minced fresh parsley
12 oz. fresh crabmeat
2 tbs. lemon juice
salt and white pepper to taste

With a food processor or blender, combine egg yolks, butter, mayonnaise, garlic, mustard, horseradish, green onion and parsley and process until smooth. Place mixture in a bowl and add crabmeat, lemon juice, salt and white pepper. Stir gently to combine. Taste and adjust seasonings. Place in a covered container and refrigerate until ready to serve.

Crabmeat Spread

Makes 2 cups

This quick and elegant dish goes well with special crackers, crusty bread rounds or melba toast. If desired, save a few whole crab legs for garnish.

8 oz. cream cheese, softened
2 green onions, finely chopped
2 tbs. lemon juice
1/4 tsp. paprika
1/4 tsp. white pepper
1/8 tsp. cayenne pepper
1/4 tsp. salt
12 oz. crabmeat

Place all ingredients, except crabmeat, in a food processor workbowl or blender container and process until smooth. Transfer mixture to a serving bowl and stir in crabmeat. Chill until ready to serve.

Artichoke Parmesan Dip

Makes 3 1/2 cups

This is a quick, simple and rich recipe that people are crazy about. Serve with French bread rounds, crackers or buttered, toasted pita bread wedges.

1 cup canned marinated artichoke hearts, cut into small pieces
1 cup grated Parmesan cheese
1 cup mayonnaise
1/2 cup diced green chiles
chopped red bell pepper or diced green chiles for garnish

Heat oven to 350°. Drain artichokes. Mix artichoke hearts with cheese, mayonnaise and green chiles. Pour into a small ovenproof dish and bake for 20 minutes. Serve hot garnished with red pepper.

Simple Liver Paté

A traditional way to serve paté is accompanied with cocktail onions, gherkins and of course, crusty French bread.

1 lb. bacon
1 ½ cups chopped onions
1 lb. calf's liver, cut into 1-inch cubes
1 lb. chicken livers, cut in half
2 tsp. salt, or to taste
1 tsp. pepper
3 egg yolks
2 eggs
¼ cup red wine (prefer Madeira)
¾ tsp. chervil
½ tsp. tarragon
½ tsp. nutmeg
¼ tsp. allspice

Heat oven to 375°. Line a loaf pan or a 7-inch soufflé mold with bacon slices, reserving 6 slices for cooking. Dice 6 reserved bacon slices and fry in a skillet until brown. Add onions and sauté until onions are slightly browned. Add calf's liver and chicken livers with 1 tsp. of the salt and ½ tsp. of the pepper and sauté until no longer pink.

With a food processor or blender, puree entire mixture, a little at a time, until smooth. Add egg yolks, eggs, red wine, spices, and remaining salt and pepper. Process until combined. Taste and adjust seasonings. Pour mixture into bacon-lined baking dish and cover with foil. Place pan in a water bath: set it in a larger baking pan and add water halfway up sides of filled pan. Bake for 2 hours. Remove from oven, pour off any excess oil and allow to cool. Place a weight, like a brick or heavy pottery, on top of paté and refrigerate for at least 8 hours before serving.

Cherry Almond Cheese Spread

Servings: 12

This easy, simple appetizer spread uses cherries flavored with liqueur. If you prefer a nonalcoholic spread, eliminate the liqueur-soaking step. Add cherry, almond or orange extract to the cream cheese mixture to taste.

1 cup dark cherries, pitted
½ cup amaretto or Grand Marnier liqueur
16 oz. cream cheese, softened
1 tbs. sugar, or more to taste
1 cup chopped toasted almonds
water crackers

In a bowl, cover cherries with liqueur and refrigerate for 24 hours; drain. With a mixer, beat cream cheese until light and fluffy; add sugar, soaked cherries and almonds, if desired (almonds can also be added later). Taste and adjust sweetness. Chill mixture until firm and form into a ball. If desired, roll ball in almonds until covered. Serve with crackers.

Tapas Fantásticas

Appetizers with a Spanish Flair

Bob and Coleen Simmons

What are Tapas?

Tapas are the small flavorful dishes that are a very important part of social and gastronomic life in Spain. The Spanish love to talk, eat and drink, and tapas bars and restaurants provide a convenient place to do all three. The tapas tradition, which has been developed and refined over the last hundred years, started with innkeepers providing a small nibble to accompany a glass of wine. The food was often full-flavored and salty, perhaps almonds, olives, a piece of cheese or a thin slice of ham, characteristics probably intended to stimulate the desire for another glass of wine. Tapa in Spanish means cover, and the nibble was often served on a small plate that was carried to the customer balanced on top of the wineglass.

Today, tapas are more popular than ever and are served all over Spain. Many tapas bars acquire a reputation and following for their own unique specialties, and part of the evening fun is to stop at several different places for a small plate or two, and another glass of wine before going on to dinner. Tapas bars are as varied as their clientele. Some are very small, with no seating and a limited tapas selection. A tortilla is usually available and probably a house special or two. Some of the more elaborate tapas establishments are found in Seville and Madrid where a restaurant or bar may have as many as 40 different tapas available. The traditional beverage to serve with tapas is dry sherry, but young fruity red or white wines, beer, sangria or even cocktails complement a broad range of tapas.

This enjoyable custom has now spread around the globe, including bars and restaurants in U.S cities. Tapas are used to fill the long gaps between mealtimes in Spain, but they can easily be eaten as a delicious alternative to dinner.

Preparing Tapas

Spanish cuisine is flavorful and refined, but not hot with peppers. Moorish foods and spices, as well as tomatoes, potatoes and peppers from the New World have all been assimilated to make its appetizing dishes. The ingredients for making most of these tapas are easily found in U.S. supermarkets, and recommended substitutes for some of the harder-to-find Spanish ingredients can be found in *The Tapas Pantry*, page 79.

Tapas are easy on the cook and can readily be made at home. Many tapas are better cooked a day in advance to be served at room temperature, or reheated just before your guests arrive. Tapas are party food! Serve a couple of tapas with drinks for a cocktail party, or as appetizers before a barbecue. Or serve several different tapas and make them the whole meal. Enjoy your own party! Make a tapa or two and pick up the rest at the market.

The Tapas Pantry

Simple tapas can be assembled at a moment's notice from ingredients often found in the refrigerator, or on the pantry shelf. In the refrigerator look for olives, cubes of cheese, cubes or slices of ham, caper berries, pickles, ready-to-eat sausage such as pepperoni, salami, summer sausage, or hard boiled eggs. On the pantry shelf there may be roasted almonds, hazelnuts, cashews, roasted red peppers, tins of tuna, sardines, anchovies, smoked clams, and smoked oysters.

All good cooking starts with high quality ingredients. The information below will help you select ingredients that will produce great tapas.

Almonds: Almonds, simply roasted and lightly salted, make a delicious snack and are frequently served as a tapa. They are also ground and used as a thickener for sauces or as an important ingredient in desserts. Roasting your own almonds will produce almonds with a better, fresher taste than buying them already roasted.

To blanch almonds, place in a bowl, cover with boiling water for 5 minutes, drain, then slip the skins off. Raw almond slices, slivers and whole almonds should be toasted to bring out their nutty flavor before using in recipes. Place nuts on a cookie sheet in a 325° oven, and bake until lightly browned, shaking the pan often. They require attention because once the nuts start to brown, they burn quickly. Remove them from oven when they begin to release a wonderful toasty aroma.

Toasted hazelnuts are also eaten as tapas. They are popular in cooking and desserts.

Anchovies: Many people claim that they don't like anchovies. This may be the result of their experience with the sometimes salty, fishy, dried-out bits found on pizza. Anchovies are available preserved in salt, oil-packed in jars and tins, and as a paste. When finely chopped, anchovies seem to disappear when mixed into a salad dressing or heated in a sauce, and add complexity and flavor to a dish without tasting particularly fishy.

To prepare anchovies preserved in salt, rinse the surface salt from the anchovy under running water. Pull off the head, and with a sharp knife, make a shallow cut down the backbone. Remove one fillet from the bone, and then pull the bone from the other fillet. Rinse the fillets again under running water and place in a shallow bowl in one layer. Cover with milk or water and allow to marinate for one hour. Drain, pat dry with paper towels, and use as you would anchovies packed in oil.

Anchovies in oil come both in jars and the familiar 2-ounce tin. Those in jars are usually higher quality, so seek them out. Briefly rinsing oil-packed anchovies under cool running water removes some of the saltiness and gives the anchovies a fresher taste.

Anchovy paste packaged in a tube is very easy to use. A small amount in a recipe adds saltiness and boosts other flavors.

Capers: Capers are the flower bud of a hardy plant that grows all around the Mediterranean. They range from petite pea-size to ones that are as large as the tip of a little finger. Usually found packed in vinegar, capers should be well drained and rinsed in cool water before using. Capers are also preserved in salt, and these should be rinsed and soaked in cool water for a few minutes to reconstitute them. Caperberries are the fruit that develops after the bud flowers. They are about the size of a small olive and have a long stem, and are also packed in vinegar. They are found in jars and on some supermarket olive bars. Skewer them on a bandiera or use them in salads. They are also currently a popular replacement for the olive in a martini.

Cheese: Spain produces many wonderful cheeses. Most are partly or wholly made from sheep's or goat's milk. Three cheeses often found in the U.S. are *manchego, cabrales* and *mahon*. Traditional manchego is made from sheep's milk. It can be identified by the basket-weave pattern on the side of the cheese wheel. Young manchego is mild and creamy, aged manchego has a firmer texture and a more assertive flavor. Both are delicious for eating and cooking. Older manchegos are often grated and added to dishes as one would Italian Parmesan. Aged manchego is often thinly sliced and served with membrillo, or quince paste, both as a tapa, and at the end of a meal with the last of a glass of red wine. A young Italian pecorino Romana can be substituted for manchego.

Cabrales is a creamy blue sheep's milk cheese that is wrapped in chestnut leaves before aging. It is creamier than Roquefort and milder than Gorgonzola, both of which can be substituted. A mahon is similar to a Dutch Gouda, which makes a wonderful substitute for it. Goat cheeses are produced throughout Spain, but they are not often found in the U.S. Goat cheese is at its best when young and creamy. Use domestic or imported French goat cheese as a substitute.

Garlic: The Romans brought garlic to all the Mediterranean countries they conquered, and Spain has loved it ever since. It is used raw, rubbed over toasted bread slices, and as an important ingredient in many cooked sauces and dishes. Fresh garlic is preferred over dried powders and salts. Buy firm, plump bulbs and store them in a cool, dark place. Cut fresh cloves in half lengthwise, and if there is a green shoot running from root to stem, remove it before slicing or mincing because it tends to be very bitter. Mincing or finely chopping garlic releases more pungent and assertive flavors than thinly slicing the cloves. Roasting whole heads of garlic produces a mellow sweet garlic paste that pairs wonderfully with potatoes, tomatoes or eggplant, or it can simply be spread on toast.

Ham: Ham is frequently used in tapas. The most flavorful is the Spanish jamon Serrano, which is salted and cured in a manner similar to Italian prosciutto. It is very thinly sliced with the grain and served on a slice of toasted bread or wrapped around a ripe fig. Spanish Serrano ham is becoming more available in the U.S., but at a very high price. More readily available imported or domestic prosciutto can be substituted. Other cooked hams such as jamon York are often used. Substitute Black Forest ham or Virginia baked ham.

Olive Oil: Many tapas depend on a wonderful, fruity, full-flavored olive oil. Buy imported oil from Spain that is labeled "extra virgin." Italian and California extra virgin oils can be substituted. Buy the best oil you can afford. It will make a noticeable difference in the taste of your tapas. Store tightly covered in a cool, dark place.

Olives: Spain is the world's largest producer of green olives, both stuffed and unpitted. Any olive, brine-cured or oil-cured makes a wonderful tapa. Spanish black olives are seen less frequently than the green in U.S. markets, but the more readily available Greek kalamata or French niçoise olives are delicious as well. If your supermarket or deli has an olive bar, buy an assortment. Warming olives briefly in a little olive oil with spices brings out the best olive flavor.

Onions: The large yellow Spanish onions have a high sugar content and turn sweet and mellow when slowly cooked in a little olive oil. They lend flavor interest to a wide variety of tapas. Shallots which are milder than onions are used in some recipes, as are green onions which can be eaten raw or only slightly cooked.

Paprika and Chile Powder: Chile pepper cultivation began in Spain soon after Columbus' voyages. Two pepper varieties were developed to be allowed to fully ripen and then be dried and ground into paprika. The milder variety adds deep color and earthy flavors but is not hot. It makes an attractive garnish when it is sprinkled over deviled eggs, potato salad or other less colorful dishes. It is also used in large quantities in sauces and meat dishes. The hotter variety is less commonly found in the U.S. It is spicy, but still milder than hot Hungarian paprika or Indian chile powder. A good substitute is mild New Mexico chile powder that also can be used to replace mild paprika if you like spicier food. Do not use prepared chili powder as it contains cumin, garlic and sometimes salt in addition to chile.

Peppers, Bell: Spanish food is robust and full-flavored, but not nearly as chile-laden as Mexican or Southwestern food. Extensive use is made of green, yellow and particularly red peppers, which are roasted, peeled and marinated in a little olive oil and vinegar. Pimiento peppers are large, heart-shaped, thick-walled red peppers with a wonderful sweet flavor. This pepper is commonly used for stuffing green olives. Pimientos are found fresh in some specialty markets or farmers' markets, but more often are found processed in cans or jars.

Roasting your own peppers is easy. Line a shallow baking pan with foil for easy cleanup and place a small rack on the foil. Preheat broiler. Wash and dry peppers and place on rack. Broil about 8 inches from heat source, turning peppers as they roast so all sides are slightly blackened. Remove peppers from broiler, place in a bowl and cover with foil, or wrap each pepper in foil. Allow to steam for 10 or 15 minutes. Do not rinse under cold water. After steaming, the pepper skins slip off easily. Remove seeds and core. Store in an airtight container in the refrigerator until ready to use.

Pine Nuts: Pine nuts are delicious when lightly toasted. They can be eaten by themselves or added to finished dishes, sprinkled over salads or incorporated into desserts. To toast pine nuts, place on a cooking sheet in a 325° oven and bake until lightly browned, shaking the pan often. Watch carefully because they burn easily. Pine nuts can also be toasted in a dry nonstick skillet over low heat. Shake pan often until the pine nuts are golden brown.

Saffron: Known as the world's most expensive spice, saffron is added to many Spanish dishes, particularly those containing rice or chicken. Avoid inexpensive saffron powders, and buy saffron threads. Crush the threads just before using. A little goes a long way to give a dish both a lovely golden color and a distinctive taste. Using too much saffron will give foods a medicinal taste. When used judiciously, there should be just enough to taste. Sprinkle it over a little hot chicken broth and let it soak for a few minutes before adding to the dish. It can also be added directly to a dish that contains some liquid.

Salt Cod: The Spanish developed a taste for *bacalao*, as they call salt cod, long before refrigeration was available. Cod, salted and dried in the cold dry climate of the North Atlantic and then imported, keeps well for months, even in a warm climate. Salt cod must be soaked for a day in several changes of water to leach out the salt. It is then boiled to soften before being used in a recipe. Salt cod pairs especially well with potatoes.

The most manageable way to buy salt cod is in 1-pound wooden boxes. The fish has already been boned and skinned, and the pieces are fairly uniform in thickness. If buying a whole unpackaged piece, choose a thicker one. The thin end pieces tend to resist softening when soaked.

Sausage: Spain has a wonderful variety of cured pork sausages. Chorizo, an air-dried sausage, is made of pork, cumin, garlic and powdered chiles. It can be found at Spanish markets and in some meat shops. It is sold both when young and moist, and aged and drier. Slice it and eat it raw or incorporate it into cooked dishes. Do not substitute Mexican chorizo, which is an altogether different product that must be removed from the casing and cooked before using. If chorizo is not available, substitute Italian pepperoni or soppressa, or Portuguese linguica. We have provided a recipe for a homemade chorizo that, while not at all authentic, has some of the flavor and character of the real thing.

Wine Vinegar: A few drops of vinegar provide a flavor boost and balance to many dishes. Your pantry should include sherry wine vinegar, an aged red wine vinegar and a good white wine vinegar. Spain produces delicious mellow sherry wine vinegars with a hint of sweetness. Seek out an aged one from Jerez. Use it in salad dressings, in sauces and to brighten up other dishes. Or sprinkle a few drops over roasted asparagus or a grilled steak. Store vinegar in a cool, dark place with your olive oils.

Parties and Menus

Tapas are party foods! A variety of delicious and attractive dishes can be assembled to serve your friends. To make the party fun for the cook, select one or two dishes that can be made a day or two ahead, and a couple to cook on the day of the party. Then fill in with nuts, olives, cheese and bread. The tapa party allows you to cater to your guests' tastes by serving a variety of vegetable and seafood dishes, as well as more hearty fare. Spanish-style desserts are simple. In addition to the classic Spanish flan, fruit banderillas, sliced fruit, ice cream, an orange or lemon cake, or cookies with coffee and a little brandy or sweet sherry all make a delicious finale.

Drinks, too, are easy. Chilled Spanish dry sherry, white and red wine, beer, pitchers of Sangria, or margaritas are all delicious with tapas. Offer a selection of beverages or serve your friends' favorite drinks.

Tapas can be served as predinner appetizers or as a complete meal. As the number of guests increases, add another dish or two. If you are running short of time, stop at the deli or market and pick up some sliced meats, marinated vegetables or salad greens to augment the menu. Buy a roasted chicken, carve it and serve with *Parsley Sauce.* Pick up some cooked shrimp and serve with *Romesco* or *Seafood Cocktail Sauce.*

Tapa parties should be colorful! Use bright tablecloths and attractive serving platters. Arrange tapas and drinks on separate tables for easier circulation. Food can be served buffet-style on one table, or placed on several smaller tables. Provide small bread or salad plates, forks and napkins for your guests. For easy clean-up, have a stack of small paper plates, napkins, toothpicks and plastic forks at each food area. Place several waste receptacles at strategic locations. Suggest that your guests take one or two tapas at a time and come back to try another dish. If tapas are being served as the main meal, have seating for everyone and use dinner plates. Set up a warming tray for the dishes that need to be served warm or reheat for a few seconds in the microwave and pass the hot food.

Traditional tapas parties are similar to a stand-up cocktail party, but make your guests comfortable by providing some seating and places to put down glasses and plates. For a small party of 4 to 8 people, seat them around the dining table and serve tapas buffet-style.

In using the following menus, don't hesitate to reduce the number of dishes, substitute other recipes or select favorite foods to fit your group. Inviting friends in to share good food, drink and conversation is one of life's great pleasures.

Tapas Menu for 6

Nibbles
almonds
olives
sliced cured sausage

Tapas
Wine and Garlic Chicken Nuggets, page 142
Marinated Mushrooms, page 113
Marinated Artichokes, page 106
Deviled Eggs, page 100
Oven-Roasted Baby Back Ribs, page 151
Warm Potato and Leek Salad, page 118

Dessert
fresh fruit platter
cookies

Drinks
wine, beer, sangria

Party Plan
One day ahead: Prepare *Wine and Garlic Chicken Nuggets, Marinated Mushrooms* and *Marinated Artichokes*. Refrigerate.

Party day: Early in day prepare *Deviled Eggs, Oven-Roasted Baby Back Ribs* and refrigerate. Remove mushrooms, artichokes and eggs from refrigerator about 1 hour before serving. Make *Warm Potato and Leek Salad*. Reheat *Wine and Garlic Chicken Nuggets* and sauce, and bake *Oven-Roasted Baby Back Ribs* just before serving.

Tapas Menu for 6

Nibbles
almonds
olives
banderillas: ham, cheese and sweet pickle chunks; small cooked shrimp, cherry tomato, roasted pepper square; tuna chunk, cherry tomato, caper berry

Tapas
Escabeche, page 129
Meatballs in Almond Sherry Sauce, page 150
Peppers with Tomato and Potato Stuffing, page 115
Sherried Chicken Wings, page 143
Garbanzo Bean Salad, page 107

Dessert
sorbet and cookies

Drinks
wine, sangria, beer

Party Plan
One to two days ahead: Make *Escabeche, Meatballs with Almond Sherry Sauce* and stuffed peppers. Start marinating *Sherried Chicken Wings*. Refrigerate.

Party day: Make *Garbanzo Bean Salad*. Bake *Sherried Chicken Wings* and remove *Escabeche* from refrigerator about 1 hour before your guests arrive. Assemble banderillas. Reheat meatballs and sauce.

Tapas Menu for 6

Nibbles
almonds
olives
cubes of manchego cheese

Tapas
Beef and Potato or *Mushroom Empanadas*, pages 146 or 112
cooked shrimp with *Romesco* or *Seafood Cocktail Sauce*, pages 157 or 158
Bagna Cauda, page 68
Classic Tortilla Espanola, page 101

Dessert
chilled melon slices

Drinks
Wine, beer, sangria

Party Plan
One to two days ahead: Bake and refrigerate empanadas and *Romesco* or *Seafood Cocktail Sauce*.

Party day: Prepare vegetables for *Bagna Cauda* and refrigerate. Cook shrimp if necessary and refrigerate. Make *Classic Tortilla Espanola*. About 1 hour before party prepare *Bagna Cauda* mixture. Prepare melon slices and chill.

Tapas for 8

Nibbles
Oven-Roasted Almonds, page 92
Warm Marinated Olives, page 95

Tapas
Asparagus and Ham Rolls, page 107
Fava Bean Salad Cups, page 111
Chicken, Artichoke and Oven-Roasted Tomatoes, page 138
Scallops with Oranges and Black Olives, page 134
Mini-Stuffed Potatoes, page 116
Lentil and Duck Salad, page 144
Lamb Meatballs in Tomato Sauce, page 149
1 or 2 Spanish cheeses such as manchego and cabrales (blue)
baguette slices or crackers

Dessert
almond, lemon or orange cake and cream sherry for dessert

Drinks
wine, beer and sangria

Party Plan
One day ahead: Prepare *Lentil and Duck Salad, Lamb Meatballs* and *Warm Marinated Olives.* Make *Oven Roasted Tomatoes.* Refrigerate. Blanch and peel the fava beans and refrigerate.

Party day: Cook and assemble *Asparagus and Ham Rolls* and *Mini-Stuffed Potatoes* in the morning and refrigerate. Remember to remove the lentil salad and cheese from the refrigerator at least 1 hour before serving. *Chicken, Artichoke and Oven-Roasted Tomatoes* and *Scallops with Oranges and Black Olives* can be done just before your guests arrive. Reheat the meatballs and bake the potatoes just before serving. Warm the olives. Dress the fava beans and place in lettuce cups at the last minute.

Tapas Menu for 8 to 10

Nibbles
almonds
olives
smoked oysters

Tapas
Hot Garlic Shrimp, page 135
Marinated Cauliflower, page 105
Rainbow Peppers, page 114
Oven-Roasted Baby Potatoes with Garlic, page 117
Sherry-Glazed Eggplant, page 110
Pork Tenderloins with Prune and Olive Compote, page 147
Chorizo-Stuffed Mushroom Caps, page 148
Mini-Tortillas, page 102
Marinated Goat Cheese Rounds, page 97
French baguette slices

Dessert
cookies and cream sherry for dessert

Drinks
wines, beer, sangria

Party Plan
One to two days ahead: Make *Marinated Cauliflower, Rainbow Peppers* and *Sherry Glazed Eggplant* and *Prune Olive Compote* for the pork and refrigerate. *Mini-Tortillas* can also be baked ahead.

Party day: Prepare *Chorizo-Stuffed Mushrooms* a few hours ahead but bake the mushrooms and *Roasted Baby Potatoes with Garlic* at the last minute and serve warm. *Marinated Goat Cheese Rounds* can be made 1 to 2 hours ahead. Time *Pork Tenderloins* and *Hot Garlic Shrimp,* and warm the *Mini-Tortillas* so that they will be done just before your guests arrive.

About Tapas Nibbles

The tapas tradition is based on providing a small mouthful of flavorful food to accompany a glass of wine or beer. To complement the wine and perhaps sell more, the food morsels are often salty or piquant. Small dishes of olives and nuts or popcorn are just as welcome as more elaborate appetizers. Supermarkets and delis abound with prepackaged and prepared ingredients that can be arranged attractively on colorful plates, skewered on toothpicks or poured into bowls. The refrigerator often yields cheese, ham, roast meat, pickles and olives for banderillas or canapés. Add some crackers or rounds of toasted bread spread with a little soft cheese and top with a strip of roasted pepper or dollop of olive paste.

We've included some favorite combinations and suggestions for banderillas and canapés. Try the easy *Oven-Roasted Almonds*. They have a delicious toasted flavor and can be done ahead, put in an airtight jar and kept for a week. A little high-quality olive oil and gentle heating make a world of difference to the flavor and taste of *Warm Marinated Olives*. Serve easy and delicious tapas for your next gathering.

Tapas Canapés

Canapés and tostas are the Spanish equivalent of Italian crostini and bruschetta. Thin slices of baguette are toasted, sometimes rubbed with garlic, and topped with a flavorful ingredient or two. Assemble them just before serving so the toasts stay crisp. Serve warm or at room temperature.

Leftover bread can be sliced, tightly wrapped and stored in the freezer. When you want to serve, just toast the slices without defrosting.

When you want to make canapés, toast the slices in a 275° or 300° oven until crisp and lightly browned. Spread toast with cream or goat cheese, and top with colorful and tasty roasted red or yellow peppers or tapenade. Green or black olive paste or tapenade can be found at an Italian deli or the specialty food section of your supermarket.

See the next page for ideas for delicious canapé toppings.

Quick and Easy Canapé Toppings

- Goat or cream cheese topped with a little tapenade, a strip of pimiento or roasted red pepper and parsley. Serve at room temperature.

- Goat or cream cheese under a thin slice of ham, topped with 1 or 2 thin slices of fresh fig. Sprinkle figs with a little lime juice and generous grinds of black pepper. Serve at room temperature.

- Prepare *Rainbow Peppers*, page 114, with a pinch of dried oregano, salt and pepper. Arrange a few strips over a thin layer of goat cheese. Sprinkle with parsley or cilantro. Serve at room temperature.

- Layer toast with 1 or 2 small thin slices grilled eggplant and a few ribbons of fresh basil leaves and top with 2 or 3 *Rainbow Peppers*, page 114. Sprinkle with grated manchego or Parmesan cheese and heat under a broiler or in a hot oven until cheese melts. Serve warm.

- Cut thin slices of ham the same size as toasts. Place ham on the toast and top with 1 or 2 small cooked asparagus spears and a thin slice of manchego or fontina cheese. Heat under a broiler or in a hot oven until cheese melts. Serve warm.

- Cut thin slices of ham to the same size as toasts. Place ham on the toast, spread with a thin layer of Dijon mustard. Top with 1 or 2 small cooked asparagus spears and a thin slice of manchego or fontina cheese. Heat under broiler or in a hot oven until cheese melts. Serve warm.

- Combine cubes of leftover roast pork or beef in food processor bowl with a few pimiento stuffed olives or capers, prepared mustard and mayonnaise. Pulse until meat is coarsely chopped and mixture holds together. Spread on toast and garnish with 1 to 2 stuffed olive slices or 1 to 2 capers. Serve at room temperature.

- Spread toasts with a thin layer of *Aioli*, page 155, and top with a thin tomato slice and 2 or 3 small cooked shrimp. Season with salt and pepper. Garnish with a few ribbons of fresh basil leaves. Serve at room temperature.

- Spread toasts with a thin layer of *Aioli*, page 155, and top with thin slices of cooked, marinated artichoke hearts and 1 or 2 strips of roasted red pepper. Sprinkle tops with grated manchego or Parmesan cheese. Heat in a hot oven until just warm.

Oven-Roasted Almonds

Almonds are an essential ingredient of the tapas table. Popcorn salt is more finely ground than table salt, and adheres better to the nuts. This recipe doubles or triples easily.

1 cup raw, unblanched whole almonds
1 tsp. full-flavored olive oil
popcorn salt or *Seasoned Salt*

Heat oven to 275°. Place nuts in a small bowl, add olive oil and stir to coat almonds evenly. Spread almonds in a single layer in a shallow baking pan. Roast for 25 to 30 minutes, until almonds are fragrant and a deeper shade of brown, but not burned. Sprinkle with salt. Turn off oven and cool almonds with oven door ajar for 5 to 10 minutes. Almonds will crisp as they cool. If not used immediately, store in an airtight container.

Seasoned Salt

Makes about ¼ cup

Sprinkle a little of this zesty salt mixture over almonds, popcorn or eggs. If available, substitute Spanish smoked paprika for the chile powder.

2 tbs. kosher salt
1 tbs. New Mexico mild chile powder
1 tbs. ground cumin
1 tsp. hot dry mustard powder
1 tsp. ground coriander
¼ tsp. cayenne pepper, optional

Blend mixture in a spice grinder or pulverize with a mortar and pestle until very finely ground. Store in a small spice shaker or airtight jar.

Banderillas

Banderillas are several compatible foods served on a cocktail pick or tooth-pick. The name comes from the decorated barbed sticks used by banderilleros in the bullfight to anger the bull before the matador comes in for the kill. Banderillas typically have streamers on the end, so using toothpicks with col-ored frills adds a nice touch. The custom is to pull off all the morsels of food at one time and eat them all together.

Banderillas can be quickly assembled from items on the pantry shelf or in your refrigerator. Here are some suggested combinations:

- chunks of ham, cheese and sweet pickle
- cherry tomato, small cooked shrimp, caper berry without stem
- small quail egg, rolled anchovy fillet, cherry tomato
- cooked pork or beef chunk, stuffed green olive, marinated mushroom
- pickled herring, cube of cooked potato, cocktail onion or green onion
- stuffed green olive, cooked sausage slice, cube of cooked potato
- smoked oyster or mussel, piece of roasted red pepper, cherry tomato
- small piece of sardine, cheese, dill pickle slice
- chunk of solid pack tuna, quail egg half, piece of roasted red pepper
- pitted black olive, cheese, piece of roasted red pepper
- marinated mushroom, sausage slice, cherry tomato
- cube of cooked chicken, marinated artichoke piece, cherry tomato
- cooked asparagus tip, ham, piece of roasted pepper
- cooked shrimp, asparagus tip, cherry tomato
- cooked carrot, pitted black olive, sausage piece
- chunk of solid pack tuna, caperberry, piece of roasted red pepper
- sausage slice, cheese cube, pepperoncini
- quarter of ripe fig, sausage slice or cube of ham
- cube of ripe melon wrapped in prosciutto

Sherried Chicken Liver Banderilla

Servings: 1

Sherry wine vinegar adds a piquant taste and attractive glaze to these chicken livers.

2-3 chicken livers
salt and pepper to taste
2 tsp. olive oil
1 tbs. sherry wine vinegar
1 caperberry
1 cherry tomato or fresh fig

Lightly flour chicken livers and season with salt and pepper. Heat oil in a skillet over high heat. Add chicken livers and sauté until lightly browned on all sides. Add sherry wine vinegar to pan and continue to cook for 1 to 2 minutes to glaze chicken livers. Cut cooked livers into bite-sized pieces and skewer on a toothpick with a caperberry and a cherry tomato or piece of fresh fig. Serve warm.

Fresh Fig and Prosciutto Banderillas

Servings: 8

The sweetness of the figs complements the rich, salty flavor of the ham. Warming the figs enhances their flavor.

4 fresh ripe figs
2 tsp. lime juice
freshly ground pepper to taste
8 thin strips prosciutto
1 tsp. olive oil
toothpicks

Cut figs into halves and sprinkle with lime juice and freshly ground pepper. Wrap each fig half with a thin strip of prosciutto. Heat oil in a small skillet over high heat. Sauté fig bundles for 1 minute, or until warmed through. Skewer with toothpicks and serve warm.

Fresh Pear and Anchovy Toasts

Choose a perfectly ripe pear and use good-quality oil-packed anchovies. Prepare toasts just before serving so they stay crisp and pears do not turn brown.

10-12 baguette slices, about ½-inch thick
2-3 tsp. full-flavored olive oil
1 clove garlic, peeled
1 ripe Comice, Bartlett, or Peckham pear
2 tbs. lemon juice
freshly ground black pepper
10-12 anchovy fillets

Heat oven to 350°. Place bread slices on a baking sheet. Brush each slice with a little olive oil. Bake for 10 to 12 minutes, or until lightly browned and crisp. Cut garlic in half and rub the top of each slice with the cut surface of garlic clove. Peel and core pear, quarter and cut each quarter into 5 thin slices. Pour lemon juice into a shallow pan, add pear slices and gently toss to coat. Grind fresh black pepper over pear slices. Rinse anchovies with water, drain and pat dry with paper towels. To assemble, place 1 or 2 pear slices on each garlic-rubbed toast and top with a strip of anchovy.

Warm Marinated Olives

Warmed marinated olives are very enticing. Combine 2 or 3 different kinds and colors of unpitted olives such as kalamata, manzanilla and other favorites. Imported black olives have more character than domestic ones.

1 cup assorted unpitted olives
2 tbs. full-flavored olive oil
¼ tsp. cumin seeds, lightly cracked
¼ tsp. anise seeds, lightly cracked
1 bay leaf
6-8 black peppercorns
2 cloves garlic, thinly sliced
8-10 caperberries, optional
3-4 drops red or green Tabasco Sauce
1 tsp. coarsely grated orange zest

Rinse olives under cold water and pat dry. With tip of a sharp knife cut 2 or 3 small slits through to the pit in each olive. In a small saucepan over low heat, heat olive oil, add cumin and anise seeds, bay leaf, peppercorns and garlic. Cook until garlic softens, about 3 to 4 minutes. Add caperberries, Tabasco, orange zest and olives. Stir briefly, remove from heat and cool to room temperature. Cover tightly and refrigerate for several hours or overnight. Just before serving, place olive mixture in a small saucepan over low heat and heat until warm to touch. Remove bay leaf, pour into a serving bowl and serve immediately.

Cheese and Egg Tapas

If you have some cheese and eggs in the refrigerator, it is easy to put together some savory tapas. A few cubes of cheese alone serve as tasty tapas, and with some ham or prosciutto slices, a few olives, and a glass of wine, your guests will be content. Don't hesitate to substitute one of your favorites in these recipes. Quesadillas can also be assembled quickly from other tapas ingredients. Deviled eggs are easily dressed up with capers or olives and make great party fare. The Spanish are known for their classic potato and egg tortilla. Included are recipes for a *Classic Tortilla Espanola* and *Mini-Tortillas*. They can be made ahead and reheated in the microwave for a breakfast or company brunch.

Apple, Walnut and Blue Cheese Balls   *Makes 14-16 pieces*

These can be made an hour or two ahead and refrigerated until ready to serve. Arrange the cheese balls on a few lettuce leaves or some watercress and accompany with crackers. Serve with red wine.

4 oz. blue cheese, crumbled, softened
1/3 cup chopped, toasted walnuts
1 Gala or Golden Delicious apple, about 7 oz.
2 tsp. lemon juice
1/2 cup finely chopped parsley
crackers

In a small bowl, combine blue cheese and walnuts. Set aside. Peel and core apple and grate coarsely in food processor or with a grater. Toss in a small bowl with lemon juice. Add walnuts and cheese mixture to apples and mix well. Form into 1-inch balls, roll in parsley and arrange on a serving platter.

Hot Goat Cheese Toasts

Small toasts are topped with a savory fresh goat cheese mixture and heated under the broiler. Serve immediately.

5 oz. fresh mild goat cheese
½ tsp. fresh thyme leaves
1 tbs. coarsely chopped capers
1 tbs. finely chopped sun-dried
   oil-packed tomatoes

⅛ tsp. mild New Mexico chile powder
generous grinds black pepper
1 day-old baguette, 2- to 3-inch
   diameter

Preheat broiler. Position oven rack about 6 inches below heat source. Line a cookie sheet with aluminum foil. In a small bowl, combine goat cheese, thyme, capers, sun-dried tomatoes, chile powder and pepper; mix well. Spread each toast round with about 2 teaspoons goat cheese mixture. Place under broiler and heat until cheese is hot and slightly puffy, about 2 minutes. Watch carefully as these brown quickly. Remove toasts and place on serving plate.

To make toasts: Heat oven to 300°. Slice baguette into ¼-inch slices. Place on cookie sheet and toast for about 15 minutes, or until lightly browned. Turn slices over and bake for another 10 minutes until crisp. Store in an airtight container until ready to use.

Marinated Goat Cheese Rounds

Makes 10 pieces

Tangy fresh goat cheese is complemented with olive oil, garlic and spice. Make this an hour or two ahead, cover and keep at cool room temperature until ready to serve. Serve with a small basket of baguette slices or crackers.

8 oz. fresh goat cheese log, cut into
   ½-inch rounds
5 slices *Rainbow Peppers*, page 114,
   cut in half, or roasted red pepper
   or pimiento pieces
10 black olives, pitted, quartered

3 tbs. full-flavored olive oil
pinch dried red pepper flakes
4 cloves garlic, thinly sliced
¼ tsp. ground cumin
2 tsp. lemon juice
generous grinds black pepper

Place goat cheese rounds in one layer on serving plate. Place a strip of pepper on each slice and scatter olive pieces over cheese. In small saucepan, over low heat, add olive oil, hot pepper flakes and garlic slices. Cook, stirring, for 2 to 3 minutes until garlic softens and is lightly browned. Add cumin and remove from heat. Cool to room temperature. Pour olive oil over cheese slices and sprinkle them with a little lemon juice. Grind some black pepper over each round and dust with paprika. Serve at room temperature.

Baked Olive Balls

Pimiento-stuffed olives or cubes of melted cheese form the centers for these savory tapas.

1 ¼ cups all-purpose flour
½ tsp. baking powder
¼ tsp. salt
1 tsp. paprika
½ tsp. ground cumin
pinch cayenne pepper, optional
¼ cup grated Parmesan or pecorino cheese
¼ cup olive oil
1 large egg
2-3 tbs. ice water
25 small Spanish olives stuffed with pimiento

Heat oven to 350°. Line a large baking sheet with parchment paper. Place flour, baking powder, salt, paprika, cumin, cayenne and Parmesan cheese in a food processor bowl. Pulse once or twice to mix ingredients. Add olive oil, egg and ice water. Process until dough comes together. Dry olives with paper towels.

Flatten a scant 2 teaspoons of the dough with your fingers into a 2-inch diameter disk. Place olive in middle and enclose in dough. Roll between your palms to seal the seams and make a uniformly smooth ball. Place on baking sheet. Bake for 20 minutes, or until lightly browned. Serve warm. If made ahead, these can be reheated in the oven for 5 minutes.

Variation

Fill balls with ½-inch cubes of sharp cheddar or hot pepper Jack cheese.

Grilled Swiss Chard and Cheese Packages   *Makes 10 pieces*

Blanched Swiss chard leaves are wrapped around a piece of firm cheese topped with a little tapenade or slivers of sun-dried tomatoes. Assemble ahead and grill when ready to serve. These are best served warm.

8 cups water
10 Swiss chard leaves
6 oz. manchego, Gruyère or Gouda cheese
2 tbs. tapenade or olive paste
olive oil

Bring water to a boil in a large saucepan. Wash chard and blanch in boiling water for about 30 seconds to soften. Remove from water and drain on paper towels. With a sharp knife, cut out the tough stem. Cut large leaves in half horizontally and trim to make approximate $3\frac{1}{2}$- to 4-inch squares. Overlap leaves where stem was removed.

Cut cheese into $1\frac{1}{2}$-inch squares, about $\frac{1}{4}$-inch thick. Place a piece of cheese in center of each leaf and top cheese with about 1 teaspoon tapenade. Fold in sides of leaf to make a compact package. Lightly brush both sides of package with olive oil.

When ready to serve, grill for about 1 minute each side, or until cheese feels soft to the touch through the leaf.

Filling Variations

- Replace tapenade with 5 or 6 oil-packed sun-dried tomatoes. Cut tomatoes into slivers.

- Cut full-flavored, thinly sliced ham into $1\frac{1}{2}$-inch pieces, spread lightly with mustard and top with cheese.

- Place a $\frac{1}{4}$-inch slice of spicy cooked sausage on top of cheese.

Deviled Eggs with Capers

Makes 8 pieces

Stuffed hard-cooked eggs are popular Spanish tapas. Double or triple this recipe depending on size of your party. Refrigerate until ready to serve.

4 hard-cooked eggs
1 tbs. mayonnaise
½ tsp. anchovy paste
1 tbs. Dijon mustard
1 tbs. coarsely chopped capers, rinsed and drained
salt and freshly ground pepper
paprika for garnish
16-20 whole capers for garnish

Cut cooked eggs in half. Carefully remove yolks and place in a small bowl. Mash yolks with a fork and combine with mayonnaise, anchovy, mustard, capers, salt and pepper. Divide filling among cooked egg white halves. Sprinkle with paprika and garnish with several whole capers.

Deviled Eggs with Olives

Makes 8 pieces

Use pimiento-stuffed Spanish olives, imported black olives, or some of each. Refrigerate until ready to serve.

4 hard-cooked eggs
1 tbs. mayonnaise
1 tbs. Dijon mustard
4-5 large olives, chopped
salt and freshly ground pepper
1 tbs. finely chopped parsley or cilantro for garnish

Cut cooked eggs in half. Carefully remove yolks and place in a small bowl. Mash yolks with a fork and combine with mayonnaise, mustard, chopped olives, salt and pepper. Divide filling among eggs. Sprinkle with parsley.

Classic Tortilla Espanola

This delicious potato omelet is found in all regions of Spain. A wedge is eaten as a mid-morning snack, a light lunch, or to accompany an evening glass of wine. Follow the recipe exactly and you will have an authentic tortilla. Be sure to save the drained oil from the cooked potatoes — it has a wonderful flavor and can be used to sauté vegetables or seafood.

½ cup full-flavored olive oil
1 clove garlic, peeled and halved
1 medium onion, halved and thinly sliced
1 ½ lb. boiling potatoes, peeled, cut into ⅛-inch slices
6 large eggs
salt and freshly ground white pepper
Tabasco Sauce, optional

Heat oil in a 9- or 10-inch nonstick skillet over medium heat. Add garlic and cook until lightly browned. Remove and discard garlic. Add onion slices and simmer in oil for 2 to 3 minutes. Slide potato slices into oil a few at a time to keep them from sticking together. Cover pan and simmer potatoes over medium heat for 25 to 30 minutes. Gently move potatoes around several times during cooking. Test with a fork for doneness. When potatoes are cooked through, but not browned, pour them into a large strainer over a heatproof bowl and allow them to drain for several minutes. Reserve oil.

Break eggs into a large bowl. Season well with salt and pepper. Add a few drops of Tabasco Sauce if desired. Whisk eggs. Spoon potato onion mixture into eggs and gently combine, keeping potato slices as whole as possible. Wipe out skillet with a paper towel and place over medium heat. Add 2 table-spoons of the reserved oil and heat until hot. Pour in egg-potato mixture and reduce heat to medium. Shake the pan frequently to keep eggs from sticking to the pan. When eggs have set on sides of pan and have started to brown, place a flat lid or plate over the pan. Over the sink or an easily cleanable sur-face, deftly invert pan onto the lid or plate and then slide tortilla back into pan to cook the other side. A perfectly cooked tortilla is barely set in the center, with a lightly browned surface on both sides.

Turn out onto a serving plate and cool before serving. Cut into wedges or squares. Serve warm or at room temperature.

Variations

Add a favorite vegetable or cooked meat to the potato mixture. Try diced green chiles, diced ham, chopped well-drained and squeezed dry spinach, flaked tuna, green peas or crumbled cooked sausage.

Mini-Tortillas

Makes 12 individual tortillas

This is a variation on the savory Spanish potato and egg dish baked in a muffin tin. The individual small tortillas are easy for a party or a lunchbox.

1 tbs. full-flavored olive oil
1 medium onion, diced, about 1 cup
2 cloves garlic, minced
2 cups diced, cooked potatoes, cut
    into 1/4-inch dice

7 large eggs
1/2 tsp. salt
1/4 tsp. ground white pepper
1/2 cup diced pimiento or roasted
    green chiles

Heat olive oil in a medium skillet over medium heat. Add onion and reduce heat to low. Cover and cook onions until tender and translucent, but not browned, about 5 minutes. Add garlic and cook for an additional 1 to 2 minutes. Add cooked potatoes and toss to coat with onion and oil mixture. Set pan off heat and cool for a few minutes.

Heat oven to 350°. In a large bowl, whisk eggs until well combined. Add salt, pepper and pimiento. Add cooled potato onion mixture and any remaining olive oil to eggs. Gently stir to combine. Lightly oil a 12-cup nonstick muffin pan with 3-inch diameter cups. Distribute potato egg mixture evenly among the muffin cups. Bake for 18 to 20 minutes, until lightly browned on the top and just set in the center. Remove tortillas from pan while hot and place on a serving platter. Serve warm or at room temperature.

Marinated Manchego Cheese

Makes 25-30 pieces

Manchego cheese takes on a nutty character after a few days of marinating.

1/2 lb. aged manchego cheese
1/3 cup full-flavored olive oil, or to barely cover cheese
dried red pepper flakes, thyme or rosemary, optional

Remove rind from cheese. Cut cheese into triangles about 1-inch on a side and 1/8-inch thick. Place in a small container with a tight fitting lid. Add enough olive oil to cover cheese. Sprinkle with red pepper flakes or herbs, if desired. Refrigerate, covered, shaking container occasionally, for 4 to 5 days. Marinated cheese can be kept in the refrigerator for 1 month.

Serve at room temperature. Place cheese and some of the oil in a shallow serving bowl. Provide a small fork or toothpicks to spear the cheese, and accompany with small pieces of bread or unflavored water crackers.

Portobello and Goat Cheese Quesadilla *Makes 16 pieces*

Mexican-style tortillas stuffed with a flavorful filling, while not Spanish, make satisfying tapas. Quesadillas can be made in a skillet, but it is easier to bake several at one time in the oven.

4 flour tortillas, 7-8-inch
olive oil
1 cup *Sautéed Portobello Mushrooms*, page 113
⅓ cup diced roasted red peppers or pimiento
1-2 tbs. capers, rinsed and patted dry
1 cup crumbled fresh goat cheese
⅓ cup grated Parmesan or pecorino cheese
dried red pepper flakes

Heat oven to 450°. Line a baking sheet with foil. To assemble: brush one side of each flour tortilla with a little olive oil. Place two tortillas oiled-side down on baking sheet. Arrange mushrooms, peppers and capers over tortillas, and top with goat and Parmesan cheese. Sprinkle with red pepper flakes and top with remaining flour tortillas, oiled-side up. Bake 8 to 10 minutes, or until lightly browned. Cut each into 8 wedges and serve immediately.

To cook in a skillet, place assembled quesadilla in a nonstick skillet. Heat over medium heat for 3 to 4 minutes, or until bottom tortilla is lightly browned. Using a large spatula, turn quesadilla over to brown the other side. Cook for 2 to 3 minutes until cheese melts and bottom tortilla is lightly browned. Slide quesadilla out onto a cutting board and cut into 8 wedges. Serve hot.

Chicken and Rainbow Peppers Quesadillas   *Makes 16 pieces*

Use thin slices of leftover roasted chicken or pork in this appetizing quesadilla.

4 flour tortillas, 7-8-inch
olive oil
⅓ cup *Romesco Sauce*, page 157
¾ cup grated mozzarella or manchego cheese
4-6 slices chicken, cut into 2-inch pieces
½ cup *Rainbow Peppers*, page 114, cut into 2-inch pieces
¼ cup grated pecorino or Parmesan cheese

Heat oven to 450°. Line a baking sheet with foil. Brush one side of each tortilla with olive oil and place 2 tortillas oiled-side down on baking sheet. Spread each with *Romesco Sauce* and sprinkle with cheese. Distribute chicken slices and peppers over cheese, and sprinkle with Parmesan. Top with second tortilla, oiled-side up. Bake for 8 to 10 minutes, until lightly browned. Place on a cutting board and cut each into 8 wedges. Serve immediately.

To cook in skillet, place assembled quesadilla in a nonstick skillet. Heat over medium heat 3 to 4 minutes, or until bottom tortilla is lightly browned. Using a large spatula, turn the quesadilla over to brown the other side. Cook for 2 to 3 minutes until cheese melts and bottom tortilla is lightly browned. Slide out onto a cutting board and cut into 8 wedges. Serve hot.

Quesadilla Ideas

- Combine thin slices of *Roasted Pork Tenderloins*, page 147, and *Prune and Olive Compote*, page 152, with grated manchego cheese and some dried red pepper flakes.

- Fill tortillas with some homemade chorizo sausage from *Chorizo-Stuffed Mushroom Caps*, page 148, *Oven-Dried Tomatoes*, page 119, and grated mozzarella and Parmesan cheese.

- Make a quesadilla with 2 or 3 different kinds of grated cheese and spoon a little *Parsley Sauce*, page 156, over cheese.

- Layer thin slices of roasted chicken or pork over grated mozzarella, top with small spoonfuls of *Olive Paté*, page 111, and peeled, seeded, chopped tomato patted dry in a paper towel.

- Layer fresh goat cheese, *Rainbow Peppers*, page 114, or pimiento strips and dot with prepared tapenade or olive paste.

- Sprinkle grated Monterey Jack cheese with cooked small shrimp, diced green chiles and chopped fresh cilantro.

Vegetable-Based Tapas

Vegetables contribute a sparkle, texture and lightness to the tapas table. Gorgeous red and yellow roasted peppers, crisp bright green asparagus and fava beans, flavorful tomatoes, potatoes and garlic all serve to complement heartier meat-based tapas. Versatile vegetables adapt well to roasting, grilling, broiling and baking. Vegetables are terrific served alone, or when used to top pizzettes, fill empanadas or combine in savory salads. If there is only time or place for one vegetable dish, be sure to make *Rainbow Peppers* or *Roasted Pepper Strips*.

Another traditional tapas vegetable is the potato. You will find several tempting recipes including *Mini-Stuffed Potatoes*, which can be cooked, stuffed ahead of time and baked just before serving. *Hot Spicy Baked Potato Wedges* accompanied with a spicy tomato sauce, and *Oven Roasted Baby Potatoes with Garlic* are easy oven dishes.

Bagna Cauda with a variety of fresh or lightly cooked vegetables ready to dip into the warm garlicky sauce is a perfect focal point of a tapas party. This dish also goes nicely with grilled chicken or steaks as the featured main course. Try some of these flavorful vegetable dishes on your tapas table.

Marinated Cauliflower
Servings: 4-6

Steamed cauliflower florets are lightly dressed with a lemon and olive oil vinaigrette. This can be done a day ahead and refrigerated. Remove from the refrigerator about 30 minutes before serving. Serve with toothpicks.

1 large head cauliflower, cut into florets
2 tbs. lemon juice
2 tbs. full-flavored olive oil
salt and freshly ground pepper
pimiento pieces and a few black olives for garnish

Steam cauliflower florets over boiling water for about 3 to 4 minutes until crisp-tender. Remove from heat and pour into a shallow serving bowl. Whisk together lemon juice, olive oil, salt and pepper in a small bowl, and pour over florets. Gently toss to combine florets with dressing. Garnish with pimiento and olives. Serve at room temperature.

Marinated Artichokes

Artichokes are a favorite tapas item. In this recipe, the artichokes are cut into quarters with an inch or two of tender stem left attached. Prepare this dish a day ahead so flavors have time to blend.

2 lemons, divided
4 medium artichokes, about 3-inch diameter
1/2 cup white wine vinegar
1/4 cup full-flavored olive oil
2 cloves garlic, chopped
1/8 tsp. red pepper flakes
10-12 fresh mint leaves, finely chopped
salt and freshly ground black pepper

Juice lemons. Reserve 2 tablespoons juice for cooking artichokes. Place remaining juice and lemon halves in a large bowl with 4 to 5 cups cold water. Remove top 1 inch of each artichoke by cutting across tips with a sharp knife, and discard. Trim the stem leaving 3/4 to 1 inch of bottom stem. Remove 3 to 4 layers of tough outside leaves until you reach tender light green leaves underneath. Cut each artichoke into quarters. With a small sharp knife or potato peeler, peel stem and evenly trim area where leaves were removed. Cut out any sharp or prickly areas in center of artichoke.

Immediately submerge trimmed artichokes in bowl with lemons and water to prevent them from turning dark. Bring 3 cups water to a boil in a 3-quart saucepan and add reserved lemon juice and wine vinegar. Remove artichokes from acidulated water and place in a saucepan. Reduce heat and gently boil uncovered for 15 to 20 minutes. Stir occasionally. Start checking at 15 minutes, piercing artichoke bottom with a knife blade. When artichokes are tender, carefully remove them to a strainer and drain for a few minutes.

Heat oil in a small skillet over medium heat. Add garlic and red pepper flakes. Cook for 2 to 3 minutes, until garlic softens. Place drained artichokes in a bowl, pour over garlic and oil, and add mint, salt and pepper. Toss gently to combine. Cover and refrigerate until 30 minutes before serving. Serve on small plates with forks.

Asparagus and Ham Rolls

Asparagus spears are wrapped in a mustard-glazed ham slice about 3 by 4 inches. Tuck in a strip of Rainbow Peppers, page 114, for a colorful and delicious variation. Serve at cool room temperature.

1 lb. large asparagus spears
2 tbs. Dijon mustard
1 tbs. sour cream or heavy cream
½ lb. thin Black Forest or boiled ham slices
freshly ground pepper

Trim asparagus spears so they are slightly longer than ham pieces. Combine mustard with sour cream in a small bowl. With a pastry brush or knife lightly spread a little mustard mixture on one side of ham slices. Place asparagus on ham with asparagus tip slightly above top of ham slice. Roll so that asparagus tip shows. Arrange on serving plate.

Note: To make more servings or if using thin asparagus, use 2 spears per roll. Position one spear with tip showing at top of ham slice and one tip showing at bottom of slice. Roll up and cut in rolls in half.

Garbanzo Bean Salad

Garbanzo beans were brought to Spain by the Moors and remain very popular today. Canned garbanzo beans are readily available and work perfectly in this hearty salad.

1 can (15 oz.) garbanzo beans, drained
1 cup peeled, seeded, chopped tomatoes
4-5 green onions, white part only, thinly sliced
½ cup diced ham pieces, about ¼-inch dice, optional
½ tsp. dried oregano
2 tbs. full-flavored olive oil
1 tbs. plus 1 tsp. sherry wine vinegar
salt and freshly ground pepper

Rinse drained garbanzo beans with cold water and drain well. Pat dry and place in a serving bowl. Add tomatoes, onions, ham and oregano and mix well. In a small bowl, whisk together olive oil, vinegar, salt and pepper. Pour over beans and toss gently to coat with dressing. Serve on small plates at room temperature.

Bagna Cauda

This dish originated in Italy, but it incorporates basic Spanish flavors of garlic, anchovy and olive oil. It means "hot bath" and makes a zesty dip for raw, cooked or grilled vegetables.

1 can (2 oz.) flat anchovy fillets
½ cup full-flavored olive oil
½ cup butter
6 cloves garlic, finely chopped
½ tsp. salt
⅛ tsp. red pepper flakes
raw and cooked vegetables
1 ½-inch French bread cubes

Drain oil from anchovies into a saucepan with oil and butter. Finely chop anchovies. Heat oil until butter starts to melt. Add garlic, chopped anchovy fillets, salt and red pepper flakes. Cook gently for 10 minutes, stirring occasionally, until garlic is soft but not browned and anchovies are dissolved. Pour sauce into a small serving bowl and keep warm on a warming tray, over a candle, or use a fondue pot. Stir sauce occasionally to redistribute garlic from the bottom.

Arrange raw and cooked vegetables and cubes of bread on a platter with a container of skewers nearby. Spear vegetables on wooden skewers or fondue forks and dip into warm oil. Catch drops of oil from vegetables on a cube of bread.

Good raw vegetables for dipping are red, green, yellow pepper strips, carrot slices or strips, fennel or celery strips, zucchini or yellow squash slices, small mushroom caps.

Blanch asparagus, snow peas, broccoli or cauliflower florets for 1 minute in boiling water or microwave briefly. Small cooked creamer potatoes, celery root cubes, parsnip slices or grilled baby leeks are delicious dippers as well.

Eggplant and Tomato Tartlets

Eggplant and garlic are roasted together in the oven to make a filling for small pastry shells.

1 medium eggplant, about 1 lb.
2 tsp. olive oil
salt and freshly ground pepper
1 bulb garlic, unpeeled
½ cup *Oven-Dried Tomatoes*, page 119, or ¼ cup chopped oil-packed
    sun-dried tomatoes
½ tsp. chopped fresh thyme leaves
1 tbs. chopped fresh mint leaves
2 tbs. crumbled blue or goat cheese
16 tartlets from *Basic Tartlet Pastry* shells, page 161, baked and cooled

Heat oven to 350°. Cut eggplant in half lengthwise and with a sharp knife make several diagonal cuts about ½-inch deep in flesh. Drizzle with olive oil and season with salt and freshly ground pepper. Line a cookie sheet with foil and place eggplant on foil, cut sides up. Cut off about ½ inch from the top of garlic bulb, slicing off a little of the individual cloves. Place on a small sheet of aluminum foil and drizzle with olive oil. Wrap garlic tightly in foil and place on baking sheet with eggplant. Bake eggplant and garlic until tender, about 35 to 40 minutes.

When eggplant is cool enough to handle, scoop flesh from shells, place in a strainer and allow to drain for 10 minutes, and place in a medium-sized bowl. Squeeze pulp from 4 or 5 roasted garlic cloves, chop or mash with a fork until smooth, and add to eggplant. Chop tomatoes into ½-inch pieces, and add to eggplant with thyme and mint leaves. Stir in cheese and season with salt and pepper. Fill tart pastry shells with about 1 tablespoon of filling just before serving.

Sherry-Glazed Eggplant

Servings: 4-6

Sauced eggplant cubes make quick and easy tapas. Use long slender Asian eggplants since they retain their shape and have an excellent flavor.

1 lb. Asian eggplants, 1- to 2-inch diameter, about 4-5
2 tbs. olive oil
½ cup finely chopped onion
2 large cloves garlic, finely chopped
1 tsp. Spanish paprika
⅔ cup chicken broth
⅓ cup cream sherry
1 tbs. sherry wine vinegar
1 tbs. tomato paste
salt and freshly ground pepper
2 tbs. chopped fresh cilantro for garnish

Trim eggplant; cut in half lengthwise and cut each half into ¾-inch slices. Heat oil over high heat in a large sauté pan until it is almost smoking and add eggplant. Cook, stirring, for 2 to 3 minutes. Add onion, garlic and paprika to skillet and cook for 1 minute. Add chicken broth, sherry, sherry wine vinegar and tomato paste. Season with salt and pepper and mix well. Reduce heat to low, cover and braise for 10 minutes, stirring once or twice, until eggplant is tender and the sauce has thickened slightly. Remove from heat. Garnish with cilantro just before serving. Serve warm or at room temperature with toothpicks.

Sweet and Sour Pearl Onions

Servings: 6-8

Frozen pearl onions work beautifully in this dish and don't need any peeling. Serve warm or at room temperature with toothpicks.

1 tbs. full-flavored olive oil
1 pkg. (10 oz.) frozen petite whole onions
2 tbs. water
2 tsp. brown sugar
¼ cup apple cider vinegar
salt and freshly ground pepper

Heat olive oil in a medium skillet over medium-low heat. Add onions and water. Cover, lower heat and simmer for 10 minutes, shaking pan occasionally. Add sugar, vinegar, salt and pepper. Uncover, increase heat to medium-high, and continue to cook for 5 minutes, shaking pan frequently, until onions are tender and liquid has evaporated. Pour into a small serving bowl.

Fava Bean Salad Cups

Fresh fava beans are one of the first harbingers of spring and have a delightful taste. It takes a little labor to peel them, but their special flavor pairs well with ham or prosciutto and cheese. You can substitute baby green lima beans for the favas.

1 lb. fava beans in the pod
¼ cup diced ham, cut into ¼-inch
   dice
¼ cup coarsely grated manchego or
   Parmesan cheese
4-5 mint leaves, finely chopped
2 tsp. full-flavored olive oil

½ tsp. Dijon mustard
1 tsp. red wine vinegar
salt and freshly ground pepper
12-14 nicely shaped small butter
   lettuce or romaine leaves
fresh mint leaves for garnish

Remove fava beans from large outer pod. Blanch favas in boiling water for 1 minute and drain. When cool enough to handle, remove the thick skin from each bean and discard. There will be about ⅔ cup of peeled fava beans. In a small bowl, combine peeled fava beans, ham, cheese and mint leaves. In another small bowl, whisk together olive oil, mustard, red wine vinegar, salt and pepper. Toss fava beans with dressing and adjust seasoning. Spoon a little of the bean mixture into small lettuce leaves and arrange on a platter. Garnish with a few mint leaves. Serve at room temperature.

Olive Paté

Spread this colorful paté on crackers or jicama slices, or use it to stuff cherry tomatoes. This will keep for several days in the refrigerator.

1 cup pimiento-stuffed green olives, drained, about 6 oz.
1 hard-cooked egg, chopped
1-2 green onions, white part only, finely chopped
1 tbs. capers, rinsed and drained
½ tsp. dried marjoram
freshly ground pepper
1½ tbs. mayonnaise
1 tbs. whipped cream cheese
1 tbs. cream sherry

Rinse olives under cold water and dry on paper towels. Place olives in a food processor workbowl with egg, onions, and capers. Pulse 5 to 6 times until mixture is coarsely chopped, about size of small peas. Spoon into a small bowl and add marjoram, pepper, mayonnaise, cheese and sherry. Combine well. Refrigerate until ready to serve.

Mushroom Empanadas

Small savory mushroom empanadas are popular tapas. Make the filling first so it has time to cool before filling the dough. Use the more flavorful brown cremini mushrooms.

1 tbs. full-flavored olive oil
¼ cup finely chopped large shallots, about 4
1 lb. white or brown mushrooms, finely chopped
salt and freshly ground pepper
½ cup grated Monterey Jack or Gruyère cheese
¼ cup finely diced flavorful ham, optional
1 tsp. dried tarragon
2 tsp. lemon juice
a few drops Tabasco Sauce
1 recipe *Basic Empanada Pastry*, page 159
1 egg white for glaze

Heat olive oil in a medium skillet over medium low heat. Add shallots and cook for 1 to 2 minutes to soften. Increase heat; add mushrooms, salt and pepper. Cook, stirring, for 3 to 4 minutes until mushroom juice is released and the mixture is quite dry. Remove from heat and cool for 15 minutes. Stir in cheese, ham, tarragon, lemon juice, and Tabasco.

Assemble and bake empanadas as instructed in *Basic Empanada Pastry* recipe.

Baked empanadas can be frozen. Heat oven to 350°. Place frozen empanadas on a cookie sheet and bake for 15 to 20 minutes, until hot. If empanadas have been refrigerated, reheat for 7 to 10 minutes, until warm to the touch.

Marinated Mushrooms

Servings: 4-6

Small white button mushrooms about 1-inch in diameter are perfect for tapas. Or use larger ones and cut into them into halves or quarters.

½ lb. small mushrooms	½ tsp. brown sugar
2 tbs. olive oil	dash Tabasco Sauce
2 cloves garlic, finely sliced	salt and freshly ground pepper
2 tbs. sherry wine vinegar	freshly chopped parsley or small
2 tbs. water	pieces of pimiento for garnish
½ tsp. dried tarragon	

Cut off mushroom stems flush with mushroom caps. Clean mushroom caps and set aside. Heat olive oil in a small saucepan over low heat. Add garlic and cook for 1 to 2 minutes to soften. Add mushrooms and stir to coat with oil. Continue to cook 1 to 2 minutes. Add vinegar, water, tarragon, sugar, Tabasco, salt and pepper. Cover pan and simmer over low heat for 5 minutes, stirring once or twice. Cool mushrooms in marinade. These can be refrigerated for 3 to 4 days. To serve, lift from marinade, place in a serving bowl, and garnish with parsley or pimiento. Serve at room temperature with toothpicks.

Sautéed Portobello Mushrooms

Servings: 4-6

Meaty and flavorful portobello mushroom strips make a wonderful topping for Pizzettes, page 122, or Portobello Mushroom and Goat Cheese Quesadillas, page 103, or serve with Wine and Garlic Chicken Chunks, page 142.

2 medium portobello mushrooms, about 4 oz. each
1 tbs. olive oil
1 clove garlic, minced
salt and freshly ground pepper
½ cup chicken broth
2 tsp. lemon juice
chopped fresh parsley for garnish

Remove stems from mushrooms and discard. Use a sharp spoon to gently scrape out black gills and discard. Cut mushrooms into ⅛-inch strips. In a large skillet over medium heat, add oil and garlic. Cook garlic for 1 to 2 minutes to soften but do not brown. Add mushrooms. Toss for 2 to 3 minutes until mushrooms are soft. Season with salt and a generous amount of black pepper. Add chicken broth and continue cooking mushrooms until liquid has almost evaporated. Remove from heat, sprinkle with lemon juice and serve warm or at room temperature.

Rainbow Peppers

Keep some of these on hand in your refrigerator. Serve them in a shallow bowl, or with soft cheese on toast. Or add few strips to a sandwich or salad.

1 large red bell pepper	salt and freshly ground pepper
1 large yellow bell pepper	2 cloves garlic, thinly sliced
1 large orange or green bell pepper	1/3 cup water
2 tbs. olive oil	2 tbs. sherry wine vinegar

Cut peppers in half, remove stems and ribs, and cut into 1/2-inch strips. If peppers are quite long, cut the strips in half. Heat olive oil in a large skillet over medium-high heat. Add pepper strips and sauté for 2 to 3 minutes. Season with salt and pepper. Add garlic slices and toss to coat with oil. Pour in water and vinegar. Reduce heat to low, and simmer covered for 20 to 25 minutes, until peppers are soft. Uncover and cook over high heat for 2 to 3 minutes, or until liquid has reduced to a syrup. Serve at room temperature.

Roasted Pepper Strips

Makes about 16 pieces

Red or yellow bell peppers are baked with a savory garlic and breadcrumb topping. Serve warm or at room temperature, on small plates or as finger-food.

2 large red or yellow bell peppers, about 6-8 oz. each	1/2 tsp. dried marjoram
1 tbs. full-flavored olive oil	1 1/2 tsp. sherry wine vinegar
1/4 cup finely minced onion	salt and freshly ground pepper
2 cloves garlic, finely chopped	1/2 cup finely chopped fresh parsley or cilantro
2 tbs. fresh fine breadcrumbs	1/4 cup grated manchego or Parmesan cheese, optional
1 tsp. paprika	
1/2 tsp. dry mustard powder	

Line a jelly-roll pan or cookie sheet with aluminum foil. Lightly oil foil. Divide peppers into sections by cutting along the natural depressions, usually 4 or 5 pieces. Remove ribs, seeds, and curved ends to produce fairly flat strips. Gently flatten pepper strips with the palm of your hand. Place pepper strips on prepared pan skin-side down.

Heat oven to 325°. Over medium heat, heat olive oil in a small skillet, add onion and cook until soft, about 5 minutes. Add garlic and cook for 1 minute. Remove pan from heat and add breadcrumbs, paprika, mustard, marjoram, wine vinegar, salt, pepper and parsley. Mix well. Spoon a little onion mixture down the length of each pepper strip. Bake peppers for 35 to 40 minutes, until very soft. Remove from oven and cut each strip into 2 or 3 pieces. Sprinkle with cheese if desired. Serve warm or at room temperature.

114   Tapas Fantásticas ~ Vegetable-Based

Peppers with Tomato and Potato Stuffing

Yellow and red bell peppers make a colorful platter. These can be made ahead and reheated just before serving. Serve warm or at room temperature on small plates.

4 small or 2 large red and yellow bell peppers, about 1 lb.
3 cups salted water for blanching
3 tbs. full-flavored olive oil
½ cup finely chopped onion
2 cloves garlic, minced
½ cup peeled, seeded, chopped tomatoes
1 cup diced cooked potatoes, in ¼-inch dice
1 tsp. dried marjoram
1 tbs. chopped fresh parsley
salt and freshly ground pepper
2 tbs. grated Parmesan cheese

Cut small peppers in half lengthwise and then cut across each half. Remove stem, seeds and cores. Cut large peppers into quarters lengthwise along natural divisions and cut each piece in half horizontally. Bring water to boil in a medium saucepan. Blanch pepper pieces for 2 to 3 minutes to soften. Drain peppers and set aside.

Heat oven to 375°. Heat olive oil in a medium skillet, add onion and cook for 5 to 6 minutes until soft. Add garlic and tomatoes and cook for 2 to 3 minutes. Remove from heat and add potatoes, marjoram, salt and pepper. Mix well. Stuff each pepper piece with about 2 tablespoons potato mixture and sprinkle with Parmesan cheese. Place peppers in one layer in an oiled shallow baking pan. Bake peppers for 20 to 25 minutes until topping is lightly browned.

Crisp Potato Slices

Baked potato slices are an easy tapa. Use the thin slicing blade on the food processor to make thin, even slices. Arrange potatoes on cookie sheets ahead of time and just pop them into the oven about 30 minutes before serving.

2 large baking potatoes
3 tbs. full-flavored olive oil
salt and freshly ground pepper

Heat oven to 350°. Line 2 large cookie sheets with aluminum foil and spray foil with nonstick cooking spray or oil lightly. Scrub potatoes. Cut off a thin slice from end of potato, and trim the sides if necessary to fit into food processor tube. Slice into 1/8-inch slices. Pour olive oil, salt and pepper in a shallow pan or pie pan. Dip both sides of each slice in olive oil and place on prepared baking sheets. Bake for about 35 to 40 minutes until slices are nicely browned and crisp. Remove slices as they start to turn dark brown. Serve hot or warm on a platter or in paper-napkin-lined basket.

Mini-Stuffed Potatoes

Small cooked red or Yukon gold potatoes are filled with a savory onion and bacon stuffing. Cook potatoes and cool or refrigerate for easier handling. Stuff these ahead and bake just before serving. Serve on small plates or as fingerfood.

1 lb. boiling potatoes, about 6
2 tbs. olive oil
1/3 cup finely chopped onion
1 tbs. sherry wine vinegar
2 tsp. Dijon mustard
salt and freshly ground pepper
3 slices cooked, crisp bacon, crumbled

Scrub and cook unpeeled potatoes in boiling water until just tender. Drain and cool. Cut potatoes in half. Using a small spoon or melon baller, scoop out potato centers, leaving a 1/4-inch shell. Chop potato centers into pea-sized pieces and reserve.

Heat oven to 375°. Heat olive oil in a medium skillet over medium-low heat. Sauté onion for 5 to 6 minutes until very soft but not browned. Add vinegar, mustard and chopped potato centers to skillet, and season with salt and pepper. Cook for 2 to 3 minutes, stirring, until mixture is well combined. Remove from heat and stir in crumbled bacon. Divide stuffing among potato halves. Place in one layer on a cookie sheet or baking pan. Bake for 30 to 35 minutes, or until filling is hot and shells are lightly browned and crisp.

Oven-Roasted Baby Potatoes with Garlic

Makes about 10 potatoes

These very low fat, vegetarian tapas can be served hot or warm. Have your guests squeeze the roasted garlic onto their potatoes.

1 tbs. full-flavored olive oil
1 lb. small creamer potatoes, about 1½-inch diameter
2 heads garlic, divided into cloves, unpeeled
1 tsp. coarse salt
freshly ground pepper

Heat oven to 400°. Line a shallow baking pan with foil and add olive oil. Wash and dry potatoes and roll in olive oil to coat. Add garlic cloves and toss to coat with oil. Sprinkle potatoes and garlic with salt and pepper, rolling to coat all sides. Bake for about 35 to 40 minutes, or until potatoes are tender. Shake pan occasionally while roasting. Arrange on a serving plate with garlic cloves.

Spicy Baked Potato Wedges (Papas Bravas)

Makes 16-20 pieces

This version of tapas is suggestive of French fries but has less fat and more flavor. Dip the hot potato chunks in Spicy Tomato Sauce, page 158, or garlicky Aioli, page 155, or as the Spaniards do, a little of each.

2 large baking potatoes, about 1½ lb., unpeeled
2 tbs. olive oil
2 tsp. mild chile powder, cumin or paprika
1 tsp. kosher or coarse sea salt
generous grinds black pepper

Heat oven to 400°. Line a large cookie sheet with aluminum foil. Scrub potatoes and cut each in half horizontally. Place cut side down on cutting board and cut each half into 8 to 10 equal-sized wedges. In a large bowl, mix together olive oil, chile powder, salt and pepper. Toss potatoes with seasoned olive oil mixture, coating wedges evenly. Place wedges skin-side down on prepared baking sheet. Bake for 35 to 40 minutes until potatoes are lightly browned, tender and lightly puffed. Serve on a heated platter with a bowl of sauce, or serve a few wedges on small plates with a spoonful of dipping sauce.

Warm Potato and Leek Salad

Creamy, buttery Yukon gold potatoes are marvelous in this salad. Pour the dressing over warm potatoes for more flavor. Serve warm or at room temperature on small plates.

1 lb. small new potatoes, 1- to 1½-inch diameter
3 small leeks, or 1 large leek, about 8 oz.
¼ cup full-flavored olive oil, divided
2 tbs. sherry wine vinegar, divided
salt and freshly ground pepper
2 tbs. chopped parsley for garnish
paprika for garnish

Scrub potatoes and place in a saucepan. Cover potatoes with water, bring to boil, and cook covered for 30 to 35 minutes, until tender. When potatoes are tender, drain and place pot back over heat for another minute to dry out potatoes. As soon as potatoes are cool enough to handle, cut into quarters or slices and place in a serving bowl.

While potatoes are cooking, cut leeks in half lengthwise and wash well to remove any sand. Remove top 4 inches of green tops and save for the stockpot or discard. Cut leek stalks into 1-inch pieces. Heat 1 tablespoon olive oil in a medium skillet over low heat, add leeks and cook for 5 minutes. Add 1 tablespoon wine vinegar, salt and pepper. Cover and continue to cook for 5 to 10 minutes until tender. Remove from heat and place in serving bowl.

Whisk together remaining 3 tablespoons olive oil, 1 tablespoon vinegar, salt and pepper and pour over warm potatoes and leeks. Toss gently to keep potatoes in whole pieces. Sprinkle with parsley and paprika.

Variation

Add 2 or 3 strips crisp bacon, crumbled.

Russian-Style Vegetable Salad

Servings: 6-8

Ensaladilla Rusa is a popular tapa in Spain, probably brought in by the many Frenchmen living in Spain about the time of the Napoleonic wars. The basic salad always has potatoes, carrots and peas. Beets, beans, cauliflower and other cooked vegetables can be added.

1 cup diced cooked potatoes, 1/2-inch dice
1 cup diced cooked carrots, 1/2-inch dice
1 cup frozen green peas, defrosted and cooked for 2 minutes
1 cup diced cooked turnip or celery root, 1/2-inch dice
1 cup 1/2-inch pieces cooked green beans
5-6 green onions, white part only, finely chopped
salt and freshly ground pepper
1/4 cup mayonnaise
2 tbs. sour cream
1 tbs. Dijon mustard
1 tbs. lemon juice
chopped fresh parsley for garnish
black olives or roasted red pepper strips for garnish

In a large bowl, combine cooked vegetables with green onions. Season with salt and pepper. In a small bowl, Combine mayonnaise, sour cream, mustard and lemon juice. Pour dressing over vegetables and toss until well coated. Cover and refrigerate until ready to serve. Spoon salad into a serving bowl or platter and sprinkle with parsley. Garnish with black olives or roasted red pepper strips.

Oven-Dried Tomatoes (Basic Recipe)

Makes about 1/2 cup

Oven-dried tomatoes become sweeter and their flavor intensifies when roasted in the oven. Use them for Chicken, Artichokes and Oven-Dried Tomatoes, page 138, Pizzettes, page 122, or Banderillas, page 93.

1 lb. plum tomatoes, about 4-5
salt and freshly ground pepper

Heat oven to 250°. Line a shallow baking pan with aluminum foil. Remove core from tomatoes. Cut each in half and then each half lengthwise into 3 or 4 pieces. Remove tomato seeds and any hard centers. Place tomatoes on baking pan, skin-side down, and season with salt and pepper. Bake for about 2 hours, or until tomatoes are dried but still pliable. Remove from oven. When cool, store covered in refrigerator for up to 4 or 5 days.

Mixed Grilled Vegetable Salad

Grilled vegetables or escalivada make appetizing tapas. Charcoal grilling gives eggplant and peppers a nice smoky flavor, but they can be cooked under the broiler as well. Serve on a platter, or layer a piece or two on a slice of toasted bread and top with a little bit of cheese.

3 red or yellow bell peppers
1 medium eggplant or 4-5 Asian eggplants, about 1 lb., trimmed, cut into ¼-inch slices
1-2 portobello mushrooms, stem and gills removed
1 large red onion, cut into ½-inch slices
6-8 green onions, trimmed to include 3 to 4 inches of green top
3-4 zucchini or yellow squash, trimmed and cut into ¼-inch slices
¼ cup full-flavored olive oil, divided
salt and freshly ground black pepper
2 tsp. sherry wine vinegar
1 large ripe tomato, peeled, seeded and chopped

When ready to grill, place peppers over hottest area and char on all sides. Remove peppers and wrap in foil to steam for a few minutes before peeling. Brush eggplant, mushrooms, onions, and squash slices generously with olive oil.

Grill vegetables over medium heat until nicely browned and tender. Depending on heat source, eggplant slices will take about 10 to 12 minutes, onions 15 to 20 minutes, green onions and squash 8 to 10 minutes. Remove vegetables as they are cooked.

Peel and seed peppers and cut into thin strips or 1-inch squares. Place in a serving bowl. Cut grilled vegetables into strips or squares and add to pepper. Season with salt and pepper. Add remaining olive oil, vinegar and tomato pieces and toss to mix well. Serve warm or at room temperature.

Tip: If vegetables are browning too fast without becoming tender, remove from grill and microwave for 1 to 2 minutes to finish cooking.

Spinach and Egg Empanadas

Fills 16 small or 30 large empanadas

Fill tender pastry rounds with this savory spinach mixture. Serve warm or at room temperature. These reheat well.

1 pkg. (10 oz.) frozen chopped spinach
2 tbs. butter
2 tbs. flour
1/2 cup milk
pinch nutmeg
1 tbs. Dijon mustard
salt and freshly ground pepper
pinch cayenne pepper
2 tsp. lemon juice
1/2 cup grated manchego or Gruyère cheese
2 hard-cooked eggs, chopped
5-6 green onions, white part only, thinly sliced
1 recipe *Easy Empanada Pastry*, page 160

Defrost spinach and drain well. Squeeze spinach with your hands to press out liquid, making spinach as dry as possible. Set aside in a bowl.

Melt butter in a medium saucepan over medium heat. Add flour, stir to combine and cook for 1 minute. Add milk gradually and stir until sauce thickens. Add nutmeg and mustard, stirring to combine. Add spinach and cook for another 1 to 2 minutes. Season with salt, pepper and cayenne. Add lemon juice. Sauce will be quite thick. Remove from heat and stir in cheese, eggs and onions. Set aside to cool.

Assemble and bake empanadas as instructed in *Easy Empanada Pastry* recipe.

Pizzettes with Vegetable Toppings

A thin, freshly baked bread crust provides a perfect foundation for many typical Spanish ingredients. The unbaked pizza crust in a tube from the supermarket refrigerator section makes a quick and easy base for a large variety of toppings.

1 tube (10 oz.) unbaked pizza crust
garlic-flavored olive oil, follows
2/3 cup grated cheese, or topping from following list

Heat oven to 375°. Remove dough from tube and carefully unroll. Place crust on the back of a lightly oiled cookie sheet or jelly-roll pan, and gently press the dough into a 10- by 15-inch rectangle. With a pizza wheel or sharp knife, cut dough into six 5-inch squares. Push in edges of the pieces to form a slight ridge. This will result in six 4-inch squares. Bake squares for 5 to 6 minutes, until crust is firm but not browned. Top pizzettes with any of the toppings below, or create your own. A little olive oil, a thin layer of cheese and 2 or 3 slices of vegetables are perfect for the crisp thin crust. Do not overload.

Final baking: Heat oven to 425°. Bake for 7 to 10 minutes, until crust is brown around the edges and topping is bubbling. Cut each pizzette into 4 squares and serve immediately.

Vegetable and Other Toppings

- **Garlic-flavored olive oil:** Heat 2 tbs. olive oil and 1 large clove garlic, minced, in a small skillet over medium-low heat. Cook for 1 to 2 minutes; do not allow
garlic to brown. Or heat oil and garlic in a small bowl in the microwave for 30 seconds.

- Goat cheese, cream cheese, grated Monterey Jack, grated manchego or grated mozzarella.

- *Sautéed Portobello Mushroom* slices, page 113

- *Rainbow Peppers*, page 114

- Grilled eggplant

- *Wine and Garlic Chicken Nuggets*, page 142

- Thin slices of cooked sausage

- Anchovies

- *Spicy Tomato Sauce*, page 158, or *Romesco Sauce*, page 157

Seafood Tapas

Seafood ranks high on the list of favorite Spanish tapas and there are innumerable ways to prepare shrimp, calamari, clams and other fish. In addition to its wide availability and popularity, seafood cooks quickly. It is important to always buy the freshest and highest quality available, and to not overcook it. Some of our favorite tapas include *Stuffed Clams with Spinach, Steamed Mussels with Parsley Sauce, Scallops with Oranges and Black Olives* and *Hot Garlic Shrimp.*

Salt cod is a typical Spanish ingredient and must be soaked for at least 24 hours to remove excess salt and soften. Try *Salt Cod and Potato Cakes* and *Garlicky Salt Cod-Topped Potato Slices* when the cod has been prepared for cooking. There are several flavorful sauces in the *Basic Sauces and Pastry* chapter to complement cooked fish and shellfish, so make some delicious seafood tapas for your next party.

Fried Calamari
Servings: 4

Crisp, hot fried calamari is a popular tapa. Serve with Aioli, page 155, Seafood Cocktail Sauce, page 158, or Romesco Sauce, page 157. The squid can be cleaned and prepared ahead of time but should be floured and fried at the last minute then served immediately.

1 lb. calamari or squid, cleaned
½ cup cake flour
1 tsp. paprika
½ tsp. dry mustard powder
salt and freshly ground pepper
3 cups canola oil

Cut calamari into ½ -inch rings. If using tentacles, remove and discard any hard pieces in the middle. On a large shallow plate, combine flour, paprika, mustard, salt and pepper. Dredge calamari lightly in flour mixture and shake off excess flour.

Heat oven to 275°. Heat oil in a heavy pan until oil reaches 375° on thermometer. Add about ¼ of the calamari to hot oil and fry for 1 to 2 minutes until calamari is a light golden brown. Remove to a paper towel-lined platter and place in oven until next batch is fried. Allow oil temperature to return to 375° and continue frying calamari. Serve hot.

Steamed Clams

Serve these clams warm or at room temperature with Red Pepper Mayonnaise, page 157, Sherry Vinegar and Shallot Sauce, page 158, or Parsley Sauce, page 156. Or use them for Stuffed Clams with Spinach, page 125. Double this recipe if you are serving a larger group.

2 lb. cherrystone or Manila clams, about 20
½ cup water
½ cup dry white wine
3 cloves garlic, coarsely chopped

Rinse clams in a bowl of cold water. Fill a bowl with cold water, add 1 tablespoon kosher or sea salt and allow clams to stand for 1 hour to release any sand. Lift clams from water and discard any clams that are not tightly closed.

To steam clams, add water, wine and garlic to a deep saucepan with a tight-fitting lid. Bring liquid to a boil and add clams. Cover tightly and steam over high heat. After 3 to 4 minutes remove the clams that have opened to a plate or bowl and continue to steam remaining clams. Check again in 2 to 3 minutes, removing opened clams. Re-cover pan and turn off heat. After 5 minutes, discard any unopened clams and save cooking liquid. When clams are cool enough to handle, discard top shell. Serve clams in a small bowl with sauce on the side, or take a small knife and loosen the clam from its bottom shell. Spoon a dollop of sauce on each clam, or serve sauce in a small bowl with a spoon.

Stuffed Clams with Spinach

Makes about 20 pieces

A good way to keep clams upright during baking is to place a layer of rock salt in the baking pan.

Steamed Clams, page 124, about 20, with strained juice
1/4 cup butter, divided
3 green onions, white part only, finely chopped
1 tbs. flour
1/4 cup milk

1 pkg. (10 oz.) defrosted spinach, squeezed very dry and finely chopped
salt and freshly ground pepper
pinch nutmeg
1 cup fresh breadcrumbs
2 cloves garlic, finely chopped

Remove clams from shells, coarsely chop and set aside. Strain any liquid from bottom of pan through a coffee filter to remove any sand and garlic pieces; reserve 1/4 cup liquid. Melt 2 tablespoons of the butter in a small saucepan over medium-high heat. Sauté onions for 2 to 3 minutes to soften. Stir in flour and cook for 1 minute. Add 1/4 cup reserved clam liquid and milk and bring to a boil. Stir in spinach, chopped clams, salt, pepper and nutmeg. Mix well. Fill each clam shell half with spinach filling and place in a baking pan.

Heat oven to 400°. In a small skillet, melt remaining 2 tablespoons butter. When foamy, add fresh breadcrumbs. Cook over medium heat until bread-crumbs turn light brown in color. Add garlic and cook for another minute. Sprinkle a few toasted crumbs over each stuffed clam. Bake for about 15 minutes until hot. Serve immediately or place on a warming tray.

Calamari Cocktail

Servings: 4-6

Cook calamari or squid only for a couple of minutes, or it tends to toughen.

2-3 quarts water
1 tsp. salt
1 lb. cleaned calamari, cut into thin rings and dried with paper towels
1/2-3/4 cup Seafood Cocktail Sauce, page 158

chopped fresh cilantro or parsley for garnish.
8-10 small black olives for garnish
small lettuce leaves

Bring 2 to 3 quarts water to a boil in a large saucepan. Add salt and squid rings and blanch squid for 2 to 3 minutes. The squid is cooked when it turns white and loses its translucent look. Immediately drain and pat dry with paper towels. Place squid in a serving bowl, pour cocktail sauce over and mix well. If not serving immediately, cover and refrigerate. Remove from refrigerator about 30 minutes before serving. Garnish with cilantro or parsley and olives. Serve at room temperature. Roll filling in lettuce leaves.

Basic Salt Cod Preparation

One pound dried salt cod makes approximately 2 cups cooked, flaked fish.

Start soaking the dried salt cod a day before you want to cook it. After soaking it will keep in the refrigerator for 3 or 4 days. Rinse pieces under cold running water for a few minutes to wash off as much salt as possible.

Place cod pieces in a large bowl, cover with cold water and soak for 10 minutes. Drain, cover with cold water and soak again for 10 minutes. Repeat this process 4 or 5 times. Cover cod with fresh cold water, cover bowl and refrigerate for 24 hours. Change water 1 to 2 times during this soaking period. Water should only taste slightly salty after this soaking.

Drain cod, place in large saucepan, cover with cold water and bring to a boil. Reduce heat, cover and simmer for 20 to 25 minutes, until fish flakes easily. Drain. When cool enough to handle, flake or chop fish as directed in recipe.

Salt Cod and Potato Cakes

Makes 16 cakes

Serve these small hot crispy cakes on small plates with Aioli, page 155, or Parsley Sauce, page 156. Leftover mashed potatoes or instant mashed potatoes work well in this dish. The cakes can be made ahead and kept warm in the oven, or reheated for several seconds in the microwave.

2 tbs. olive oil plus more for frying
1/4 cup finely chopped green onions, white part only
1 cup finely chopped prepared cooked salt cod, about 1/2-inch pieces
3/4 cup prepared mashed potatoes
white pepper and salt
1 egg yolk
fine dry breadcrumbs

Heat oil in a medium skillet over medium heat. Sauté onion for 3 to 4 minutes until soft, but do not brown. Remove from heat and reserve. In a bowl, combine cod and potatoes. Taste for seasoning and add white pepper and salt if needed. Stir in egg yolk, onions and oil from skillet. Mix well. Form into small patties, about 1 1/2-inch diameter and 1/2-inch thick. Lightly coat each cake with breadcrumbs.

Add enough olive oil to cover bottom of skillet, about 1/4 inch deep. Heat oil over medium-high heat. When hot, fry cakes until lightly brown and heated through. Drain on paper towels. Serve immediately.

Garlicky Salt Cod-Topped Potato Slices

This goes together quickly when you have cooked potatoes and some soaked cooked salt cod in the refrigerator. It is easier to slice potatoes after they have cooled and been refrigerated.

4-5 small boiling potatoes, red, Finnish or Yukon gold, about 1½-inch diameter
salt
1 cup flaked, cooked salt cod, page 126, about 5 oz.
¼ cup *Aioli*, page 155
finely chopped fresh parsley or cilantro for garnish
roasted red pepper or pimiento strips for garnish

Scrub potatoes but do not peel. Boil in salted water until tender, but not mushy. Drain potatoes and cool. Slice cooked potatoes into rounds about ⅜-inch thick. In a small bowl, combine flaked cod with *Aioli* and parsley. Top each potato slice with a generous tablespoon of salt cod mixture and garnish with a thin strip of roasted red pepper.

Variation

Cut 2 hard-cooked eggs into thin slices. To assemble, place an egg slice on top of each potato slice, lightly season with salt and pepper and top with salt cod mixture.

Monkfish in Tomato Almond Sauce

Monkfish is a flavorful, dense-textured fish that some find to be similar to lobster. Halibut, swordfish or cod make good substitutes. Prepare the tomato sauce first and bake the fish for a few minutes. Serve hot on small plates or spear chunks with a toothpick.

2 tbs. full-flavored olive oil
1 slice bread, about ¾-inch thick, crust removed
10 blanched almonds
1 clove garlic, chopped
2 large ripe tomatoes, peeled, seeded and chopped, about 1 cup
pinch saffron threads or powder
2 tbs. lemon juice
⅓ cup water
salt and white pepper
1 lb. monkfish or other firm-fleshed fish, cut into 1-inch cubes
chopped fresh parsley for garnish

Heat oven to 375°. Heat olive oil in a medium-sized ovenproof skillet over medium heat. Tear bread into several pieces and add to skillet. Add almonds and sauté, stirring, until bread and almonds are lightly browned. Add garlic and cook for 1 minute, but do not allow to brown. Add tomato, saffron and lemon juice, reduce heat and simmer for a few minutes. Pour into food processor or blender bowl with ⅓ cup water and process until fairly smooth. Taste for seasoning and add salt and pepper to taste.

Pour sauce back into skillet. Sauce will be thick but monkfish liquid will be released as it cooks. Bring to a boil and remove from heat. Salt and pepper monkfish chunks and add to skillet. Toss to coat fish with sauce. Place skillet in oven and bake for 15 minutes, turning fish over about halfway through cooking time. Sprinkle with parsley and serve hot.

Escabeche

This piquant seafood dish can be prepared a day or two ahead of time. Firm-fleshed fish such as halibut, orange roughy or sea bass can be substituted. Serve on small plates with forks, or cut fish into bite-size pieces and serve with toothpicks.

1 lb. fresh red snapper fillets
salt, pepper and flour
3 tbs. olive oil, divided
1 medium onion, thinly sliced
1 small carrot, peeled and thinly sliced
3 cloves garlic, peeled and thinly sliced
1/8 tsp. dried red pepper flakes
1/2 cup cider vinegar
1/4 cup water
1 tsp. brown sugar
1 tbs. lemon juice
2 sprigs fresh thyme, or 1/2 tsp. dried
2 tbs. white raisins
1 tbs. capers, drained, rinsed
black olives for garnish

Cut each fish fillet into 2 to 3 medium pieces. Season with salt and pepper and dust lightly with flour. Heat 2 tablespoons of the olive oil in a large skillet over medium heat. Quickly sauté fish for 3 to 4 minutes on each side, until lightly browned and cooked through. Remove fish and place in one layer in a deep-sided glass or nonreactive pan.

Discard hot oil, wipe out skillet, add remaining 1 tablespoon olive oil to skillet and heat over medium heat. Add onion, carrots, garlic cloves and red pepper flakes. Cook for 2 to 3 minutes until onion and carrot soften. Add vinegar, brown sugar, lemon juice, thyme, raisins, salt and pepper to skillet. Bring to a boil and cook 2 to 3 minutes. Pour over fish. Sprinkle with capers, cool to room temperature, then cover and refrigerate for a few hours or overnight. Bring to room temperature before serving.

Seafood Salad

This simply cooked and lightly dressed dish is totally dependent on the quality of the seafood and tomatoes. Serve on small plates at cool room temperature.

3 tbs. olive oil
1 tbs. sherry wine vinegar
1 tbs. lemon juice
salt and white pepper to taste
1 tbs. finely chopped capers
1 tbs. kosher salt
¼ lb. small white shrimp, peeled and deveined
¼ lb. small bay scallops
¼ lb. calamari, cleaned and cut into ¼ -inch rings
¼ lb. firm fleshed white fish (halibut, flounder, sole) cut into ½-inch cubes
1 tbs. chopped fresh parsley
1 hard-cooked egg, finely chopped
½ cup peeled, seeded, chopped ripe tomato

Prepare dressing in serving bowl by whisking together olive oil, wine vinegar, lemon juice, salt and pepper. Add capers. Bring at least 2 quarts water to boil in a large pot. Add kosher salt. On a tray or cookie sheet, place 2 or 3 layers of paper towels. Place shrimp in a basket or strainer with a handle and hold in the boiling water for 1 to 2 minutes just until shrimp turn opaque.

Shake and drain shrimp and pour onto paper towels. Drain on paper towels for a minute and place in a serving bowl with the dressing. Toss to combine.

Repeat cooking with scallops, calamari and white fish, draining before placing in serving bowl. Just before serving, add parsley, egg, tomato and taste. Add salt and pepper if necessary and toss to combine.

Basic Steamed Mussels

Mussels in their striking black shells make attractive as well as delicious tapas. Steamed mussels can be served in small bowls with a little of the strained cooking broth, or loosen them from their shells.

1 lb. mussels
1 lemon, thinly sliced
1 large shallot, finely chopped
1 bay leaf
dried red pepper flakes
2-3 fresh parsley sprigs
1 sprig fresh thyme
1/3 cup dry white wine or vermouth
1 1/2 cups water

To prepare live mussels, place them in a bowl of cold water and soak them for 10 to 15 minutes. Wash shells under cold running water and scrub mussels with a small brush. Pull off "beards" which are small strings protruding from the shells. Squeeze the shell of any open mussel and if it does not close tightly, discard it. If a mussel seems particularly heavy for its size, it may be full of sand, so discard it as well. In a tall pot large enough to hold all mussels, combine lemon slices, shallots, bay leaf, red pepper flakes, parsley, thyme, wine and water. Bring to a boil, cover and simmer for 3 to 4 minutes. Add cleaned mussels, cover and steam over high heat 3 to 5 minutes until most of the mussels have opened. The pot has a tendency to boil over, so watch carefully and lift lid for a few seconds once or twice during cooking. Discard any mussels that do not open. Remove mussels from pot, place in small bowls or a large bowl, and strain broth over mussels. Serve hot.

Steamed Mussels with Parsley Sauce

Steamed mussels are topped with a vibrant, piquant green sauce and served warm or at room temperature. The precooked, frozen New Zealand green-lipped mussels can be substituted in this recipe. Defrost and heat them according to package directions and top with sauce.

1 lb. cleaned *Basic Steamed Mussels*
1/2 cup *Parsley Sauce*, page 156

Remove steamed mussels from pot. Discard top shell and loosen mussels from bottom shell with a small knife. Top with a teaspoon of *Parsley Sauce* and arrange on a serving platter. Serve warm or at room temperature.

Mussels Stuffed with Garlic and Breadcrumbs

Make a savory topping of garlic and breadcrumbs and broil the mussels for a few minutes before serving. Serve on small plates with forks. Be sure to loosen the mussels from their shells for easier eating.

1 lb. *Basic Steamed Mussels*, page 131
1 tbs. olive oil
1 clove garlic, finely chopped
1/8 tsp. dried red pepper flakes
1/2 tsp. dried marjoram or thyme
1 cup fresh breadcrumbs
grated zest from 1 lemon
1 tbs. chopped fresh parsley
salt and freshly ground pepper
1/4 cup dry white wine

Preheat broiler. Discard top shell and with a small knife loosen each mussel from the bottom shell. Place on a baking sheet. In a medium skillet, heat olive oil and sauté garlic and red pepper flakes over low heat for 2 to 3 minutes until garlic softens. Add marjoram, breadcrumbs, lemon zest and parsley. Season with salt and pepper and mix well. Firmly press about 2 teaspoons breadcrumb mixture onto each mussel. Sprinkle each mussel with about 1/2 teaspoon white wine. Position broiler rack about 6 inches from heat source. Broil mussels for 3 to 5 minutes, or until topping has lightly browned. Serve warm or at room temperature.

Bacon and Green Onion-Stuffed Mussels

Omit olive oil and garlic in *Mussels Stuffed with Garlic and Breadcrumbs.* Substitute 1 slice of bacon cut into 1/4-inch pieces. Sauté in a skillet until crisp. Remove bacon and add 2 finely chopped green onions until soft. Continue with basic recipe.

Pesto-Topped Mussels

Makes about 25 pieces

Mix 2 tablespoons prepared pesto with 1 cup fresh breadcrumbs. Press mixture over mussels, sprinkle each with a little white wine and broil.

Smoked Salmon and Cucumber Tartlets

Makes about 12

Spread this savory filling on crackers if you don't have time to make tart shells. Make filling a day ahead and remove from refrigerator at least 30 minutes before filling shells.

½ cup diced peeled, seeded
   cucumber, in ¼-inch dice
4 oz. smoked salmon, cut into ¼-inch
   dice
3 tbs. whipped cream cheese
1 tsp. lemon juice

½ tsp. dried tarragon
1 tbs. finely chopped fresh mint
   leaves
pinch white pepper
12 tartlets from *Basic Tartlet Pastry*,
   page 161, baked and cooled

Drain diced cucumber on paper towels for 10 minutes to absorb any liquid. In a small bowl, combine cucumber, smoked salmon, cream cheese, lemon juice, tarragon, mint and white pepper. Stir until well combined. Spoon mixture into baked tart shells and serve immediately.

Sardine and Egg Empanadas

Fills 16 small or 30 large empanadas

Serve this piquant sardine- and egg-filled empanada slightly warm or at room temperature. A copita or glass of dry sherry is a perfect accompaniment.

1 can (5 oz.) oil packed sardines, drained and flaked
2 hard-cooked eggs, chopped
1 tbs. coarsely chopped rinsed, dried capers
4 tsp. Dijon mustard
generous grinds black pepper
1 recipe *Easy Empanada Pastry*, page 160, or *Basic Empanada Pastry*,
   page 159

In a small bowl, combine sardines, eggs, capers, and mustard; stir well. Season with pepper. Fill and bake empanadas as directed in pastry recipe.

Baked empanadas can be frozen. Heat oven to 350°. Place frozen empanadas on a cookie sheet and bake for about 15 to 20 minutes, or until hot. If empanadas have been refrigerated, reheat on cookie sheet for 7 to 10 minutes, until warm to the touch.

Tapas Fantásticas ~ Seafood   133

Lemon Scallops

Serve medium-sized sea scallops hot on small plates with forks or toothpicks.

1 lb. sea scallops
salt and freshly ground pepper
2 tbs. olive oil
½ cup minced shallots

zest and juice of 1 lemon
3 tbs. dry white wine
1 tbs. rinsed, dried capers
¼ cup chopped fresh Italian parsley

Remove and discard tough muscle on sides of scallops. Wash and pat dry and season with salt and pepper. Preheat a large nonstick skillet over medium heat. Add olive oil. Place scallops in skillet, sauté for 2 minutes and turn over. Add shallots to pan and cook for 2 minutes. Add lemon juice, zest, white wine and capers. Increase heat to high and reduce liquid to a thin sauce, about 2 minutes. Sprinkle with parsley and serve in a heated bowl.

Scallops with Oranges and Black Olives

Servings: 6

Orange segments and red onion slices add color to these shellfish tapas. Serve on small plates with forks.

2 navel oranges
1 lb. large sea scallops, about 10-12
1 tsp. olive oil
salt and freshly ground black pepper
2 tbs. frozen orange juice concentrate, undiluted

2 tsp. white wine vinegar or lemon juice
1 small red onion, thinly sliced into rings
½ cup kalamata black olives for garnish

Use a citrus zester to cut long strips of orange zest from 1 orange, or use a potato peeler to remove strips and cut them into long matchsticks with a sharp knife. Set aside. Cut a thin slice from top and bottom of each orange. With a sharp, thin-bladed knife, cutting from top to bottom, remove the peel and membrane under it to expose the fruit. Cut down on each side of the separating membranes to release the segments. Set segments aside. Squeeze any juice remaining in membranes into a small bowl. Add zest, orange juice concentrate and vinegar to bowl.

Remove small tough muscle from sides of scallops and discard. Wash and dry scallops and generously season with salt and pepper. Heat a nonstick skillet over high heat. Add oil and scallops and sear for 1 to 2 minutes on each side until lightly browned. Remove to a plate. Add orange juice, zest mixture and onion rings to pan and stir for 1 minute. Add orange segments and combine. Return scallops to pan and cook for 1 to 2 minutes. Pour into a serving dish. Taste for seasoning and garnish with black olives. Serve warm or at room temperature.

Hot Garlic Shrimp

Make these tapas with the highest quality shrimp you can find. This recipe works well with any size shrimp — just cook larger shrimp a minute or two longer. Serve warm or at room temperature in a shallow bowl with toothpicks.

3 tbs. lemon juice
1/4 tsp. green or red Tabasco Sauce
2 tsp. sugar
salt
3 tbs. full-flavored olive oil

1 lb. medium white shrimp, peeled
  and deveined
3 cloves garlic, finely chopped
1 tbs. chopped fresh parsley or
  cilantro for garnish

Combine lemon juice, Tabasco, sugar and salt in a small bowl. Set aside. Add olive oil to a nonstick skillet over medium heat. Add shrimp and garlic. Stir-fry for 1 to 2 minutes. When shrimp start to turn opaque add lemon juice mixture. Continue to cook, stirring, until shrimp are barely cooked through. Remove shrimp with a slotted spoon to serving dish. Reduce pan juices over high heat until thick and syrupy. Pour over shrimp, sprinkle with parsley or cilantro and serve.

Shrimp a La Plancha

After marinating for a few minutes, these shrimp are sautéed in a hot skillet.

1 lb. large shrimp, about 30-35, peeled and deveined
2 tbs. olive oil
3 tbs. lemon juice, divided
2 cloves garlic, finely minced
salt and freshly ground pepper

Dry and skewer shrimp pinwheel style. With a cocktail pick or a short 3-inch skewer, pierce the tail of one shrimp, go through the thick end of the second shrimp, then through the thick end of the first shrimp and then the tail of the second to make a circular form that has almost uniform thickness. Mix together olive oil, 2 tablespoons lemon juice, garlic, salt and pepper on a large plate. Dip shrimp in marinade, coating both sides, and marinate on plate for about 15 minutes. Heat a large cast iron or heavy skillet over high heat until very hot. Shrimp should sizzle loudly when placed in pan. Lift shrimp skewers from marinade and place in skillet. Press shrimp down firmly with a spatula and cook for about 2 minutes on each side until just barely cooked through. Sprinkle with remaining lemon juice and serve immediately.

Note: To serve shrimp in their shells, cut down the back of each shrimp with a sharp knife and fish out dark vein. Line up 2 or 3 shrimp on each skewer, marinate and sauté as directed above.

Grilled Shrimp with Bacon

Makes about 25

Here is another party favorite. The shrimp can be prepared ahead and broiled at serving time. Use very thinly sliced bacon to wrap the shrimp and secure with toothpicks if bacon does not stay in place. Serve hot or warm with toothpicks.

1 lb. large shrimp, about 25-30, peeled, deveined
1/4 cup Dijon mustard
freshly ground pepper
8 strips bacon, thinly sliced

Dry shrimp. Spread a little mustard on each side of shrimp and season with ground pepper. Cut each bacon slice into 4 pieces by first cutting the slice in half, then cut each piece in half length-wise to make thin strips. Wind a bacon piece around each shrimp and place on broiler rack. Heat broiler. Position shrimp about 6 inches from heat source and broil for 3 minutes, then turn shrimp over and cook for another 2 minutes or until bacon is crisp and shrimp just barely cooked. Do not overcook.

Smoked Trout in Endive Leaves

Makes 20-24

Endive leaves are filled with a horseradish-flavored cream and topped with pieces of smoked trout for elegant, light tapas. If they are available, use both red and white endive. Smoked salmon can be substituted for the trout.

1/2 cup sour cream or crème fraiche
1 tsp. prepared horseradish
salt and a generous grind white pepper
5 oz. smoked trout
20-24 red or white endive leaves, about 2 heads
1 tbs. chopped fresh parsley or small watercress leaves for garnish

Combine sour cream with horseradish, salt and pepper. Remove any skin or bones from trout and cut or break into 1-inch long by 1/2-inch wide pieces to fit into the endive leaves. Cut off bottom core of endive head and separate leaves. Spoon a little horseradish cream into the larger flat end of endive, top with a piece of trout, and put a little more cream on top of trout. Repeat with remaining endive leaves. Garnish with parsley or watercress. These can be done 1 hour ahead and refrigerated until ready to serve.

Tuna and Egg Tartlets

Bake tartlet shells a day or two ahead and keep them in an airtight container. The filling can also be made ahead and refrigerated. Anchovy paste is available in tubes at most supermarkets.

1 can (6½ oz.) oil-packed tuna, drained
1 hard-cooked egg, chopped
3 tbs. coarsely chopped rinsed, dried capers
2 tsp. Dijon mustard
2 tsp. mayonnaise
1 tsp. anchovy paste
freshly ground pepper
2 tbs. chopped fresh parsley
½ recipe *Basic Tartlet Pastry*, page 161, baked into shells

Place tuna in a medium bowl and add egg, capers, mustard, mayonnaise and anchovy paste. Mix well, season with pepper and stir in parsley. If filling has been refrigerated, remove it from the refrigerator about 30 minutes before assembling tarts. Fill each tartlet shell with about 1 tablespoon of filling. Serve at room temperature.

Poultry

Chicken dishes are a delicious and popular entrée in most households and are found on the tapas table as well. Many favorite recipes can be served as tapas if the meat is cut into smaller pieces and served with toothpicks or forks, or as finger foods. Chicken salads, grilled chicken legs or wings and chunks of chicken cooked in a savory orange, tomato or barbecue sauce are all candidates for the tapas table. Whether you start from scratch or buy already-prepared ingredients, include at least one poultry dish on your tapas table.

Chicken, Artichoke and Oven-Dried Tomatoes

Servings: 4-6

This tapas dish is colorful and flavorful. Serve warm or at room temperature on small plates with forks. The chicken is more easily sliced if placed in the freezer for 30 minutes.

2-3 boneless, skinless, chicken breast halves, about 1 lb.
2 tbs. full-flavored olive oil
2 tbs. lemon juice
½ tsp. dried marjoram
1 pkg. (8 oz.) frozen artichoke hearts
½ cup *Oven-Dried Tomatoes*, page 119, cut into ½-inch pieces
3 green onions, white part only, minced
salt and freshly ground pepper

Wash and dry chicken breasts. With a sharp knife, slice chicken on the diagonal across the grain to yield ¼-inch-thick medallions about 1-inch square. Mix together olive oil, lemon juice and marjoram in a medium bowl, add chicken pieces and marinate for 15 minutes. Cook artichoke hearts according to package directions, drain and set aside.

Heat a large nonstick skillet over medium high heat. Add chicken, marinade, salt and pepper to pan and sauté, stirring often, until chicken is cooked through but not brown, about 3 minutes. Add artichokes, tomato pieces and green onions and toss to combine. Arrange on a serving platter. Adjust seasoning, adding more lemon juice or olive oil if desired. Serve warm or at cool room temperature.

Velvet Chicken Breast Chunks

Everyone loves these succulent morsels and they only take a few minutes to prepare. Sauce the chunks with Almond Sauce, page 156, Romesco Sauce, page 158, or Parsley Sauce, page 156.

2-3 boneless, skinless, chicken breast halves, about 1 lb.
½ cup flour
1 tbs. paprika
½ tsp. salt
⅛ tsp. white pepper
1 tbs. olive oil
½-¾ cup *Almond* or *Romesco Sauce*
fresh parsley for garnish

Heat oven to 375°. Cut chicken into 20 to 24 equal chunks and pat dry with paper towels. Combine flour, paprika, salt, and pepper in a paper bag. Add chicken and shake to coat pieces evenly. Heat a large nonstick skillet over medium heat and add olive oil. Shake excess flour from chicken pieces and place in skillet. Lightly brown on one side, turn, and brown other side. Place skillet in oven for 7 to 8 minutes until chicken is barely cooked through, 7 to 8 minutes.

While chicken is in the oven, add *Almond* or *Romesco Sauce* to a medium saucepan over medium heat. The sauce should have a pourable consistency, so thin with a little stock or water if necessary. Lift chicken pieces from skillet and place in sauce. Stir gently to combine and simmer for 1 to 2 minutes. Turn into a warm serving dish and garnish with parsley. Serve hot or warm on small plates with forks or with toothpicks.

Chicken and Carrots with Orange Sherry Sauce

It takes just a few minutes to stir-fry the chicken breasts and finish in a delicious orange sherry sauce. Serve on small plates with forks or toothpicks.

½ lb. baby carrots or 3 medium carrots
1 tsp. salt for cooking water
2-3 boneless, skinless, chicken breast halves, about 1 lb.
1 tbs. olive oil
salt and freshly ground pepper
¼ cup minced shallots
zest from 1 orange
¼ cup orange juice
1 tsp. sherry wine vinegar
¼ cup medium dry sherry
½ tsp. dry mustard powder

Peel, trim tops and tail, and cut baby carrots into 1-inch lengths, or cut whole carrots into diagonal slices about ½-inch thick. Bring water to a boil in a small saucepan, add salt and blanch carrots for about 2 to 3 minutes until crisp-tender. Drain carrots and reserve.

Trim any remaining fat from chicken breasts and cut into 20 to 24 equal pieces. Pat dry with a paper towel. Heat oil in a large nonstick skillet over medium-high heat, add chicken, season with salt and pepper and sauté for 2 to 3 minutes until chicken pieces turn opaque. Add shallots and cook for 1 minute, and add orange zest, orange juice, vinegar, sherry, mustard and carrots. Reduce heat, cover and cook for 6 to 8 minutes until chicken is cooked through and sauce has reduced. Pour into a serving bowl. Serve hot or warm.

Goat Cheese, Eggplant and Tomato-Stuffed Chicken Breasts

Makes 16-18 pieces

Chicken breasts are pounded flat and stuffed with a colorful, zesty filling. Cooked carrots or potatoes can be substituted for the eggplant. These can be done ahead of time and refrigerated until 30 minutes before serving. Serve on small plates with forks.

3 small boneless, skinless, chicken breast halves, about 1 lb.
¼ cup creamy goat cheese
¼ cup coarsely chopped cooked eggplant
3-4 green onions, white part only, minced
3 tbs. chopped *Oven-Dried Tomatoes*, page 119, or
   oil-packed sun-dried tomatoes
salt and freshly ground pepper
1 tsp. full-flavored olive oil
¼ cup medium dry sherry

Trim any fat from chicken breasts. If still attached, remove the tenderloin and save for another purpose. Place each breast half between two sheets of waxed paper and flatten with a meat mallet until it is a uniform ¼-inch thickness, about 4-by-8-inches in size.

Combine goat cheese, eggplant, onions and tomatoes in a small bowl. Season mixture and chicken breasts with salt and pepper. Spread each flattened breast with ⅓ of the filling, bringing it to within 1 inch of the straightest long edge. Start rolling up the long side like a jelly roll. After the first turn, fold in the two ends and continue rolling tightly. Pin with toothpicks at each end to hold roll together.

Heat olive oil in a medium skillet just large enough to hold all 3 rolls over medium-high heat. Place chicken rolls seam-side down in skillet and brown on all sides, about 5 minutes total. Add sherry to skillet, cover tightly, reduce heat and braise for 10 minutes. Remove to a plate and allow cool for 15 minutes. Slice into ¾-inch slices. Serve warm or at room temperature.

Wine and Garlic Chicken Nuggets

Makes 45-50 pieces

Chunks of chicken thighs are stir-fried with lots of garlic to make this succulent quick tapa.

2 lb. chicken thighs, about 6
1 tbs. full-flavored olive oil
6 cloves garlic, thinly sliced, about
   3 tbs.
½ cup full-bodied red wine

¼ tsp. Tabasco Sauce
salt
1 tbs. lemon juice
¼ cup chopped fresh cilantro or
   parsley for garnish

Remove bone, skin and excess fat from chicken thighs and save to make chicken stock. Cut each thigh into 6 to 8 equal pieces. Heat oil in a medium skillet over medium heat. Add garlic slices and soften in oil for 2 to 3 minutes, but do not brown. Add chicken pieces and increase heat to high. Stir chicken until it firms and changes color. Add wine, Tabasco and salt. Cover, reduce heat to medium and simmer for 2 to 3 minutes. Remove cover, increase heat to high and reduce sauce to a thick glaze. Add lemon juice and parsley. Serve warm on small plates or in a shallow bowl with toothpicks.

Rice and Chicken-Stuffed Tomatoes

Servings: 8

If you have cooked chicken and rice in the refrigerator, this savory dish goes together quickly. Serve warm on small plates with forks.

4 medium tomatoes, about
   2½- to 3-inch diameter
1 tbs. olive oil
⅓ cup finely chopped onion
pinch saffron or turmeric
1 clove garlic, finely chopped

½ tsp. dried marjoram
¾ cup cooked rice
¾ cup diced, cooked chicken
2 tbs. chopped parsley
salt and freshly ground pepper

Cut tomatoes in half through stem. Carefully trim stem end. Scoop out centers and seeds of each tomato half. Discard seeds and chop removed tomato pulp into ¼-inch pieces. Lightly salt tomato shells and turn upside down to drain for a few minutes.

Heat oven to 350°. Heat olive oil in a medium skillet over medium-low heat. Sauté onion for 4 to 5 minutes until soft but not brown. Add saffron, garlic and marjoram and cook for 1 minute. Stir in rice, chicken, tomato pulp and parsley and mix well. Season with salt and pepper. Divide stuffing among tomato halves. Place tomatoes in an oiled shallow baking pan. Bake tomatoes for about 15 minutes, until hot. Place on a serving platter and serve warm.

Sherried Chicken Wings

Succulent chicken wings are definitely finger food tapas that everybody loves. Serve with plenty of napkins. These marinate in the refrigerator for 3 to 4 hours before baking.

10 chicken wings, about 2 lbs.
2 cloves garlic, coarsely chopped
2 tbs. full-flavored olive oil
2 tbs. honey
¼ cup cream sherry
½ tsp. dry mustard
1 tsp. paprika
a few drops Tabasco Sauce
½ tsp. salt
freshly ground pepper

Prepare chicken wings. Cut each wing into 3 pieces. Save the wing tips for the stockpot. Trim off any excess skin and fat from the drumette and wing piece. Wash and pat dry. Place chicken pieces in zipper-top plastic bag. In a small bowl, combine, garlic, olive oil, honey, sherry, paprika, mustard, Tabasco, salt and pepper. Pour over chicken pieces. Close bag and shake to distribute marinade, coating each piece. Refrigerate for 3 to 4 hours, turning bag occasionally.

Heat oven to 400°. Line a rimmed cookie sheet with aluminum foil. Spray a rack with nonstick cooking spray and place on foil. Remove chicken from marinade and arrange on baking rack. Discard marinade. Bake chicken for 25 minutes, turn pieces over and continue to bake for another 25 minutes until chicken is cooked through and nicely browned. Serve immediately, or refrigerate. Remove from refrigerator about 30 minutes before serving.

Lentil and Duck Salad

If you have a local Chinese market or restaurant that roasts fresh ducks, buy a half duck for this salad. If roast duck is not available, substitute Sherry-Glazed Sausage Chunks, page 153, smoked chicken, or ham. This salad can be made a day ahead and refrigerated. Bring to room temperature before serving.

1 cup lentils, brown or green
2 cups water
2 whole cloves
1 onion, peeled and cut in half
1 bay leaf
3 carrots, peeled and cut into $\frac{1}{8}$-inch dice, about 1 cup
3 tbs. full-flavored olive oil, divided
$\frac{1}{2}$ cup finely chopped onion
2 cloves garlic, finely chopped
$\frac{1}{4}$ tsp. dried red pepper flakes
1 cup diced roasted duck meat, in $\frac{1}{4}$-inch dice
2 tbs. sherry or balsamic wine vinegar
$\frac{1}{2}$ tsp. salt
freshly ground pepper
$\frac{1}{4}$ cup chopped fresh parsley

Pick over lentils, rinse and drain. Place in a medium saucepan with water. Stick cloves in onion halves and add to pan with bay leaf. Bring water to boil, reduce heat, cover and simmer for about 20 minutes. Start checking to see if lentils are tender but not mushy at 15 minutes. Do not overcook. Remove pan from heat, drain lentils in a sieve and transfer to a serving bowl. Discard onion, cloves and bay leaf. Bring 2 cups water to a boil in a small saucepan. Blanch diced carrots 2 to 3 minutes, until crisp-tender. Drain and add to serving bowl.

Heat 1 tablespoon of the oil in a small skillet over medium-low heat. Sauté onion for 3 to 4 minutes until soft. Add garlic and red pepper flakes and cook for 1 minute. Add onion mixture and duck meat to serving bowl. In a small bowl, whisk together remaining 2 tablespoons olive oil, vinegar, salt and pepper. Pour over warm lentils and gently toss to combine. Garnish with parsley. Serve warm or at room temperature.

Meat Tapas

Include at least one of these beef, lamb or pork dishes to create a nice balance at your next tapas table. Here are some delicious meat tapas to tempt you. Savory empanadas, flavorful meatballs, sausage chunks and baby back ribs all can be made ahead and reheated at the last moment.

Good chorizo is sometimes hard to find, so we have included a flavorful homemade recipe. Use it to stuff mushroom caps or as a filling for quesadillas or tacos. A light fruity red or rosé wine complements these hearty meat tapas.

Anticuchos

Makes 6-8 servings

These zippy chunks of beef heart are really from Peru and Ecuador. If heart isn't available, top sirloin makes a nice substitute. The meat needs to marinate overnight, so start this the day before. This dish goes well with beer or sangria.

2 lb. beef heart or sirloin steak
¾ cup red wine vinegar
2 tsp. dried red pepper flakes
1 tbs. paprika
2 cloves garlic, finely chopped
4 jalapeño peppers, stemmed, seeded and finely chopped
½ tsp. dried oregano
1 tbs. ground cumin
1 tsp. salt
2 tbs. olive oil

Trim meat to remove any fat or veins and cut into 1-inch cubes. Process vinegar, red pepper flakes, paprika, garlic, jalapeño, oregano, cumin, salt and olive oil with a food processor or blender until smooth. Place meat cubes in a zipper top plastic bag and pour marinade over meat. Exclude most of the air from bag and close tightly. Place bag in the refrigerator and marinate overnight, turning bag once or twice.

If using bamboo skewers, soak in water for 30 minutes before using. When ready to grill, remove meat from refrigerator and bring to room temperature. Drain and reserve marinade. Skewer 4 or 5 chunks of meat on each skewer. Grill over hot coals or place under a preheated broiler and grill for 2 to 3 minutes. Brush with reserved marinade, turn over, and grill for an additional 1 to 2 minutes. The meat should be cooked no more done than medium-rare. Serve hot.

Beef and Potato Empanadas
Fills 16 small or 30 large empanadas

Make these tender-crusted pies a day or two ahead and reheat them in the oven just before serving. Turkey, veal or lean pork can be substituted for ground beef if you like.

1 tbs. full-flavored olive oil
½ lb. ground round
¾ cup minced onion, 1 small
1 jalapeño pepper, stemmed, seeded and finely chopped
1 clove garlic, minced
1 small uncooked potato, peeled and cut into ¼-inch dice, about ½ cup
1 medium carrot, cut into ¼-inch dice
2 tsp. ground cumin
1 tbs. tomato paste
1 cup beef broth or water
1 tsp. salt
freshly ground black pepper
1 tbs. minced fresh cilantro
1 recipe *Basic Empanada Pastry*, page 159, or *Easy Empanada Pastry*, page 160
1 egg white for glaze

Heat olive oil in a medium skillet over high heat. Crumble beef into skillet and cut into small pieces with a spatula. Add onion, jalapeño and garlic. Cook, stirring until beef is cooked through but not browned. Add potato, carrot, cumin and tomato paste. Stir to combine. Add broth, salt and pepper. Reduce heat to medium and simmer uncovered until potatoes are tender, about 15 minutes. If there is any liquid remaining in bottom of pan, increase heat and cook until liquid has evaporated. Allow mixture to cool before filling empanada pastry. Allow mixture to cool and stir in cilantro before filling empanada pastry.

Assemble and bake empanadas as instructed in *Basic Empanada Pastry*.

Baked empanadas can be frozen. Remove from freezer and reheat on cookie sheet in 350° oven for 15 to 20 minutes, or until hot. If empanadas have been refrigerated, reheat on cookie sheet for 7 to 10 minutes, until warm to touch.

Roast Beef Rolls

Spread deli roast beef slices with your favorite blue-veined cheese for a savory tapa. These can be made a day ahead and sliced just before serving.

2 oz. blue-veined cheese — cabrales, Roquefort, Maytag or Danish Blue
2 oz. whipped cream cheese
generous grinds black pepper
6 oz. thin sliced roast beef, about 5-6 slices
2 tbs. finely chopped fresh parsley

In a small bowl, combine blue and cream cheeses and mix well. Season with pepper. Spread a thin layer of cheese on each beef slice. Start from the small end and roll each slice up into a compact roll. Refrigerate until ready to serve. To serve, cut each roll into ¾-inch slices, wiping knife clean between cuts. Dip top cut side of each roll into chopped parsley and arrange on serving plate.

Roasted Pork Tenderloins

Mustard glazed pork tenderloins roast quickly. To serve, top thin slices of roasted pork with a little Prune and Olive Compote, page 152, or Romesco or Parsley Sauce, pages 157 or 156.

2 pork tenderloins, about ¾ lb. each
2 tbs. Dijon mustard
2 tbs. honey
2 tbs. medium amontillado sherry
salt and freshly ground pepper
Prune and Olive Compote
watercress or parsley leaves for garnish

Heat oven to 400°. With a sharp knife, trim tenderloins of fat and silverskin. Combine mustard, honey and sherry in a small bowl and spread half over each tenderloin. Place tenderloins on a rack in baking pan. Roast pork for 20 to 25 minutes, or until internal temperature reaches 160° on a meat thermometer. Remove from oven and allow to cool. To serve, slice into ½-inch medallions, top with a little *Prune and Olive Compote* and garnish with a watercress or parsley leaf. Serve at cool room temperature.

Chorizo-Stuffed Mushroom Caps

Makes about 20

Authentic Spanish chorizo is sometimes difficult to find in this country. Try easy homemade chorizo and use as a filling for bite-sized mushrooms. Eat as finger food or serve on small plates with forks.

½ lb. lean ground pork
1 small clove garlic, finely chopped
1 tbs. prepared chili powder
¼ tsp. ground coriander
2 tbs. red wine vinegar
½ tsp. salt
generous grinds black pepper
20 mushroom caps, brown or white, 1 ½-inch
⅓ cup water
1 tbs. tomato paste
2 tbs. grated manchego or Parmesan cheese

In a small bowl, combine pork, garlic, chili powder, coriander, vinegar, salt and pepper. Cover and refrigerate for 1 to 2 hours. While mixture is chilling, clean and trim mushroom caps. Twist out mushroom stems, chop finely and reserve. With a melon baller or small sharp spoon, enlarge mushroom cap stuffing area by digging out some of the gills.

Remove meat from refrigerator. Heat a medium skillet over medium heat. Crumble pork into skillet and add mushroom stems. Stir as mixture browns and break into small pieces with a spatula. When browned, add water and tomato paste and continue to cook until mixture is almost dry, about 5 minutes.

Heat oven to 375°. In a shallow baking pan large enough to hold mushrooms in one layer, add enough water to cover ½-inch of the bottom of pan. Spoon a little of the stuffing mixture into each mushroom cap, pressing mixture down lightly but firmly. Sprinkle with cheese. Bake, uncovered for about 20 minutes, or until mushroom caps are tender when pierced with a knife. Remove from liquid, drain on paper towels and arrange on serving plate. Serve warm.

Lamb Meatballs with Tomato Sauce   *Makes about 30 servings*

These cilantro-scented meatballs are browned in the oven and simmered in an aromatic tomato sauce. Make them ahead and reheat before serving. Serve with toothpicks or on small plates with forks.

½ cup fresh breadcrumbs
2 tbs. medium amontillado sherry
3 cloves garlic
¾ tsp. kosher salt
¾ lb. lean ground lamb
1 large egg
¼ cup finely minced onion

¼ cup finely chopped fresh cilantro
   leaves, plus some for garnish
½ tsp. ground cumin
¼ tsp. ground coriander
1 tsp. paprika
generous grinds freshly ground pepper

Tomato Sauce

1 tbs. olive oil
½ cup finely chopped onion
1 tbs. flour
1 can (14 oz.) beef broth
2 tbs. tomato paste
½ tsp. ground cumin
2 tsp. Dijon mustard
fresh cilantro leaves for garnish

Heat oven to 450°. Line a large shallow baking pan or jelly-roll pan with aluminum foil. Spray foil with nonstick cooking spray. Add sherry to bread-crumbs and set aside to soak. Mince garlic on a cutting board and sprinkle salt on top. Use the side of your knife to reduce garlic to a paste. Place lamb in a bowl; add soaked breadcrumbs, garlic and salt, egg, onion, cilantro, cumin, coriander, paprika and black pepper. Mix until well combined. Form into 30 meatballs about 1¼-inches in diameter. Place meatballs on prepared baking sheet and bake for 15 minutes, until nicely browned.

While meatballs are browning, prepare the sauce. Heat olive oil in a heavy 3-quart saucepan and sauté onion over medium-high heat for 4 to 5 minutes, until lightly browned. Stir in flour and cook for 1 minute. Add beef broth, tomato paste, cumin and mustard. Simmer for a few minutes until thick and smooth. Add browned meatballs to sauce and bring to a boil. Cover and sim-mer over very low heat for 30 minutes. Spoon into a serving bowl, garnish with fresh cilantro leaves and serve hot.

Meatballs in Almond Sherry Sauce *Makes about 70 meatballs*

Albondigas, or meatballs, are a classic Spanish tapa. They are even better the next day, so make them ahead and reheat before serving. Serve on small plates with a fork or with toothpicks.

¾ lb. ground veal
¾ lb. lean ground pork
1 cup finely chopped onion
3 cloves garlic, finely chopped
1 large egg, lightly beaten
½ cup fresh breadcrumbs
½ tsp. salt
½ tsp. freshly ground black pepper
¼ cup chopped fresh parsley, divided
flour for coating meatballs
3 tbs. olive oil

Place veal, pork, onion, garlic, egg, breadcrumbs, salt, pepper and 2 table-spoons parsley in a large bowl and stir to combine well. Place flour on a large plate or pie pan. Form meat mixture into 1-inch meatballs and lightly roll each one in flour. Add olive oil to a large skillet over medium-high heat and lightly brown meatballs on all sides. Do this in 2 or 3 batches, depending on size of skillet. Remove browned meatballs to a plate with a slotted spoon and set aside.

Almond Sherry Sauce

additional olive oil if needed
2 tbs. flour
½ cup finely ground almonds
1 can (14½ oz.) beef broth
⅓ cup dry sherry
salt and freshly ground pepper

Heat same skillet used for meatballs. If necessary, add enough olive oil to make 3 tablespoons of liquid. Stir in flour and almonds and cook over medium low heat for 1 to 2 minutes, but do not brown. Gradually stir in beef broth, sherry, salt and pepper, mixing well. Increase heat to medium and stir until sauce thickens. Reduce heat to low and add meatballs to sauce. Cover and simmer meatballs in sauce for 30 minutes, turning meatballs 2 or 3 times during cooking. If sauce becomes too thick, thin with a little water. Spoon into a heated bowl, sprinkle with parsley just before serving and serve warm.

To keep meatballs warm during serving, use a warming tray, or place in a small microwavable bowl and reheat in the microwave as needed.

Oven-Roasted Baby Back Ribs

These delectable morsels take very little work and can be roasted ahead and heated just before serving. Cut into individual ribs and serve as finger food.

2 racks baby back ribs, about 4 lb.
1½ tbs. paprika or mild New Mexico chile powder
1½ tsp. dry mustard powder
1½ tsp. ground coriander
1½ tsp. garlic powder
1½ tsp. ground cumin
1½ tsp. salt
½ tsp. freshly ground black pepper

Basting Sauce

⅓ cup cream sherry
2 tbs. sherry wine vinegar
¼ tsp. Tabasco Sauce, or to taste
½ tsp. salt

Trim any surface fat from ribs. In a small bowl combine paprika, mustard, coriander, garlic powder, cumin, salt and pepper. Sprinkle spice mixture evenly over both sides of ribs and gently massage into meat. Allow meat to stand at room temperature for 1 to 2 hours.

Heat oven to 325°. Line a large baking sheet with aluminum foil. Place ribs meaty side up on foil. Add ⅓ cup water to pan. Loosely cover meat with another sheet of foil and bake for 1 hour. Remove foil, turn ribs over and continue to bake uncovered for 30 minutes. Pour off accumulated fat from pan and turn ribs over again. Continue to roast for another 40 to 45 minutes. Meat should be very tender and beginning to pull away from the bone. Remove ribs from oven and cool.

In a small bowl, combine cream sherry, wine vinegar, Tabasco and salt. Just before serving, heat oven to 450°. Place ribs on baking sheet. Brush with basting sauce or your favorite barbecue sauce, and place in oven to heat through for about 15 minutes. Liberally baste with sauce and turn every few minutes. Cut into individual ribs for easy eating and serve immediately.

Prune and Olive Compote

Use this piquant mixture to top roast pork tenderloin slices or smoked ham squares. Or put a spoonful on a crisp cracker spread with a little creamy goat cheese. This keeps for several days refrigerated.

⅓ cup softened prunes
⅓ cup kalamata olives
1 tsp. sherry wine vinegar
1 tsp. Dijon mustard

1 tsp. brown sugar
salt and freshly ground pepper
2 tbs. chopped cilantro
1 tbs. capers, rinsed and drained

Remove pits from prunes and olives and chop into small pieces on a chopping board. Scrape mixture into a small bowl and add vinegar, mustard, sugar, a little salt and pepper. Stir well. Spread a small amount of mixture on each pork slice. Garnish with a cilantro leaf and 1 or 2 capers.

Savory Pork Chunks

Makes 4-6 servings

Cubes of tender braised pork are coated with spices and broiled briefly to give them a nice crusty coating. Serve hot with toothpicks.

1 lb. pork shoulder, trimmed of fat, cut into 1½-inch cubes
1 cup chicken broth
2 cloves garlic, peeled
1 tsp. tomato paste
1 tsp. sherry wine vinegar
1 tsp. paprika
½ tsp. kosher salt
⅛ tsp. cayenne pepper
freshly ground black pepper

Trim surface fat from pork cubes and place in a saucepan. Add chicken broth and garlic. Bring to a boil, lower heat and simmer covered for 30 minutes. Remove pork from broth and place on a foil-lined baking pan. Discard garlic, skim fat from braising liquid and reduce over high heat to about ⅓ cup. Add tomato paste and sherry wine vinegar.

Preheat broiler. In a small bowl mix together paprika, salt, cayenne and pepper. Sprinkle half of the spice mixture over the pork pieces. Place under broiler about 6 inches away from heat source and broil for 2 to 3 minutes, or until pork is lightly browned. Remove pork from broiler, turn pieces over and sprinkle them with remaining spice. Broil for 2 to 3 minutes until brown and crisp on the second side. Do not overcook. Reheat broth, add pork pieces and toss to coat with sauce. Pour into a serving dish.

Sherry-Glazed Sausage Chunks

Makes 20-25 pieces

Fully cooked sausages such as Polish or kielbasa can be used without poaching. Italian, garlic and other raw sausages must be poached before slicing and cooking in sherry.

1 lb. cooked sausage: kielbasa, Polish, chorizo, or linguica
½ cup cream sherry

Cut sausages into ¾-inch pieces. Pour sherry into skillet, add sausages and cook over medium-high heat for 4 to 5 minutes, until sherry evaporates and sausages are lightly browned. Stir frequently during cooking. Serve warm with toothpicks. Sausages can be cooked and reheated in the microwave for 1 minute before serving.

Note: For fresh, uncooked Italian sausages, turkey or other specialty sausages, poach sausages first in water. See method in *Sausages and Figs In Orange Sherry Sauce*.

Sausages and Figs in Orange Sherry Sauce

Makes 4-6 servings

Dried Calimyrna or Mission figs pair deliciously with sausage cooked in a little orange juice and sherry. Make ahead and reheat just before serving. Serve warm on small plates or with toothpicks.

1 lb. uncooked mild Italian sausages
1 cup water
1 medium onion, thinly sliced
zest and juice from 1 orange
⅓ cup medium amontillado sherry

1 tsp. sherry wine vinegar
8 oz. dried Calimyrna figs, stemmed
 and cut in half or quarters
generous grinds black pepper

Place sausages in a medium skillet with water. Bring to a boil, cover, lower heat and simmer for 8 to 10 minutes, turning sausages over halfway during cooking. Drain liquid from sausages and increase heat to medium-high. Cook sausages until lightly browned on both sides, about 2 to 3 minutes. Remove sausages from skillet and place on a cutting board. When cool enough to handle, cut into ¾-inch slices. Add onion to skillet and cook over medium heat for about 2 minutes. Add orange juice and zest, sherry, wine vinegar and figs to skillet. Cover and cook for 2 minutes to soften figs.

Return sausage slices to skillet, cover and cook for 2 more minutes. Uncover, increase heat to high and reduce liquid in pan to about ¼ cup. Turn sausages into a heated serving dish and finish with a generous grind of black pepper. Serve hot.

Veal, Raisin and Pine Nut Empanadas

Fills 30 small or 16 large empanadas

Cinnamon and allspice give these savory empanadas a Moorish touch. Cool mixture before filling empanada pastry.

1 tbs. full-flavored olive oil
½ lb. lean ground veal
1 cup finely chopped onion, about 1 medium
¼ tsp. cinnamon
⅛ tsp. ground allspice
½ tsp. salt
½ cup water
2 tbs. amontillado sherry or brandy
¼ cup golden raisins, coarsely chopped
¼ cup pine nuts, toasted
1 recipe *Basic Empanada Pastry*, page 159, or *Easy Empanada Pastry*, page 160
1 egg white for glaze

Heat olive oil in a medium skillet over medium heat. Crumble in veal and break up large pieces with a spatula. Add onion and continue to cook until veal is cooked through. Add cinnamon, allspice and salt, and stir to combine. Add water, sherry and raisins. Continue cooking until moisture has completely evaporated, about 15 minutes. Remove from heat and cool. Stir in pine nuts.

Assemble and bake empanadas as instructed in *Basic Empanada Pastry*.

Baked empanadas can be frozen. Heat oven to 350°. Remove from freezer and reheat on a cookie sheet 15 to 20 minutes, or until hot. If empanadas have been refrigerated, reheat on cookie sheet for 7 to 10 minutes, until warm to touch.

Basic Sauces and Pastry

Sauces add vivid color, texture and complementary flavors to simply pre-pared foods. Romesco and tomato sauces are probably the most widely used sauces in Spain, followed closely by the garlicky mayonnaise-based aioli. Prepare one or two of these sauces, keep them in the refrigerator, and spoon some over steamed vegetables, grilled meats or simply prepared seafood. It will be easy to taste the magic of sauces with foods on your tapas table.

Empanadas and tartaletas have a definite place on the tapas table. Here are two empanadas pastries, a traditional crust and an *Easy Empanada Pastry* that requires no chilling and can be made in the food processor. Both have an excellent flavor and are easy to handle.

Aioli
Makes 1 cup

This is a sauce for garlic lovers. Serve it with grilled vegetables or fish, Fried Calamari, page 153, Oven-Roasted Baby Potatoes with Garlic, page 117, or as a base for bruschetta toppings. Use a mortar and pestle to mash the garlic with the salt, or put it through a garlic press to make it very fine. This will keep in the refrigerator for 2 to 3 days.

4-5 cloves garlic
½ tsp. kosher or coarse salt
1 cup prepared mayonnaise
2 tsp. lemon juice
2 tbs. full-flavored olive oil
⅛ tsp. white pepper

Peel garlic cloves, coarsely chop and place in a mortar with salt. Crush gar-lic with pestle until very smooth. If you have a large mortar, add mayonnaise, lemon juice, olive oil and pepper to garlic and mix until well combined. Otherwise scrape garlic into a small bowl, add remaining ingredients and whisk until well combined. Refrigerate if not using immediately.

Almond Sauce

Makes 1 cup

Serve this quick, versatile sauce with cooked asparagus, green beans, steamed new potatoes or broccoli, grilled fish, or with Velvet Chicken Breast Chunks, page 139. This sauce tends to thicken when refrigerated. Add more chicken broth or water to thin it before serving.

½-¾ cup chicken broth
3 tbs. chopped shallots
1 cup toasted almond slices, about
   3 oz.
2 tbs. lemon juice

2 tbs. dry sherry
1 tsp. sherry wine vinegar
2 tbs. full-flavored olive oil
salt and freshly ground pepper
paprika for garnish

Bring ½ cup chicken broth and shallots to a boil in a small saucepan. Cook for 3 to 4 minutes to soften shallots. Remove from heat. Place almonds in a food processor workbowl and process until mixture resembles coarse meal. With motor running, add lemon juice, sherry, wine vinegar, olive oil, chicken broth and shallots. Process until well combined. Season with salt and pepper. Thin sauce with more chicken broth if needed to produce a pourable sauce. Sprinkle with paprika. Spoon over vegetables or fish, or serve in individual dishes and use as a dipping sauce.

Parsley Sauce

Makes ⅔ cup

Serve this vibrant green, piquant sauce with Basic Steamed Mussels, page 131, Steamed Clams, page 124, or grilled seafood, chicken or sausages. This keeps in the refrigerator for 3 or 4 days.

2 cloves garlic, peeled
2 green onions, white part only, cut
   into 1-inch lengths
⅓ cup full-flavored olive oil
¼ cup capers, drained, rinsed and
   patted dry on paper towels
1 tbs. anchovy paste, or 3 oil-packed
   anchovy fillets

2 tsp. Dijon mustard
2 tsp. sherry wine vinegar
½ tsp. sugar
⅛ tsp. white pepper
⅓ cup finely chopped fresh Italian
   parsley, packed
salt

Into a food processor workbowl, with motor running, drop garlic and onion pieces through feed tube and process until finely chopped. Scrape down sides of bowl. Add oil, capers, anchovy, mustard, vinegar, sugar and pepper. Process until smooth. Add parsley and pulse 2 to 3 times to combine. Add salt to taste. Refrigerate until ready to serve.

Red Pepper Mayonnaise

Makes ½ cup

This vibrant red sauce pairs deliciously with any cold seafood or chicken.

½ cup prepared mayonnaise
¼ cup roasted red pepper pieces
¼ tsp. paprika
1 tbs. brandy or cognac

Place ingredients in a small blender container or food processor workbowl and process until smooth. Chill until ready to use.

Romesco Sauce

Makes about 3 cups

Serve this mildly spicy Spanish sauce with hot grilled shrimp, scallops, chicken, baby leeks or green onions. It is also delicious in quesadillas or ham or roast beef sandwiches. Make it 2 or 3 days ahead and refrigerate until ready to serve.

½ cup full-flavored olive oil, divided
2 slices French-style bread, ½-inch
   thick, about 1 oz., crusts removed
2 large red bell peppers
1 small onion, peeled, cut into ½-
   inch slices
3 cloves garlic, peeled

2 tomatoes
¼ tsp. dried red pepper flakes
1 tsp. paprika
⅓ cup toasted almonds
2 tbs. red wine vinegar
2 tbs. water
salt and freshly ground pepper

Heat 1 tablespoon of the olive oil in a medium skillet over medium heat and sauté bread on both sides until nicely browned. Remove bread, cut into 3 or 4 pieces and set aside. Preheat broiler. Line a shallow baking pan with foil. Place red peppers, onion slices and garlic on foil. Cut tomatoes in half, cut out cores and remove seeds. Place in baking pan cut-side down. Brush onion, garlic and tomatoes with a little olive oil. Broil vegetables about 8 inches from heat source for 8 to 10 minutes. Rotate peppers as they char. Turn vegetables over and continue to cook for another 5 to 7 minutes, or until vegetables are lightly charred. Wrap peppers in foil and steam for 10 minutes.

Pull off skin from peppers and place peppers in a food processor workbowl with onions, garlic and tomatoes. Add bread pieces, red pepper flakes, paprika, almonds, vinegar, water and remaining olive oil. Process until quite smooth. Season with salt and pepper. Remove from refrigerator about 30 minutes before serving. The sauce should be the consistency of heavy cream; stir in a little water if it gets too thick.

Seafood Cocktail Sauce

Makes ¾ cup

Serve this bright sauce with boiled shrimp, grilled scallops, Shrimp a la Plancha, page 135, Calamari Cocktail, page 125, or Fried Calamari, page 123.

¾ cup bottled chili sauce
1 tbs. creamy horseradish
1 tbs. lemon juice

½ tsp. brown sugar
salt and freshly ground pepper

In a small bowl, combine chili sauce with horseradish, lemon juice, brown sugar, salt and pepper. Use immediately or refrigerate for several days.

Sherry Vinegar and Shallot Sauce

Makes about ⅓ cup

Serve this piquant dipping sauce with clams or oysters.

⅓ cup sherry wine vinegar
3 small shallots, finely chopped
salt and freshly ground pepper

Combine ingredients in an attractive small bowl and serve with prepared shellfish.

Spicy Tomato Sauce

Makes about 2 cups

This sauce eclipses any ketchup. Serve it warm with Spicy Baked Potato Wedges, page 117, Mini-Tortillas, page 102, boiled or grilled shrimp, or Fried Calamari, page 123, or just spoon it on a grilled hamburger.

Heat oil and onions in a small heavy saucepan over medium heat. Reduce heat and cook onion for 4 to 5 minutes until translucent and soft, but not brown. Add garlic and cook for 1 minute. Add wine and vinegar to pan, bring to a boil and cook over high heat for 2 to 3 minutes. Add tomato sauce and paste, paprika, sugar, cayenne and salt. Bring to a boil, reduce heat to low and simmer for about 15 minutes, until sauce thickens slightly. Stir several times during cooking. Taste carefully and add more cayenne or some Tabasco if desired.

Basic Empanada Pastry

Makes pastry for 30 small or 16 large empanadas

This traditional tender, flaky pastry is perfect for any empanada filling. It requires an hour in the refrigerator before rolling and cutting.

3 cups all-purpose flour
1 tsp. salt
½ cup cold vegetable shortening, butter or lard, cut into cubes
2 large eggs
3-4 tbs. ice water
1 egg white for glaze

Place flour and salt in a food processor workbowl. Pulse a few times to combine. Add shortening and pulse several times until mixture resembles small peas. With processor running, add eggs and ice water. Process until dough forms a ball. Divide dough in half, flatten each to a disk about ¾-inch thick, wrap in plastic wrap and refrigerate for at least 1 hour before rolling and cutting the dough.

Place dough between 2 sheets of waxed paper and roll out to a thickness of ⅛-inch. Cut as many 2¾-inch or 4-inch circles from the dough as possible. Combine dough scraps, roll out again and cut more circles.

Heat oven to 375°. Line a cookie sheet with parchment paper. Place a slightly rounded teaspoon of filling for small empanadas or about 2 tablespoons of filling for larger empanadas on the bottom half of each pastry circle. Brush edge of dough with a little water to help seal. Fold dough over to form a half-circle, pressing firmly along the edges. Use fork tines to finish sealing the edges of each empanada. Place on prepared cookie sheet. In a small bowl, whisk egg white until foamy and brush on top of each empanada. Prick tops with a fork to allow steam to escape. Bake for 25 minutes until pastry is firm and lightly browned. Serve warm or at room temperature.

Baked empanadas can be frozen. Heat oven to 350°. Place frozen empanadas on a cookie sheet and bake for about 15 to 20 minutes, until hot. If empanadas have been refrigerated, reheat for 7 to 10 minutes, until warm to the touch.

Easy Empanada Pastry

This pastry goes together quickly, requires no chilling and is easy to roll out.

3 cups all-purpose flour
1 tsp. salt
1 tsp. baking powder
1 tsp. paprika
2 large eggs
½ cup full-flavored olive oil
2 tbs. chilled fino or medium dry sherry
3-4 tbs. ice water

Place flour, salt, baking powder and paprika in a food processor workbowl. Pulse 1 to 2 times to combine. Separate one egg. Add 1 whole egg, 1 egg yolk and olive oil to workbowl and process until combined. Reserve egg white to glaze empanadas. Add sherry and 3 tablespoons ice water, and process for a few more seconds. Mixture will resemble coarse meal and hold together when pinched between thumb and forefinger. Add a few more drops of ice water if necessary.

Heat oven to 375°. Line a cookie sheet with parchment paper. Divide dough into 2 equal-sized pieces and roll each piece between 2 pieces of waxed paper to a thickness of ⅛ inch. Cut as many 2¾-inch circles from the dough as possible. Combine dough scraps, roll out again and cut more circles. Place a slightly rounded teaspoon of filling for small empanadas or about 2 tablespoons of filling for larger empanadas on the bottom half of each pastry circle. Lightly brush bottom edge of dough with a little water to help seal. Fold dough over to form a half-circle, pressing firmly along the edges. Use fork tines to finish sealing the edges of each empanada. Place on prepared cookie sheet. In a small bowl whisk remaining egg white until foamy and brush top of each empanada. Prick tops with a fork to allow steam to escape. Bake for 25 minutes until pastry is firm and lightly browned. Serve warm or at room temperature.

Baked empanadas can be frozen. Heat oven to 350°. Place frozen empanadas on a cookie sheet and bake for about 15 to 20 minutes, until hot. If empanadas have been refrigerated, reheat for 7 to 10 minutes, until warm to the touch.

Basic Tartlet Pastry

Use these flaky shells for Eggplant and Tomato Tartlets, page 109, or Tuna and Egg Tartlets, page 137, or with your favorite filling. These small tartaletas or pastry shells are handy to have on hand and keep well for several days when stored in an airtight container or kept frozen.

1 1/2 cups all-purpose flour
1/2 tsp. salt
1/2 cup (1 stick) chilled, unsalted butter, cut into 8 pieces
4-5 tbs. chilled dry sherry or ice water

Place flour and salt in food processor workbowl and pulse once or twice to mix well. Add butter and process until mixture resembles coarse meal. Sprinkle 4 tablespoons sherry on dough and pulse several times until mixture starts to form a ball. Add a few more drops of liquid if necessary to make dough hold together. Remove dough from workbowl and press into a flat rectangle. Wrap with plastic wrap and refrigerate for 1 hour.

Heat oven to 375°. Lightly oil back of a miniature muffin pan and inside of another pan of the same size. Roll out chilled dough to 1/8-inch thickness. Use a small fluted cookie cutter to cut circles about 1/2-inch larger than diameter of tart pans. Gently press dough onto oiled back pan and top with another pan, pressing down firmly. Bake for 20 minutes, then remove top pan and return shells to oven to bake for 3 more minutes, or until shells are lightly browned and feel dry to the touch. Cool both pans and repeat with remaining pastry dough. Cool baked shells and fill as directed.

What Do You Drink With Tapas?

The whole concept of tapas originated in Andalucia, home of sherry. It is therefore no coincidence that dry sherry pairs marvelously with classic Spanish tapas. Sherry wine production was well established before the time of Columbus, who included casks of it in the provisions for his voyages to the New World.

Wines labeled "sherry" are produced in many countries. Australia and South Africa produce some interesting sweet sherries, but the sherries found in the United States are most often from Spain, California and to a lesser extent, New York.

The sherries preferred by Spaniards to go with tapas are light and dry. Lightest of all sherries are the manzanillas. Aged in the cooler, more humid climate of San Lucar de Barrameda, manzanillas tend to be lower in alcohol, with a fresh, clean, slightly bitter taste. Manzanillas do not age well, so purchase them from a high-volume merchant, store in the refrigerator and consume soon after purchase. Some excellent Spanish manzanilla and dry fino sherries are produced under Emilio Lustau, Duff Gordon, Hartley and Gibson, Gonzales Byass, and Osborne labels.

Fino, aged in Jerez which is inland from the sea coast, has a little more body and character than manzanilla. Finos often are slightly fortified with brandy to give them a longer shelf life. They are at their best served chilled with tapas.

Amontillado sherry is heavier and has been aged longer than manzanilla or fino. It is often fortified to bring the alcohol level up to 18 to 20 percent, and sometimes is lightly sweetened. Amontillados are rich and full-bodied and are a little too powerful to accompany seafood tapas. They do pair well with tapas that contain meat or poultry in a distinctive sauce, particularly those containing garlic and tomatoes. Cream sherries are rich and sweet, and are best saved to go with dessert.

American sherries are very well made and quite enjoyable. The ones that go best with tapas are labeled "fino" and often "dry sherry." They are rarely as light and dry as those from Spain. Wines with 18 percent or less alcohol will be less cloying, and pair better with tapas. In California, Sheffield Cellars and Paul Masson produce a full range of sherries.

Sparkling wines, always festive, go very well with the whole range of tapas. Spain produces wonderful cavas, wines made by the same method as the true French champagnes. They are less expensive than their French counterparts, and readily available. Look for Freixenet or Codorniu.

California sparkling wines are also very good. Unless your budget demands, avoid the least expensive bulk process California sparklers. Spending just a few more dollars makes a world of difference in quality. Look for, Mumm's, Chandon, Piper-Sonoma, Roederer Estate and Schramsberg.

Young fruity wines — white, red and especially rosé — are also suitable for tapas. A tapas party is not the occasion to serve fine old wines. Tapas party foods generally have assertive flavors that might overpower fine vintages. Look for inexpensive young wines from Spain, California, Italy or the south of France. White, rose or red Zinfandel, and crisp Sauvignon blanc from California complement tapas flavors.

Of the three major table wine-producing areas of Spain — the Rioja, Penedes and Valdepenas — the best for serving with a broad range of tapas come from Penedes. Look for the well-made wines of Miguel Torres, which are widely available.

Beer is a favorite with tapas. Many of the lagers and lighter ales produced by micro breweries are great with tapas. Avoid heavier, maltier and sweeter ales.

Sangria
Makes 2 quarts, or 8-10 glasses

Sangria has a gorgeous red-orange color and is typically made from red wine, fruit juices, sliced fruits and sparkling water. Sometimes a small amount of brandy or other liqueur is added. This refreshing drink is served over ice. Use an inexpensive Spanish wine or a California Zinfandel or Burgundy.

2 oranges
1 bottle (750 ml.) young, fruity red wine
1 ripe peach, sliced or 1 cup frozen peach slices
¼ cup brandy, prefer Spanish or Mexican
2 tbs. sugar
1 ½ cups club soda
ice cubes for glasses

Chill all ingredients before combining with ice. Wash oranges. Thinly slice 1 orange and squeeze juice from second orange. In a large pitcher or nonreactive container, combine orange slices and juice, red wine, peaches, brandy and sugar. Stir until sugar is dissolved and refrigerate. Just before serving, add club soda and stir gently to combine. Place a few ice cubes in tall glasses and pour sangria over ice. Make certain everyone gets an orange slice and piece of fruit in their glass.

Limonada or Sangra Blanca

Makes 2 quarts, or 8-10 glasses

Limonada is not typically Spanish. It is a New World invention, but it makes a great accompaniment for tapas, especially in warm weather. Use a young, inexpensive white wine such as a Riesling, Chenin Blanc or other fruity white wine. Regular frozen lemonade concentrate works well, but frozen raspberry-flavored lemonade is particularly good.

1 bottle (750 ml.) fruity white wine
½ cup defrosted, undiluted frozen raspberry lemonade concentrate
1 lemon, washed, unpeeled and thinly sliced
½ cup vodka, optional
16 oz. club soda
1 cup raspberries
ice cubes for glasses
1 lemon, thinly sliced, for glasses
additional raspberries for glasses

Chill all ingredients. Combine white wine, raspberry lemonade, lemon and vodka in a pitcher or large bowl. Add chilled soda and raspberries just before serving, and stir gently to combine. Place a few ice cubes in tall glasses and pour *Limonada* over ice. Make certain that everyone's glass contains a lemon slice and a few raspberries.

Sherry Shrub

Makes 2 quarts, or 8-10 glasses

Shrubs have been around since Revolutionary times. They are often made with rum but also with brandy or sherry, and provide a refreshing tall drink to accompany tapas.

1 bottle (25 oz.) dry fino sherry, imported or domestic
⅓ cup undiluted frozen orange juice concentrate
2 tbs. Cointreau or Triple Sec
2 tbs. rum
2 tbs. lemon juice
3 cups club soda
ice for glasses
1 orange, thinly sliced for glasses
1 lemon, thinly sliced for glasses

Mix sherry, orange juice, Cointreau, rum and lemon juice in a large pitcher, punchbowl or nonreactive container and refrigerate until ready to serve. Just before serving add chilled club soda and stir gently to combine. Place a few ice cubes in tall glasses, add an orange and lemon slice and pour drink over.

Classic Margaritas

Classic Mexican margaritas go very well with a wide range of tapas. The best margaritas are prepared with tequila, freshly squeezed lime juice and a good quality orange liqueur. It isn't necessary to use aged golden tequila in your margaritas. The lime and orange liqueur flavors dominate and overpower the subtle complexity of finer tequilas. Cointreau, while costlier, has a more intense orange flavor and makes a better margarita than Triple Sec.

Be careful with these! They go down easy, but pack a real punch.

kosher salt for glass rim, optional
2 oz. tequila
1 oz. Cointreau or Triple Sec

1 oz. freshly squeezed lime juice
crushed ice

See note on page 166 to make a salt-rimmed glass, if desired. In a cocktail or margarita glass, combine tequila, Cointreau and lime juice with crushed ice. Makes 1 serving.

Shaker Margarita

Pour tequila, Cointreau, lime juice and crushed ice in a cocktail shaker. Shake vigorously for 10 seconds and strain into a salt-rimmed margarita or martini glass.

Blender Margarita

Double ingredients and place tequila, Cointreau, lime juice and 1 cup crushed ice into blender bowl. Blend for a few seconds on high and pour into 2 salt-rimmed glasses.

Pitcher Margaritas

Pitcher margaritas are more subtle and less alcoholic than the *Classic Margarita*. Start with a good quality margarita mix, either frozen or bottled.

In a large pitcher, combine margarita mix and tequila in the proportions directed on the mix, using the lesser amount of tequila if there is a range. Instead of water, add club soda to equal the amount of margarita mix and tequila to the pitcher just before serving. Stir gently and pour or ladle into tall salt-rimmed glasses over ice cubes.

Note: To make salt-rimmed glasses, pour a small amount of kosher or coarse salt on a piece of waxed paper or into a saucer. Rub the rim of each glass with a small piece of lime to moisten and roll the rim in salt.

The New International Fondue Cookbook

Ed Callaghan

Edited and augmented by
Coleen and Bob Simmons

Introduction

Fondue is a delightful way of sharing food with family and friends. When this, one of the earliest and most successful fondue books, was updated, recipe additions and new recipes were added, including delicious hot dips and wonderful Oriental broths.

Different Types of Fondue

From the original cheese fondue evolved the cooking of meats and seafood in hot oil (fondue bourguignonne), with all of its variations, and from America came dessert fondues. Although baked fondue, which also originated in this country, isn't at all similar to either the classic Swiss fondue or fondue bourguignonne, it is a popular make-ahead party dish and it is included in this collection of fondues. Rarebits, on the other hand, bear no similarity of name but are quite like many of the cheese fondues. The major difference between a fondue and a rarebit seems to be whether the bread goes into or under the sauce. Rarebits can certainly be served with bread cubes for dipping as well as spooned over toast in the traditional manner.

Equipment

The classic-type cheese fondues can be prepared in an earthenware pot called a caquelon, or a metal pot over a heat source, or a chafing dish, or in a dish in a microwave oven (see *Classic Fondue in a Microwave*, page 170). Some fondue mixtures and rarebits do not stand up well over direct heat, and so they must be prepared and served over hot water. Because a chafing dish can be used in much the same way as a double boiler, it is by far the best to use under these circumstances. The various pots come in different sizes, shapes and prices. Special fondue forks are not essential but make the dipping process easier and more fun. It really isn't necessary to have special fondue equipment, but inexpensive sets are available and the more decorative the pot and other elements, the more festive the effect.

Entertain with Fondue

Fondue is an excellent appetizer when you have friends in for cocktails. It's perfect when you're camping or on a trip to a ski or beach cabin. Retire to the living room after dinner with dessert fondue and steaming cups of hot coffee or tea. Or make fondue the main event for a meal or party. You may serve what you wish as long as the basic ingredients — good friends and a communal pot — are there.

Classic Fondue

How you eat is as much fun as what you eat! There are various Swiss traditions surrounding the unfortunate person who drops his bread in the fondue pot. A lady must pay her debt by kissing the man nearest her and a man pays by buying the wine; or perhaps it might mean only a loss of one's next turn.

½ lb. Emmentaler cheese
½ lb. Gruyère cheese
1 clove garlic
2 cups dry white wine
1 tbs. lemon juice
2 tbs. flour
3 tbs. kirsch
dash nutmeg and paprika

Finely dice or coarsely shred cheese. It will melt better than if finely grated. Cut garlic clove in half. Rub the fondue pot or saucepan and wooden spoon with cut side of garlic clove and then discard. Pour wine into pot and set over moderate heat. When hot (never boil), add lemon juice. Lightly toss flour with cheese. Drop by handfuls into hot wine. Stir constantly with wooden spoon. Allow each addition to melt before adding the next. Continue stirring in a figure-eight motion until cheese is melted. Add kirsch and spices and serve.

Place the fondue pot in the middle of the table over low heat. Provide each guest (not more than 4 or 5 to a pot) with a fondue fork or bamboo skewer and bread cubes to dip into the cheese mixture.

The brown crust that remains in the bottom of the pot should be removed with a knife and divided among the diners. Many people think the crust is the best part of the fondue!

If serving fondue as a main course, the rest of the menu might consist of a crisp green salad tossed with raw vegetables and a light oil and fresh lemon juice dressing, chilled fruity white wine (dry Riesling or dry Chenin blanc are particularly good choices), and for dessert a fresh fruit tray, baked apples or shortcakes topped with fresh or poached fruit.

Variations

- **Fondue Vermouth**. Use dry vermouth instead of dry white wine.

- **Fondue Gorgonzola et Tilsiter**. Use ⅓ Gorgonzola, ⅓ Tilsiter and ⅓ Gruyère cheeses.

Classic Fondue in a Microwave

Servings: 2-3

If you don't have a fondue pot, or if you are going to put the cooked fondue over a candle or other warmer that isn't hot enough to cook over, make it in the microwave in a soufflé dish, and then transfer the hot fondue to your fondue serving container. If you are using a microwavable dish, the fondue can be reheated uncovered for 1 to 2 minutes on HIGH and returned to the serving table.

¼ lb. Emmentaler cheese, coarsely grated
¼ lb. Gruyère cheese, coarsely grated
1 tbs. flour
1 cup dry white wine

1 clove garlic, cut in half
2 tsp. lemon juice
1 tbs. kirsch
dash nutmeg and paprika

Combine grated cheeses with flour and set aside. Place wine, garlic and lemon juice in a 1-quart soufflé dish or microwavable container and microwave uncovered on HIGH for 2 to 3 minutes until boiling. Remove garlic and discard. Stir in grated cheese and flour mixture. Cook uncovered on MEDIUM power for about 4 minutes until cheese is melted. Stir every 2 minutes. Stir in kirsch when mixture is almost melted and continue to cook until fondue is smooth. Sprinkle top of fondue with grated nutmeg and a dash of paprika. Transfer to a fondue pot for serving, or place a soufflé dish over a candle warmer on the table.

Pizza Fondue

Servings: 6

Serve this fondue at a winter holiday gathering. Breadsticks make perfect dippers. Any left over makes a great lunch served over toasted English muffins.

½ medium onion, chopped
1 garlic clove, minced
¼ lb. ground beef
1 jar (10½ oz.) pizza sauce
½ tsp. fennel seed
½ tsp. dried oregano
1 cup shredded cheddar cheese
½ cup shredded mozzarella cheese
breadsticks

Brown onion, garlic and ground beef in a saucepan. Drain all excess liquid and fat. Return saucepan to medium heat, add pizza sauce and herbs and stir. Add cheese and stir until smooth. Transfer to a fondue pot for serving.

Continental Fondue

Choose a lively young Soave or Pinot Grigio Italian white wine to accompany this dish. An antipasto tray of fresh vegetables, olives and thin sliced salami or other Italian deli meat is great with this.

1 clove garlic, cut in half
½ lb. Swiss cheese, minced
½ lb. Bel Paese or fontina cheese, minced
¾ cup dry white wine
2 tbs. brandy
French or Italian bread, cubed, or breadsticks

Rub bottom and sides of a fondue pot, saucepan or microwave dish with cut garlic. Add cheese and pour wine over it. Let stand at room temperature for 4 to 5 hours. A few minutes before serving time, place over low heat, or microwave on MEDIUM. Stir frequently until cheese melts and mixture is smooth. Blend in brandy. Serve with bread cubes.

Fondue Sonoma

The dry Riesling gives this fondue a distinctive taste.

1 clove garlic, cut in half
2 cups California dry Riesling wine
1 lb. Swiss cheese, diced
1 tsp. flour
freshly ground pepper to taste
pinch grated nutmeg
2 tbs. California brandy
French or Italian bread, cubed

Rub the inside of a fondue pot or saucepan and wooden spoon with cut garlic. Pour in wine and warm over low heat. Toss cheese with flour. Add to heated wine, a little at a time. Stir until melted. Blend in seasoning and brandy. Serve with bread cubes.

Fondue Chablis for Two

Servings: 2

Have a romantic supper in front of the fire with fondue, salad and a glass of wine.

½ lb. Swiss cheese, diced
½ tbs. flour
1 clove garlic, cut in half
½ cup California Chablis wine
dash nutmeg and pepper
French or Italian bread, cubed

Toss cheese with flour. Rub fondue pot and wooden spoon with cut garlic. Pour in wine. Heat, but do not boil. Add cheese and stir until melted. Add seasonings, blend well and serve with bread cubes.

Pesto Fondue

Servings: 3-4

The zesty flavors of sweet basil and garlic spice up this dish. You can also buy commercially prepared pesto in your grocer's refrigerator case. You will need about 1¼ cups.

Pesto Sauce

1 cup fresh basil leaves, well packed, about 1 bunch
2 cloves garlic
1 tbs. full-flavored olive oil
2 tbs. grated Parmesan cheese
freshly ground pepper to taste

Process all ingredients with a food processor or blender until fairly smooth.

Fondue

¼ lb. fontina cheese, coarsely grated
¼ lb. Swiss or Gruyère cheese, coarsely grated
1 tbs. flour
1 cup white wine
1 tsp. lemon juice

Combine grated cheese with flour. Bring wine and lemon juice to a boil in a fondue pot or microwave dish, stir in cheese and cook over low heat until cheese melts. Stir in pesto and heat for another minute. Serve hot with breadsticks, bread cubes or small cooked new potatoes.

Spicy Bean Dip

This simple hot dip is a favorite for summer pool parties or after skiing. The little pockets of hot pepper cheese give it some zing.

1 can (15 oz.) chili beans in sauce
2 oz. hot pepper cheese, cut into very small dice
½ tsp. ground cumin
chopped fresh cilantro for garnish
tortilla chips and crisp vegetable slices for dipping

Drain chili beans, reserving 2 to 3 tbs. liquid. Place beans and cumin in a food processor workbowl and process until smooth. Pour into a shallow microwave or soufflé dish. Stir in diced cheese. If using the microwave, heat uncovered on MEDIUM power for 2 to 3 minutes, stir and continue to cook until beans are hot but cheese is not completely melted. Or heat in a small saucepan on the stove and pour into a warmed shallow serving container. Sprinkle with chopped cilantro. Serve warm.

Variation

Top hot dip with peeled, seeded, chopped fresh tomato pieces.

Egg Fondue

This classic rich creamy fondue needs only a crisp salad and a glass of Chardonnay to complete the meal.

1 clove garlic
¾ cup dry white wine
2 cups grated Swiss cheese
2 tbs. butter
6 eggs, beaten
salt and freshly ground pepper to taste
French or Italian bread, cubed

Press garlic into wine. Pour into a saucepan and boil until reduced to half the original volume. In a fondue pot or saucepan, combine cheese, eggs and seasonings. Stir until cheese melts and mixture is smooth. Slowly blend reduced wine into cheese mixture and serve with bread cubes.

Fondue de Berne

Dip small cooked new potatoes in addition to bread cubes for a delicious variation.

1 clove garlic, cut in half
½ cup dry white wine
I lb. Emmentaler cheese, diced
4 egg yolks
⅓ cup cream
dash nutmeg and paprika
French or Italian bread, cubed

Rub the inside of a fondue pot with cut garlic. Pour in wine and heat over low heat. Add cheese gradually, stirring constantly until melted. Combine egg yolks, cream and seasonings. Slowly blend into cheese mixture. Cook, stirring, until mixture is thickened and creamy. Serve with bread cubes.

Creamy Clam Dip

Here is a savory hot dip made with light cream cheese so you can indulge a little. Serve with crackers, crisp vegetable slices or tortilla chips.

6 oz. light cream cheese (Neufchatel)
1 can (6 oz.) chopped clams, drained, juice reserved
2 green onions, thinly sliced
2-3 oil-packed sun-dried tomatoes, diced
dash red pepper flakes
⅛ tsp. dried thyme
¼ tsp. dry mustard
1 tbs. chopped fresh parsley
1 small tomato, peeled, seeded and chopped for garnish

Microwave method: In a microwave, heat cream cheese on DEFROST for 1 to 2 minutes to soften. Stir in drained clams, green onions, sun-dried tomatoes, red pepper flakes, thyme and mustard. Heat uncovered on MEDIUM for 2 minutes. Stir, add 1 to 2 tbs. reserved clam juice if mixture seems too thick, and heat for another minute. Top with parsley and fresh tomato pieces.

Conventional method: Combine all ingredients, except parsley and fresh tomato pieces, spoon into a shallow oven dish and bake at 350°F for 10 to 15 minutes until hot. Top with parsley and tomato pieces.

Fondue Jeune Fille

One or two marinated vegetable salads such as grated carrots or celery root can be done ahead and are a delicious accompaniment for this fondue. Serve with a dry Chenin blanc.

¼ cup butter
2 tbs. flour
1½ cups dry white wine, heated
1 cup grated Swiss cheese
3 egg yolks
3 tbs. cream
nutmeg, salt and cayenne pepper to taste
French or Italian bread, cubed

Melt butter in a fondue pot over moderate heat. Stir in flour and let bubble. Remove from heat. Slowly blend in wine. Return to heat and cook, stirring, until mixture is thickened. Add cheese. Combine egg yolks and cream. Carefully stir egg yolks into hot mixture until well blended. Season to taste and serve with bread cubes.

Chile Con Queso

Need a snack for the football crowd, or something to go with margaritas? This is the ticket. If there is any left, reheat and serve on English muffins for brunch.

1 tbs. vegetable oil
½ cup finely chopped onion
1 clove garlic, minced
1 tbs. flour
1 can (4 oz.) can green chiles, drained
1 large fresh tomato, peeled, seeded and chopped
1 tbs. hot taco sauce
¼ cup evaporated milk
6 oz. Monterey Jack cheese, coarsely grated
6 oz. sharp cheddar cheese, coarsely grated
tortilla chips or crisp vegetable slices for dipping

Place vegetable oil, onion and garlic in a microwavable container. Cook on HIGH, uncovered, for 1 to 2 minutes. Stir and continue to cook for 1 to 2 minutes. Add cheese, stir and cook on MEDIUM power for 2 to 3 minutes. Stir and cook for 1 to 2 more minutes until cheese is melted. Pour into a fondue pot or serving dish. Serve warm.

Fonduta

This fondue is inspired by the Piedmont region of Italy, which is famous for fontina cheese.

¾ lb. fontina cheese, diced
¾ cup milk
2 tbs. butter
3 egg yolks
½ tsp. white pepper
buttered toast fingers or Italian breadsticks

Combine cheese and milk. Refrigerate for several hours to soften cheese. When ready to prepare, transfer to a heavy saucepan. Cook over low heat, stirring constantly, for about 5 minutes or until cheese melts. It may be somewhat stringy at this point. Beat yolks lightly and gradually stir about ¼ cup of hot cheese mixture into yolks. Pour slowly back into cheese mixture, beating constantly. Continue cooking over low heat until mixture becomes smooth and finally thickens. Serve with toast fingers or breadsticks.

Fondue with Chives

Chives give this fondue a pretty green hue and a subtle flavor. Serve as an appetizer in the living room with drinks before dinner.

3 tbs. butter
3½ tbs. finely chopped chives
1 cup dry white wine
½ lb. Swiss cheese, diced
1 tbs. flour
2 egg yolks, beaten
salt, dash Tabasco Sauce and nutmeg to taste
French or Italian bread, cubed

Melt butter in a fondue pot over low heat. Lightly sauté chives. Pour in wine and heat. Toss cheese with flour. Add to wine and stir until melted. Stir 3 tbs. hot cheese mixture into egg yolks. Slowly pour egg yolk mixture back into fondue pot, stirring constantly. Season and serve with bread cubes.

Creamy Spinach Dip

This attractive green dip starts with frozen creamed spinach. Great with whole wheat toast fingers, cooked new potatoes or fresh mushrooms for dippers. Add some crumbled bacon or diced ham for a new twist.

1 pkg. (9 oz.) frozen creamed spinach
1 tsp. butter
2-3 green onions, finely chopped
1 clove garlic, minced
1/3 cup evaporated milk
1/2 tsp. dry mustard
1 tsp. dill weed
1 tsp. Worcestershire sauce
2 oz. Gruyère cheese, grated
3 tbs. grated Parmesan cheese

Defrost spinach in a microwave according to package directions or defrost unopened pouch in boiling water for 12 minutes. In a soufflé dish, put butter, green onions and garlic. Microwave uncovered for 1 to 2 minutes. Add defrosted spinach, evaporated milk and remaining ingredients. Stir well. Microwave on MEDIUM power for 1 to 2 minutes, stir, and continue to cook another 1 to 2 minutes until cheese is melted.

Simple Simon Fondue

Servings: 4

Serve a light fruity Napa Gamay or Italian Bardolino with this dish. Blanched broccoli or cauliflower pieces make terrific dippers, too.

1 garlic clove, cut in half
1 lb. mild cheddar or American cheese, diced
1/2 cup milk
1 tsp. dry mustard
salt, cayenne pepper and paprika to taste
1 egg yolk, beaten
1 egg white, beaten to stiff peaks
French or Italian bread, cubed

Rub a fondue pot with cut garlic. Add cheese. Place pot over low heat and stir cheese until melted. Combine milk, seasonings and beaten egg yolk. Slowly blend into hot melted cheese. Cook until thickened. Carefully fold in stiffly beaten egg white and serve immediately with bread cubes.

Cheddar Cheese Fondue

The mustard complements the cheddar cheese and gives this fondue a little character. Use whole wheat or rye bread for dippers and serve with a full-bodied ale.

1 tsp. dry mustard
3 tbs. butter
3 tbs. flour
freshly ground pepper to taste
2 cups diced cheddar cheese
French or Italian bread cubes

Melt butter in a saucepan over medium heat. Add flour, mustard and pepper; cook for 1 minute. Remove from heat. Slowly stir in milk; return to heat and cook, stirring, until mixture boils. Add cheese and stir until melted. Transfer to a fondue pot and serve with bread cubes.

Cider Fondue

Make this for your Little Leaguers, Girl Scouts or any group with a hearty appetite. Serve with the same nonalcoholic cider used in the fondue.

1 tsp. flour
1 tsp. dry mustard
2 cups apple cider
2 lb. cheddar cheese, diced
2 tbs. butter
salt and freshly ground pepper to taste
French or Italian bread, cubed

Mix flour and mustard together. Blend into 1/2 cup cider with a fork. Heat remaining cider in a saucepan over low heat. Add cheese and butter and stir constantly until smooth and cheese is melted. Add mustard mixture and seasonings. Pour into a fondue pot and serve with bread cubes.

Greek Shrimp Fondue

The wonderful Mediterranean flavors make this fondue perfect for dipping cooked shrimp, scallops and small creamer potatoes. If there is any left, it makes a terrific pasta sauce, or pour it over grilled polenta squares.

2 tbs. full-flavored olive oil
4-5 green onions, finely chopped
2 large cloves garlic, finely chopped
1 can (15 oz.) tomato puree
1/3 cup white wine
1 tsp. dried oregano, or 1 tbs. fresh
1/8 tsp. red pepper flakes

5-6 oz. feta cheese, crumbled
2 tbs. finely chopped fresh parsley
salt and freshly ground pepper to
   taste
1 lb. cooked medium shrimp or sea
   scallops, or combination
2-5 small cooked potatoes per person

Heat olive oil in a fondue pot. Add onion and garlic and saute for 1 to 2 minutes until onion softens. Add tomato puree, white wine, oregano and red pepper flakes; heat. Tomato sauces seem to splatter in a fondue pot, so watch carefully and keep just at a simmer. Add feta cheese and continue to cook until cheese has mostly melted. Add parsley, salt and pepper. Serve hot.

Hot Pepper Cheese Fondue

This is a simple, zesty fondue that is great with tortilla chips, whole wheat toast fingers or crisp vegetables for dippers.

2 tbs. butter
2 tbs. flour
1 1/2 cups milk
6 oz. hot pepper cheese, coarsely grated
2 tbs. grated Parmesan cheese
1/4 tsp. dry mustard

Conventional method: Melt butter in a fondue pot, add flour and cook for 2 minutes. Slowly stir in milk and cook until mixture thickens. Add both cheeses and dry mustard. Cook until cheese melts and mixture is hot.

Microwave method: Reduce milk to 1 1/4 cups and heat uncovered on HIGH until milk is steaming. Combine flour with grated cheeses and stir into hot milk mixture with mustard. Cook on MEDIUM for 2 minutes, stir, and continue to cook for another 1 to 2 minutes until cheeses are melted. Pour into a fondue pot or serving dish.

Fondue Marseillaise

This light creamy fondue makes an excellent appetizer, or it makes a lovely luncheon when served with crusty French bread and a crisp green salad. Serve with a dry Chenin blanc.

2 cups milk
1 cup grated Swiss cheese
3 tbs. flour
1 tbs. Worcestershire sauce
salt to taste
½ tsp. dry mustard
1 lb. small cooked shrimp

Blend all ingredients except shrimp in a blender container or food processor workbowl until well combined. Pour into a saucepan or a microwave dish and cook over medium heat or on MEDIUM power in the microwave, stirring constantly, until smooth and thickened. Pour into a fondue pot and serve with shrimp "dippers."

Fondue Avec Oeufs

This makes a substantial brunch or luncheon dish. Serve with Canadian bacon, toasted English muffins and a fresh fruit platter.

6 hard-cooked eggs
¾ cup breadcrumbs
3 tbs. finely chopped fresh parsley
2 tbs. finely chopped chives
¼ tsp. dill weed
salt, cayenne pepper and paprika to taste
Fondue Chablis, page 172

Cut eggs in half lengthwise. Remove yolks and mash with breadcrumbs and seasonings. Stuff egg whites with filling. Spoon heated fondue over eggs, dust with additional paprika and serve.

Hot Oil and Hot Broth Fondues

Hot oil fondue, traditionally called fondue bourguignonne, according to legend had its beginning centuries ago in the famous vineyards of the Burgundy region of France. During the harvest season, the grapes had to be picked at the precise time of ripeness; there was no time for the harvesters to eat. Someone had the idea of keeping a pot of fat boiling so each worker could quickly cook his own pieces of meat in spare moments. Whether or not the story is true, the Swiss have developed the idea to its present form and honored the Burgundy origin by naming the dish fondue bourguignonne.

The right equipment for meat fondue is extremely important. The pot must be made of metal that will tolerate high heat and keep the oil hot. It must set securely on its stand to avoid the danger of tipping. The traditional pot is wide at the base and narrow at the top to eliminate some of the spattering and retain the heat. A tray beneath the pot will help catch some of the spatters; many fondue sets come with a tray.

The heat source, over which the fondue pot sets, must be adequate enough to keep the oil hot during the entire cooking process. Those which can be adjusted are best; butane, alcohol or electric burners are preferable. Forks used for cooking should be a minimum of 10 inches in length with long tines for securing the food. Many have color-keyed handles or tips so each person can recognize his own. Special fondue plates with sections for the sauces are attractive, but sauces can be served in individual dishes as well.

Never have the pot more than half full of oil. And, unless your fondue pot is electric, it is better to heat the oil to the desired temperature on the range and then bring it to the table. The recommended temperature is about 375° F. Test with a deep fat thermometer or cubes of bread or meat. Bread will brown in the meat, which will start to brown immediately. Adjust the heat source to keep the oil as close to that temperature during cooking as possible. A good quality of oil should always be used. For extra flavor, half oil and half clarified butter are sometimes used. Be careful to keep the temperature below 400°F or the clarified butter will begin to smoke.

Hot broth recipes are found in this section, and you will find them a delightful and healthy variation to use with your fondue pot.

For the best fondue, use good cuts of high-quality meat or seafood. Remove all fat, cut into bite-sized pieces and pat dry to cut down on spattering. Take the meat from the refrigerator about 30 minutes before using. It will cook faster and it will help to maintain the temperature of the oil if the meat is not cold. Guests should be provided with dinner forks, since fondue forks become extremely hot and are not safe for eating.

Classic Fondue Bourguignonne

This is the basic hot oil fondue from which the variations have developed.

2 lb. beef filet or boneless sirloin
oil to fill ½ fondue pot
3-5 dipping sauces, pages 189-194
salt and freshly ground pepper to taste

Trim all fat from meat and cut into bite-sized pieces. Arrange on small plates so each guest may have his own. Heat oil in fondue pot to about 375°F. Place in the center of the table over a heat source. Pieces of meat should be speared on fondue forks and cooked to taste (about 50 seconds for medium-rare). Remove meat from fondue fork, season and dip into sauces as desired.

Mixed Grill Fondue

Serve with creamy scalloped potatoes, a marinated vegetable salad and a Cabernet Sauvignon.

½ lb. beef filet or boneless sirloin
½ lb. lean pork
½ lb. veal cutlets, pounded
4 chicken livers
oil to fill ½ fondue pot
salt and freshly ground pepper to taste
3-4 dipping sauces, pages 189-194

Trim all fat from meat and cut into bite-sized pieces. Arrange several pieces of each meat on a small plate for each guest. Heat oil in a fondue pot to about 375°F, maintain heat over heat source and allow each guest to cook meat to taste. Serve with seasonings and assorted sauces.

Poultry Fondue

Servings: 4

Either a full bodied Chardonnay or a Pinot Noir make perfect accompaniments. Make a spicy Oriental-style noodle salad with slivered fresh vegetables to serve with this.

2 lb. chicken or turkey breast meat
oil to fill ½ fondue pot
3-5 sauces for dipping, pages 189-194
salt and freshly ground pepper to taste

Remove skin from breast meat and cut into bite-sized pieces. Arrange on plates for guests; heat oil in a fondue pot to 375°F and allow each guest to cook meat to taste. Serve with seasonings and assorted sauces.

Lamb Fondue

Servings: 4

Ask your butcher for a tender cut. A small leg might be the best buy. Baked tomatoes stuffed with onion and thyme-scented rice, and a salad of crisp romaine leaves dressed with a light vinaigrette and sprinkled with Parmesan cheese would be perfect accompaniments. Serve with a fruity Zinfandel.

2 lb. tender lamb
oil to fill ½ fondue pot
3-5 sauces for dipping, pages 189-194
salt and freshly ground pepper to taste

Remove all fat from meat and cut into bite-sized pieces. Arrange on plates for guests; heat oil to 375°F and allow each guest to cook meat to taste. Serve with seasonings and assorted sauces.

Pork or Ham Fondue

Try this with a white Zinfandel. Cinnamon-flavored chunky applesauce and crisp potato wedges will round out this dinner.

2 lb. lean pork or ham
oil to fill ½ fondue pot
3-5 sauces for dipping, pages 189-194
salt and freshly ground pepper to taste

Cut meat into bite-sized pieces. Arrange on plates for guests; heat oil to 375° F and allow each guest to cook meat to taste. Serve with seasonings and assorted sauces.

Tempura

Be sure seafood, chicken and vegetable pieces are dry and almost room temperature before dipping them into the batter. Then simply cook in hot oil until golden. Cauliflower, snow peas, sliced carrots, red or green bell pepper strips, green beans and thin asparagus are just a few of the vegetables that are delicious this way.

½ lb. seafood, cut into bite-sized pieces
½ lb. chicken or turkey, cut into bite-sized pieces
assorted vegetables, cut into bite-sized pieces

Batter

1 egg yolk, at room temperature
1 cup ice water
1 cup flour
pinch salt
white pepper to taste
flour to coat dipping foods

Beat egg yolk with a fork, add cold water and mix well. Add flour and just stir to combine. Batter should be quite thin, about the consistency of cream. Add more ice water if necessary. Mixture should leave just a thin coating on seafood or vegetables when dipped. Blot prepared vegetables or seafood in a paper towel and then roll in flour. Dip into the tempura batter and cook immediately in hot oil. Serve with *Sweet and Sour Sauce*, page 194, or *Teriyaki Sauce*, page 193.

Bagna Cauda

Bagna cauda is a delicious Italian hot olive oil and garlic dip for fresh vegetables. The anchovies melt into the hot oil and add a zesty complex flavor to the dish. Even those who dislike anchovies have been known to enjoy this preparation. Vegetables for dipping can be prepared in advance, covered and refrigerated until you are ready to serve.

½ cup olive oil
½ cup butter
3 medium cloves garlic, finely chopped
1 can (2 oz.) flat anchovy fillets, finely chopped, with oil
½ tsp. salt
⅛ tsp. red pepper flakes
vegetables and bread cubes for dipping

Combine olive oil and butter in a fondue pot or small saucepan. Heat oil until butter starts to melt. Add garlic, chopped anchovy fillets with oil, salt and red pepper flakes. Heat gently over low heat for about 10 minutes, stirring occasionally, until garlic is soft and anchovies are dissolved. Serve warm with a colorful variety of vegetables, raw or cooked. The vegetables are speared on the fondue fork and the cube of bread in the left hand is used to catch the savory drips of oil from the vegetables.

Raw Vegetables for Dipping

Red, green and yellow pepper pieces, carrot slices or thin baby carrots, fennel or celery strips, zucchini or yellow summer squash slices, small mushroom caps, jicama slices, green onions, cucumber slices.

Cooked Vegetables for Dipping

Small creamer potatoes; snow peas, broccoli or cauliflower florets, blanched for 1 minute in boiling water or microwaved briefly.

Seafood Fondue

This dish can be served as a fondue, dipping each morsel of cooked seafood into a garlicky mayonnaise; or cook the seafood all at once in the broth, ladle over rice, and top with Aioli, French-style. Each person should have a small bowl of cooked rice to catch the drops of broth from the cooked seafood.

1 can (14½ oz.) chicken broth
1 bottle (8 oz.) clam juice
⅓ cup white wine
2 tbs. soy sauce
dash Tabasco Sauce
3-4 green onions, thinly sliced
1 thin slice fresh ginger
1 clove garlic, minced
½ cup finely diced carrots

¼ lb. sea scallops, cut in half if large
¼ lb. medium-sized shrimp, peeled
   and deveined
½ lb. ling cod, halibut, or salmon, cut
   into bite-sized pieces
1 cup green peas or 5-6 slivered fresh
   snow peas
1 cup thinly sliced mushrooms
3-4 cups hot cooked rice

Combine chicken broth, clam juice, white wine, soy sauce, Tabasco, green onions, ginger, garlic and carrots in a fondue pot or microwave dish. Bring to a boil. Arrange seafood pieces on a large platter. Each person should have a plate with a small rice bowl of hot rice, a spoonful of aioli and a fondue fork.

Cook individual pieces of seafood in the hot broth for 2 to 3 minutes until just cooked, dip in *Aioli* and eat. When most of the seafood has been cooked, add the green peas and mushroom slices to the broth with the rest of the fish. Cook 2 to 3 minutes and spoon over rice in individual bowls. Stir in a spoonful of *Aioli*.

Aioli

6-8 large cloves garlic
2 egg yolks
1½ tbs. lemon juice
1 tsp. Dijon mustard
dash cayenne pepper or Tabasco sauce
½ cup full-flavored olive oil
¾ cup vegetable oil
salt and white pepper to taste
2-3 tsp. boiling water

Mince garlic with a food processor. Add egg yolks, lemon juice, cayenne and mustard; process for a few seconds. Slowly add olive and vegetable oils, processing until mixture thickens. Stir in 1 to 2 tsp. boiling water. The sauce should be thick and shiny. Add salt and white pepper to taste. If made ahead, refrigerate until just before serving.

Beef Mizutaki

Mizutaki is a term that simply means "boiling water." It is known some-times as shabu-shabu. Ancient Mongolia gets credit for originating this sim-ple, elegant dish. It is also a friendly dish, the whole meal being served from a common bowl. Plenty of hot rice should be available. This is one meal where the soup follows rather than precedes the main course. You will be making the soup as you cook the meat. A suitable implement for cooking mizutaki is one that will keep water bubbling-hot: chafing dish, electric frying pan or fondue pot.

3-4 cups beef broth (enough to fill ½ container)
1½ lb. market or Spencer steak, sliced ⅛-inch thick
1 block tofu, cut into bite-sized pieces
8-10 fresh shitake mushrooms, or 3-4 dried, softened in warm water
1 bunch fresh spinach leaves
1 bunch green onions, cut into 2-inch lengths
1 lb. Chinese cabbage, shredded into 2-inch lengths
hot cooked rice

Bring beef broth to a boil. Add tofu and cook just long enough to warm through. Add mushrooms, spinach, green onions and cabbage. Cook for 1 to 2 minutes until wilted. Add meat and cook for 1 to 2 minutes. Remove cooked ingredients with chopsticks to individual serving bowls and serve with rice and dipping sauces. After eating the meat and vegetables, spoon out some of the stock and drink as a broth, seasoning with salt, pepper or a few drops of dip-ping sauce.

Horseradish Dipping Sauce

½ cup dark soy sauce
1 tbs. finely grated wasabi horseradish

Ginger Dipping Sauce

½ cup dark soy sauce
1 tbs. finely grated fresh ginger

Citrus Dipping Sauce

½ cup soy sauce
¼ cup lemon juice
¼ cup orange juice

Chicken Mizutaki

Servings: 4

Bite-sized pieces of chicken also make a delicious mizutaki. Arrange chicken and vegetables in an attractive pattern on a platter. Chopsticks work well to put the individual morsels into the bubbling hot broth.

5-4 cups chicken broth
1½ lb. boneless chicken breasts, cut into bite-sized pieces
1 block tofu, cut in bite-sized pieces
4-6 medium dried shitake mushrooms, softened in warm water
4-6 fresh mushrooms, thinly sliced
2 carrots, cut into ¼-inch diagonal slices
1 bunch green onions, cut into 2-inch lengths
1 lb. Chinese cabbage, cut into 1-inch squares
hot cooked rice

Bring broth to a boil, add chicken and cook until tender, about 10 minutes. Add tofu and just heat through. Cook mushrooms, carrots, watercress, green onions and cabbage until wilted, 2 to 3 minutes. Remove cooked meat and vegetables to serving bowls. Serve with rice and dipping sauce. Spoon out some of the broth and drink after eating the meat and vegetables, seasoning with salt or dipping sauce. See *Beef Mizutaki*, page 187.

Low Calorie Fondue

This version of fondue is very popular with calorie watchers. Meats and vegetables are cooked in a delicious broth instead of being deep-fried. Broth may be substituted for oil in any of the previous recipes. After the meat has all been cooked the flavorful broth can be served alone or over cooked rice or noodles as a tasty bonus.

2½ cups beef or chicken broth
1¼ cups water
½ cup dry white wine
½ bunch green onions, chopped
1 stalk celery, chopped
several sprigs fresh parsley
salt and freshly ground pepper to taste
1 tsp. fines herbes

Simmer ingredients in a saucepan for 10 minutes. Remove from heat and let stand for 2 hours. Strain into a fondue pot and bring to a boil.

Anchovy Sauce

If you love the distinctive flavor of anchovies, this sauce is for you.

1 cup mayonnaise
1 tbs. chopped fresh parsley
1 tbs. capers, drained
1 tbs. chopped anchovies
1 hard-cooked egg, finely chopped
1 tsp. dry mustard
garlic powder to taste

Combine ingredients. Chill until serving. Makes 1 ½ cups.

Avocado Sauce

This sauce adds a "south-of-the-border" flavor.

2 ripe avocados
2 tbs. minced onion
1 tbs. lemon juice
1 tbs. mayonnaise
2 drops Tabasco Sauce
salt to taste

Mash avocados. Stir in onion, lemon juice, mayonnaise, Tabasco and salt. Mix until well blended. Makes 1 ½ cups.

Easy Barbecue Sauce

This is especially good with chicken.

1 bottle (12 oz.) hot catsup
2 tsp. celery seed
3 tbs. vinegar
1 clove garlic, cut in half

Combine ingredients. Chill for several hours. Remove garlic before serving. Can also be served warm, if desired. Makes 1 ½ cups.

Spicy Catsup

This is delicious with seafood. Use any left over for cocktail sauce.

¾ cup catsup
2 tbs. vinegar
½ tsp. prepared horseradish

Combine ingredients. Chill. Makes ¾ cup.

Island Peanut Sauce

Use this spicy Indonesian dipping sauce for chicken, pork or beef.

½ cup chicken stock
¼ cup peanut butter
¼ tsp. finely minced garlic
¼ tsp. finely grated fresh ginger
2 green onions, white part only, finely minced
2 tsp. brown sugar
2 tsp. dark soy sauce
1 tsp. cider vinegar
dash Tabasco Sauce

Combine all ingredients in a small saucepan. Heat on low, stirring constantly, until mixture boils. Add a little more chicken stock or water if mixture is not thin enough for dipping. This sauce can be made ahead and reheated in a microwave on MEDIUM power when ready to serve. Makes ⅔ cup.

Sour Cream Horseradish Sauce

This classic creamy sauce goes well with everything.

1 cup (½ pt.) sour cream
3 tbs. prepared horseradish, well drained
1 tsp. lemon juice or vinegar
salt to taste
dash paprika

Combine all ingredients. Chill. Makes 1 ¼ cups.

Sour Cream Mustard Sauce

Use a Dijon-style mustard.

1 cup (½ pt.) sour cream
3 tbs. prepared mustard
2 tbs. chopped green onion
salt and freshly ground pepper to taste

Combine ingredients. Chill. Makes 1¼ cups.

Curry Mayonnaise

Here is a dipping sauce with the flavor of India.

½ cup mayonnaise
½ cup sour cream
1 tsp. lemon juice
1 tsp. curry powder

Combine mayonnaise and sour cream. Blend in lemon juice and curry. Taste. Add more seasoning if desired. Chill. Makes 1 cup.

Roquefort Butter

A French classic, this is wonderful with beef.

4 oz. Roquefort cheese, crumbled
½ cup butter, room temperature
1 tbs. prepared mustard
1 clove garlic, crushed
1 tsp. Worcestershire sauce

Blend ingredients together well. Serve at room temperature. Makes 1 cup.

Sour Cream Chutney Sauce

Use this sauce with chicken.

¾ cup sour cream
¼ cup chutney
pinch curry powder

Combine ingredients and chill to blend flavors. Makes 1 cup.

Blender Bearnaise Sauce

The blender makes this classic sauce foolproof.

4 shallots
½ cup tarragon vinegar
2 egg yolks
salt and cayenne pepper to taste
1 tsp. chopped fresh parsley
1 tsp. chopped fresh chives
1 tsp. dried tarragon
½ cup butter, melted and cooled

Place shallots and vinegar in a blender container and run at low speed for 15 seconds or until shallots are chopped. Pour mixture into a small saucepan and boil until liquid is reduced to 2 tablespoons. Strain; pour liquid back into blender container. Add egg yolks, salt, cayenne, parsley, chives and tarragon. Blend on lowest speed. Gradually pour in cooled butter and stop blending when sauce thickens. Makes 1 cup.

Piquant Sauce for Ham

It's the perfect sauce with ham. Try it with pork chunks, too.

½ cup currant jelly
2 tbs. prepared mustard
1 ½ tsp. lemon juice
⅛ tsp. cinnamon

Combine in a saucepan. Heat until jelly melts. Makes ⅔ cup.

Teriyaki Sauce

The flavor of Japan is delicious with fish or meat.

½ cup soy sauce
1 clove garlic, minced
1 tbs. brown sugar
1 tsp. grated fresh ginger
¼ cup sake or dry sherry

Combine ingredients. Makes ¾ cup.

Tangy Mint Sauce for Lamb

Mint and lamb are a classic English combination.

½ cup mint jelly
2 tbs. butter
2 tbs. cider vinegar
1 tbs. lemon juice
½ tsp. dry mustard

Combine ingredients in a small saucepan. Stir over low heat until jelly melts and mixture comes to a boil. Makes ¾ cup.

Tartar Sauce

Your favorite fish sauce is easy to prepare at home.

½ cup mayonnaise
½ cup sour cream
1 tbs. chopped stuffed green olives
1 tbs. minced fresh parsley
1 tbs. chopped capers
1 tbs. chopped sweet pickles

Combine mayonnaise and sour cream. Fold in remaining ingredients. Chill to blend flavors. Makes 1¼ cups.

Sweet and Sour Sauce

These Chinese flavors are delicious with chicken, fish, ham and pork, but not beef.

½ cup orange juice
½ cup cider vinegar
½ cup sugar
2 tbs. tomato paste
½ tsp. sesame oil
2-3 drops Tabasco Sauce
1 tbs. cornstarch dissolved in 2 tbs. water

Combine all ingredients except cornstarch in a small saucepan or microwave dish. Bring to a boil. Stir in 1 tbs. of dissolved cornstarch mixture and continue to cook for 1 to 2 minutes. Add more cornstarch if a thicker sauce is desired. Makes 1 cup.

Baked Fondues

Although baked fondues are not as spectacular as soufflés, they do have a similar texture and are sometimes thought of as simplified soufflés. Happily the fear of having a beautiful soufflé collapse on its way to the table doesn't exist with its country cousin, which originated many years ago as a practical way of using stale bread or breadcrumbs. Many variations of this nutritious and economical discovery have appeared over the years, sometimes called "strata," and they still are a favorite make-ahead dish. Baked fondues with meat or fish are perfect for main courses and lend themselves beautifully to party buffets or suppers.

A buffet supper might consist of a baked main dish fondue, your favorite tossed salad, a pretty molded salad, buttered vegetable, crusty rolls, a light fruit dessert and a beverage, most of which can easily be prepared in advance.

Easy Baked Cheese Fondue
Servings: 2

Use any full-flavored cheese for this dish — Swiss, cheddar, blue-veined or a combination.

1 cup fresh breadcrumbs
1 cup milk, warmed
1 cup (4 oz.) grated cheese
2 tbs. butter, melted
salt and cayenne pepper to taste
1 egg yolk, slightly beaten
1 egg white, beaten to stiff peaks
grated Parmesan cheese for topping

Soak breadcrumbs in milk. Stir in cheese, butter, salt and cayenne. Add beaten egg yolk. Fold in stiffly beaten egg white. Pour mixture into a well-buttered casserole. Sprinkle with Parmesan cheese. Bake at 375°F for 1 hour or until a knife inserted in the center comes out clean.

Baked Cheddar Cheese Fondue

Servings: 6

Make this the night before for an easy, satisfying company breakfast or brunch.

8 slices bread, buttered
1¾ lb. sharp cheddar, grated
6 eggs
2½ cups half-and-half
1 tbs. minced onion
1 tsp. brown sugar
½ tsp. Beau Monde seasoning
½ tsp. Worcestershire sauce
½ tsp. dry mustard
salt and freshly ground pepper to taste

Dice bread. Scatter ½ of the bread cubes on the bottom of a buttered casserole. Add ½ of the cheese, another layer of bread and finally the remaining cheese. Beat eggs. Blend with remaining ingredients and pour over cheese. Refrigerate for 1 hour. Bake in a 300°F oven for 1 hour or until a knife inserted in the center comes out clean.

Baked Fondue Maria

Servings: 2-3

To give this fondue extra zip, use some hot pepper cheese; or add ½ cup sautéed onions or a small can of crumbled onion rings before folding in the egg yolks.

1 clove garlic, cut in half
1 cup milk, warmed
1 cup fresh breadcrumbs
1 cup (4 oz.) diced cheese
1 tbs. butter
salt, cayenne pepper and paprika to taste
3 egg yolks, beaten
3 egg whites, beaten to stiff peaks

Rub bottom and sides of a casserole dish with cut garlic and then butter it well. Combine milk, crumbs, cheese, butter and seasonings in a heavy saucepan. Cook over medium heat until cheese melts and mixture is smooth. Remove from heat. Stir in beaten egg yolks. Fold in stiffly beaten egg whites and pour into prepared casserole. Bake in a 350°F oven for 35 to 40 minutes, or until a knife inserted in the center comes out clean.

Petite Baked Fondues

Almost any cheese you may have on hand will work in this recipe. For added flavor, fold in ½ cup finely diced ham or some crumbled bacon bits.

1 cup fresh breadcrumbs
2 cups milk
2 eggs, beaten
½ lb. cheese, grated
1 tbs. butter, melted
1 tsp. Dijon mustard
1 tsp. dried Italian herbs
dash Tabasco Sauce
salt and freshly ground pepper to taste
¼ cup grated Parmesan cheese

Combine breadcrumbs and milk. Add eggs, cheese, melted butter and seasonings. Pour into buttered individual ramekins or a casserole. Sprinkle with Parmesan cheese. Bake in a 300°F oven for 1 hour, or until a knife inserted in the center comes out clean.

Baked Tuna Fondue

This is a quick dish to put together for a weekday dinner. Serve it with coleslaw or a grated carrot salad. You can relax while it bakes.

1 cup fresh breadcrumbs
1 cup milk, warmed
1 can (6½ oz.) tuna, drained
3 tbs. diced pimiento
1 cup (4 oz.) grated cheese
2 tbs. butter, melted
salt and cayenne pepper to taste
2 egg yolks
2 egg whites, beaten until stiff
grated Parmesan cheese for topping

Soak breadcrumbs in milk. Add tuna, pimiento, cheese, butter, salt and cayenne. Beat egg yolks until creamy. Stir into cheese mixture. Fold in egg whites. Pour into a well-buttered casserole. Top with Parmesan cheese. Bake in a 325°F oven for 35 to 45 minutes, or until a knife inserted in the center comes out clean.

Baked Fondue with Beer

Slip a slice of ham or thin Canadian bacon into these sandwiches for a heartier dish.

8 slices bread, buttered
8 slices American cheese
3 eggs, beaten
1 tsp. Worcestershire sauce
1/2 tsp. dry mustard
1 cup beer

Make 4 sandwiches using buttered bread and 4 slices cheese. Place in a square buttered baking dish and top with remaining cheese slices. Beat eggs and seasonings together. Stir in beer and pour over sandwiches. Bake in a 350°F oven for about 40 minutes, or until set.

Baked Cheddar Beer Fondue

This is a great dish for a blustery cold evening or after skiing. Serve with beer, of course.

1 cup milk
2 tbs. chopped onion
1 cup beer
3 cups (12 oz.) grated cheddar cheese
2 1/2 cups bread cubes
salt to taste
1/2 tsp. dry mustard
4 egg yolks, beaten
4 egg whites, beaten to stiff peaks
2 tbs. butter
2 tsp. caraway seeds

Combine milk and onion in a saucepan. Scald over low heat. Add beer, cheese, 2 cups of the bread cubes, salt and dry mustard. Stir until cheese melts. Lightly beat egg yolks. Slowly add to mixture, stirring constantly. Fold in stiffly beaten egg whites and pour into a well-buttered casserole. Dot with butter; sprinkle with caraway seeds and remaining 1/2 cup bread cubes. Bake in a 325°F oven for 1 1/4 hours, or until a knife inserted in the center comes out clean.

Baked Parisian Fondue

This dish will star at a weekend brunch. Start with Bloody Marys or champagne and orange juice. Serve with a platter of fresh fruit.

1 1/2 loaves French bread, sliced
1/2 cup soft butter
1/2 cup prepared mustard
1 1/2 lb. cheddar cheese, sliced
4 eggs, beaten
5 cups milk, heated
1 1/2 tsp. Worcestershire sauce
salt, cayenne pepper and paprika to taste

Spread bread slices with butter and mustard. Cover bottom of a large, well-buttered casserole with slices of bread. Cover bread with cheese slices. Continue until bread and cheese are all used, ending with bread. Combine eggs, hot milk, Worcestershire sauce and seasonings. Pour over bread. Refrigerate for several hours or overnight. Bake in a 350°F oven for 1 1/2 hours, or until a knife inserted in the center comes out clean.

Baked Crabmeat Fondue

This recipe is equally good with cooked salad shrimp instead of crab. Serve with a Sauvignon blanc or Chardonnay for a company supper.

2 cups milk
1/4 cup butter
1 3/4 cups breadcrumbs
1 clove garlic, minced
1/2 tsp. minced onion
salt and freshly ground pepper to taste
1/4 tsp. ground ginger
5 eggs, separated
1 cup (4 oz.) grated Monterey Jack cheese
6-8 oz. fresh or imitation crabmeat, flaked

Heat milk in a saucepan. Add butter, breadcrumbs, garlic, minced onion, salt, pepper and ginger. Add beaten egg yolks. Cook over low heat, stirring constantly until thickened. Stir in cheese and crabmeat. Beat egg whites until stiff and fold into mixture. Pour into a well-buttered casserole. Bake in a 325°F oven for 1 1/2 hours, or until a knife inserted in the center comes out clean.

Baked La Fondue Hestere

Here is a new twist to tuna sandwiches, hot and savory.

1 can (6½ oz.) tuna, drained
1 cup finely chopped celery
2-3 green onions, finely sliced
¼ cup mayonnaise
1 tbs. dry mustard
½ tsp. salt
12 slices bread
6 slices cheddar cheese
3 eggs, beaten
2½ cups milk
2 tsp. Worcestershire sauce

Combine tuna, celery, onions, mayonnaise, mustard and salt. Trim crusts from bread. Spread tuna mixture on 6 slices of bread; cover with remaining bread. Place sandwiches in a buttered baking dish. Top with cheese slices.

Combine eggs, milk and Worcestershire sauce; pour over sandwiches. Bake in a 325°F oven for 45 minutes, or until a knife inserted in center comes out clean.

Baked New Orleans Fondue

This dish is a snap to make and you usually have these ingredients on hand.

1 can (8 oz.) salmon
1 cup minced celery
¼ cup mayonnaise
1 tbs. dry mustard
salt to taste
12 slices bread
6 slices American cheese
3 eggs, beaten
2½ cups milk
2 tsp. Worcestershire sauce

Drain and flake salmon, discarding skin and bones. Combine salmon, celery, mayonnaise, mustard and salt. Trim crusts from bread. Spread salmon mixture on 6 slices of bread and cover with remaining bread. Place sandwiches in a buttered baking dish and top with cheese slices. Combine eggs, milk and Worcestershire sauce and pour over sandwiches. Bake in a 325°F oven for 45 minutes, or until a knife inserted in the center comes out clean.

Baked Chicken Fondue

Serve this with a dry Chenin blanc or a light red Napa Gamay.

4 egg yolks
4 egg whites, beaten to stiff peaks
1 can (10½ oz.) cream of chicken soup
1½ cups diced cooked chicken
2-3 tbs. diced pimiento
1 cup grated cheddar cheese
2 cups fresh breadcrumbs
salt, cayenne pepper and paprika to taste

Beat egg yolks until light. Add soup, chicken, pimiento, cheese, bread-crumbs and seasonings. Fold in stiffly beaten egg whites. Pour into a well-buttered cas-serole. Bake in a 325°F oven for 1 hour, or until a knife inserted in the center comes out clean.

Baked Turkey Fondue

The green chiles give this dish a little zip. This is a great recipe for the after-Thanksgiving turkey.

1 cup milk
1 cup turkey stock
2 tbs. butter
1¾ cups fresh breadcrumbs
2 tbs. lemon juice
1 tsp. dried thyme
salt and freshly ground pepper to taste
⅓ cup diced canned green chiles
5 egg yolks, beaten
5 egg whites, beaten to stiff peaks
2 cups diced cooked turkey

Heat milk, stock and butter in a heavy saucepan over medium heat. Add breadcrumbs, lemon juice, thyme, salt, pepper and green chilies. Stir in beaten egg yolks. Cook, stirring constantly, until thickened. Stir in turkey. Remove from heat and fold in stiffly beaten egg whites. Pour into a well-buttered casserole. Bake in a pan of hot water in a 325°F oven for 1¼ hours, or until a knife inserted in the center comes out clean.

Baked Sausage Fondue

This savory dish is for sausage lovers. Use hot pork sausage if you like spicy things.

1 1/2 lb. pork sausage
2 tbs. minced green onions
1/4 cup chopped pimiento
1 tsp. dry mustard
salt and freshly ground pepper to taste
12 slices bread
6 eggs, beaten
3 cups milk
2 tsp. Worcestershire sauce

Brown sausage in a skillet, crumbling into small pieces; drain off fat. Stir in onion, pimiento, mustard, salt and pepper. Trim crusts from bread. Line a buttered baking dish with 6 slices of bread. Cover with sausage mixture and top with remaining bread slices. Combine eggs, milk and Worcestershire sauce; pour over bread. Bake in a 325°F oven for 1 1/2 hours, or until set.

Baked Rice Fondue

Serve this fondue with an apple walnut salad or stir-fried broccoli.

4 eggs, separated
1 1/2 cups milk
2 cups (8 oz.) grated sharp cheddar cheese
2 cups cooked rice
3-4 green onions, thinly sliced
2 tsp. Worcestershire
salt and freshly ground pepper to taste

Beat egg yolks well. Add milk, cheese, rice, green onions and seasonings and mix well. Beat egg whites until stiff but not dry. Fold into rice mixture and pour into a buttered casserole. Bake in a pan of hot water in a 350°F oven for 1 hour, or until a knife inserted in the center comes out clean.

Baked Asparagus Fondue

Servings: 4

This makes a great accompaniment for a baked ham or pork roast. It is even better when made with fresh, slightly cooked asparagus.

3 slices bread, cubed
1 pkg. (10 oz.) frozen asparagus, thawed
¾ cup (6 oz.) grated fontina cheese
1 egg, beaten
1 tbs. butter, melted
2 tsp. Dijon mustard
salt and freshly ground pepper to taste

Arrange layers of bread cubes, asparagus and ½ cup of the cheese in a buttered casserole. Blend together egg, milk, butter, onion, mustard, salt and pepper. Pour over casserole ingredients. Sprinkle with remaining cheese. Bake in a 350°F oven for 45 minutes, or until a knife inserted in the center comes out clean.

Baked Corn and Cheese Fondue

Servings: 4

Add 1-2 slices of crumbled cooked bacon or ½ cup diced ham to this fondue for a variation.

1 cup milk
1 cup canned corn, drained
1 cup (4 oz.) grated cheddar cheese
1½ cups fresh breadcrumbs
1 tbs. butter, melted
salt, freshly ground pepper and paprika to taste
3 egg yolks, beaten
3 egg whites, beaten to stiff peaks

Combine milk, corn, cheese, breadcrumbs, butter and seasonings. Add beaten egg yolks. Fold in stiffly beaten egg whites. Bake in a well-buttered casserole in a 350°F oven for 1 hour, or until a knife inserted in the center comes out clean.

Baked Leek Fondue

This fondue is delicious as a side dish for grilled salmon or halibut. Serve with a dry Riesling wine.

6 slices bread, buttered
1½ cups (6 oz.) grated Gruyère cheese
¾ tsp. dry mustard
3 eggs, well beaten
3 cups milk
2 tbs. butter
1 cup diced leeks
salt and freshly ground pepper to taste

Cut bread into cubes and place in a buttered baking dish. Spread cheese evenly over bread cubes. Melt 2 tbs. butter and sauté leeks for 3 to 4 minutes over low heat until soft. Combine leeks with remaining ingredients and pour over bread. Let stand for 2 hours. Bake in a 350°F oven for 40 minutes, or until a knife inserted in the center comes out clean.

Baked Spinach Fondue

This pretty green fondue makes a great luncheon dish.

1⅓ cups milk, warmed
salt, freshly ground pepper and cayenne pepper to taste
1 tsp. Worcestershire sauce
¼ cup butter, melted
½ cup finely chopped mushrooms
3-4 green onions, thinly sliced
4 eggs, separated
1 cup chopped cooked spinach
⅔ cup grated Gruyère cheese

Combine milk and breadcrumbs in top of a double boiler. Let stand for 5 minutes. Add salt, pepper, cayenne and Worcestershire. Melt butter in a small skillet. Sauté mushrooms and onions for 3 to 4 minutes. Add to breadcrumb mixture. Beat egg yolks and blend into crumb mixture. Cook over hot water until thickened. Cool. Add well-drained spinach and cheese to cooled mixture. Beat egg whites to stiff peaks and fold into mixture. Pour into a buttered casserole and bake in a pan of hot water at 350°F for 1 hour, or until a knife inserted in the center comes out clean.

Rarebits

A rarebit as it is prepared today is quite similar to fondue. Originally the bread was toasted, soaked in wine, covered with cheese and toasted again. The result was similar to a grilled sandwich. Today the cheese is melted, as with fondue, and served over toasted bread or English muffin.

There is no reason why, if you so desire, you couldn't dip the bread in the rarebit instead. Rarebits are especially nice in the winter for a cozy supper, a brunch or as a snack with crackers for a large crowd.

Quick Welsh Rarebit
Servings: 6-8

This is delicious spooned over cooked broccoli or cauliflower, too.

1 tbs. butter
2 lb. American or cheddar cheese, diced
3 tbs. grated onion
2 tsp. Worcestershire sauce

½ tsp. dry mustard
salt, freshly ground pepper and paprika to taste
1 cup ale

Melt butter and cheese in top of a double boiler over hot water, stirring constantly. Add remaining ingredients. Cook, stirring, until mixture is smooth. Serve in a chafing dish or fondue pot with bread cubes for dipping, or spoon over toast.

London Rarebit
Servings: 4

Try this with a fontina or Swiss cheese for a variation.

3 tbs. butter
3 tbs. flour
salt to taste
dash Tabasco Sauce
½ cup milk

1½ cups (6 oz.) diced cheddar cheese
¼ cup sherry
1 cup ale

Melt butter in a saucepan over low heat. Stir in flour and seasonings and let bubble a minute. Remove from heat and slowly add milk. Cook over low heat, stirring constantly, until thickened. Add cheese and sherry, stir until cheese is melted and blend in ale. Serve in a chafing dish or fondue pot with bread cubes for dipping, or spoon over toast.

Spanish Rarebit

This delicious rarebit makes a wonderful omelet topping.

3 tbs. butter
2 green bell peppers, chopped
½ cup chopped onion
1 clove garlic, crushed
2 cups (8 oz.) grated Monterey Jack cheese
1 cup beer
¼ tsp. Tabasco Sauce

Melt butter in a saucepan or chafing dish. Sauté pepper, onion and garlic for 5 minutes. Slowly add cheese, stirring constantly until melted and smooth. Blend in beer and Tabasco Sauce. Serve in a chafing dish or fondue pot with bread cubes for dipping, or spoon over toast.

Sherry Rarebit

Serve this as an appetizer with glasses of dry sherry.

⅓ cup cream
1 lb. Gruyère or fontina cheese, cubed
⅓ cup sherry
½ tsp. Worcestershire sauce
1 tsp. mustard

Combine cream and cheese in the top of a double boiler. Cook over hot water until cheese is melted and mixture is smooth. Add Worcestershire sauce and mustard and stir to blend. Serve in a chafing dish or fondue pot with bread cubes for dipping, or spoon over toast.

Rosy Rarebit

Children love this pretty pink, delicately flavored rarebit.

1 can (8 oz.) stewed or whole tomatoes
1 1/2 tbs. butter
1 lb. American cheese, diced
salt and freshly ground pepper to taste

Drain tomatoes. Melt butter in a heavy saucepan over low heat. Add drained tomatoes, breaking them into small pieces with a spoon, and simmer for 20 minutes. Slowly add cheese, stirring constantly until it is melted and mixture has thickened. Season to taste. Serve in a chafing dish or fondue pot with bread cubes for dipping, or spoon over toast.

Cream of Celery Rarebit

Lightly blanched broccoli or cauliflower florets, small raw mushrooms and small cooked potatoes make great dippers if this rarebit is served as a fondue.

1 can (10 oz.) cream of celery soup
1/4 cup dry white wine
1/2 tsp. Dijon mustard
1/2 tsp. Worcestershire sauce
1 1/2 cups (6 oz.) diced cheddar cheese
1 egg, well beaten

Combine soup, wine, mustard and Worcestershire sauce in a saucepan or chafing dish. Cook over medium heat until mixture is just beginning to boil. Slowly add cheese, stirring constantly until melted. Blend in well beaten egg and continue cooking until mixture reaches desired consistency. Spoon over toast, or serve with bread cubes or vegetables for dipping.

Eastern-Style Rarebit

Servings: 4-6

The sardines add a delicious touch to this rarebit.

Sherry Rarebit, page 206, made with cheddar cheese
1 can (4 oz.) sardines in oil
1 tbs. butter
salt and freshly ground pepper to taste
8-12 English muffin halves

Prepare rarebit according to directions. Melt butter in a skillet. Gently sauté sardines for about 10 minutes. Using a pancake turner or spatula, lay sautéed sardines on toasted muffin halves. Spoon *Sherry Rarebit* over sardines.

Western Rarebit

Servings: 4

This makes a savory Sunday supper dish.

1 jar (4-5 oz.) dried beef
2 tbs. butter
2 tbs. flour
1½ cups milk
4 oz. pimiento cheese, diced
2 eggs, beaten
freshly ground pepper to taste

Shred beef and rinse with boiling water; drain well. Melt butter in a heavy saucepan over medium heat. Add flour and blend. Let bubble a minute or two and remove from heat. Slowly stir in milk. Return to heat and cook, stirring until thickened. Add cheese and stir until melted. Mix a little of the hot mixture with the beaten eggs. Stir back into cheese sauce. Add beef and pepper and cook, stirring, until thoroughly heated. Serve over toast.

Spicy Rarebit

If you like hot food, this is for you! Serve with beer or ale.

1 tbs. butter
½ lb. cheddar cheese, diced
½ lb. hot pepper cheese, diced
1 tbs. chili sauce
½ tsp. Tabasco Sauce
½ tsp. mustard
salt and freshly ground pepper to taste
6-7 tbs. ale

Melt butter in a heavy saucepan or chafing dish over low heat. Slowly add cheese and stir until melted. Blend in chili sauce, Tabasco, mustard and seasonings. Add ale one tablespoon at a time, stirring. Cook, stirring constantly, until mixture is thickened and smooth. Serve in a chafing dish or fondue pot with bread cubes for dipping or spoon over toast.

Red and Green Rarebit

You can use fresh chopped red and green bell peppers in this dish for a little crunch.

1 lb. American cheese, diced
1 tsp. dry mustard
salt, cayenne pepper and paprika to taste
½ cup ale
2 tbs. chopped canned green chiles
2 tbs. chopped pimiento

Melt cheese in a heavy saucepan over low heat, stirring until smooth. Add mustard, salt, cayenne and paprika. Slowly blend in ale. Add green chiles and pimiento and serve with bread cubes for dipping or spoon over toast.

Frankfurter Rarebit

This quick dish is popular with all ages, but especially children.

2 tbs. butter
6 frankfurters
2 cups (8 oz.) shredded American cheese
¾ cup milk
6 slices toast, buttered
1 mild onion, sliced

Melt butter in a skillet over medium heat. Sauté frankfurters for 15 minutes, until plump and lightly browned. Combine cheese and milk in the top of a double boiler. Cook over hot water, stirring constantly, until cheese melts and mixture is smooth. Slit frankfurters lengthwise, without cutting all the way through. Place cut sides down on toast slices. Spoon cheese mixture over franks and garnish with onion slices.

Shrimp Rarebit

Here is a quick appetizer or first course. Serve with a Sauvignon blanc or Chardonnay.

1 can (10 oz.) cream of mushroom soup
½ cup small salad shrimp
1 lb. Monterey Jack cheese, diced
¼ cup sherry
¼ tsp. creamed horseradish
2-3 green onions, thinly sliced
salt and freshly ground pepper to taste

Empty soup into the top of a double boiler. Add cheese, place over hot water and stir until cheese is melted. Slowly blend in sherry and seasonings. Cook, stirring, until mixture reaches desired consistency. Add shrimp and heat through. Spoon over toast.

Tuna Rarebit

This makes a delicious supper or winter luncheon dish.

1 tbs. butter
1 tbs. diced cheddar cheese
3 tbs. minced onion
1 tsp. Worcestershire sauce
1 cup ale
½ tsp. dry mustard
salt, freshly ground pepper and paprika to taste
1 can (6½ oz.) water-packed tuna, drained and flaked

Melt butter and cheese together in the top of a double boiler over hot water. Stir constantly until mixture is smooth. Add remaining ingredients and stir until heated and thickened. Serve as a fondue with bread cubes for dipping or spoon over toast.

Dessert Fondue

A dessert fondue, a tasty blend of chocolate and other confections, is an informal, friendly way to top off a meal. Dessert fondues are also great party fun for children.

Use some of these ideas for dippers, and add your own. A little bit of care and imagination in arranging your dippers will make any of these dessert fondues a colorful and unusual way to finish a meal.

- chunks of angel food cake
- lady fingers
- macaroons
- plain cookies
- pound cake slices or chunks
- bite-sized cream puff pastry
- fresh fruits, such as strawberries, grapes, bananas, pears or papayas
- dried fruit
- crunchy pretzels

Fondue Au Creme

Servings: 4

This simple fondue is rich and delicious, a warm "frosting" for pieces of pound cake, angel food cake, plain cookies or pieces of fresh or dried fruit.

1 cup confectioners' sugar
1 cup heavy cream
$\frac{1}{2}$ tsp. flavoring, such as vanilla, almond, mint or lemon extract

Combine sugar and cream in a saucepan. Bring to a boil, stirring constantly. Boil for about $\frac{1}{2}$ minute. Pour into a fondue pot or chafing dish. Keep heat as low as possible to prevent scorching. Serve with assorted fruit or cake pieces.

Fondue Au Chocolat

Chocolate fondue is actually an American invention. It is said to have originated in a New York restaurant. There are many variations of the basic recipe.

9 oz. Swiss milk chocolate, broken into pieces
½ cup whipping cream

Combine ingredients in a fondue pot or chafing dish. Stir over very low heat until chocolate is melted and mixture is smooth. Serve with a variety of "dippers."

Variations

- Use bittersweet chocolate instead of milk chocolate.
- Use pretzels of various shapes for dipping.
- Add ½ cup crushed almonds.
- Add 2 tbs. kirsch.
- Add 1 tbs. instant coffee powder.
- Add ¼ tsp. ground cinnamon and ¼ tsp. ground cloves.
- Add mint flavoring.

Peanut Butter Fondue

This fondue is for the young crowd and for peanut butter lovers. Bananas are the thing to dip.

4 oz. peanut butter chips
2 tbs. peanut butter
¾ cup milk
½ tsp. vanilla extract
2-3 ripe bananas, cut into ¾-inch chunks

Combine ingredients and melt in a fondue pot or in a microwave on MEDIUM power. Serve hot.

Chocolate Rum Fondue

This fondue is for chocolate lovers. Strawberries make delicious dippers.

6 oz. Hershey's Special Dark Chocolate
¼ cup light cream
1 tbs. dark rum

Melt chocolate and cream in a fondue pot or in a microwave on MEDIUM power. Stir in rum and serve.

Vanilla Fondue

Dip fresh strawberries or chunks of ripe peaches or pineapple for this dessert.

6 oz. vanilla milk chips
2 tbs. light cream
1 tbs. Grand Marnier or coffee-flavored liqueur

Melt vanilla chips and cream in a fondue pot or in a microwave on MEDIUM power. Stir in liqueur and serve hot.

Butterscotch Fondue

Here is a quick dessert to satisfy a real sweet tooth. If there is any left over, it can be reheated in the microwave and used for an ice cream or dessert sauce.

6 oz. butterscotch chips
¼ cup evaporated milk
1 tbs. brandy
cubes of pound cake or lady fingers for dipping

Melt butterscotch chips with evaporated milk in a fondue pot over low heat or in a small microwave dish on MEDIUM power. Stir in brandy. Serve warm.

Cheddar Cheese Fondue with Apple

Here is a new twist to that classic combination of apples and cheese, and a refreshing alternative to sweet fondues.

3 tbs. butter
3 tbs. flour
1 cup milk
2 cups (8 oz.) diced sharp cheddar cheese
crisp green apples, cut into chunks

Melt butter in a fondue pot over medium heat. Stir in flour and allow to bubble for 1 minute. Remove from heat and slowly stir in milk. Return to heat and cook, stirring, until mixture thickens and boils. Add diced cheese and stir until melted and smooth. Serve with apple chunks.

The Best 50
Dips

Joanna White

Tips and Tricks for Serving Dips

Dips have progressed far beyond the standard onion-sour cream dip. Now they can vary from very simple to most elegant. Dips provide an ideal way to serve a large number of guests for as little money as you choose to spend. They are generally easy to prepare and easy to transport. Also, many recipes can be made in advance. So take time to plan well, use your imagination and present these dips with a flair!

Natural Containers for Dips

Hollow out some of these items to make containers to hold your dip for a unique presentation.

honeydew melon	orange
melon	bell pepper
bread loaf	zucchini
cantaloupe	pineapple
eggplant	pumpkin
grapefruit	winter squash
cabbage	watermelon
lemon	potato

Ideas for Dippers for Savory Dips

In addition to the usual chips and crackers, here are some dipper ideas.

breadsticks	cooked artichokes
baguette bread rounds	cauliflower florets
toast triangles	jicama slices
pretzels	radishes
small cooked new potatoes	cucumber slices
zucchini rounds	celery
Belgian endive	cherry tomatoes with stems
yellow crookneck squash strips	strips of beef, chicken or pork
bell pepper strips	cooked prawns
carrot slices	crisp pita triangles
cabbage wedges	

Ideas for Dippers for Sweet Dips

bite-sized chunks of fruit
strawberries with stems
pound cake chunks
lady fingers
other firm cookies
dried fruits

Ways to Reduce Fat in Dip Recipes

- Use low-fat or nonfat cream cheese in place of whole cream cheese.

- Use nonfat sour cream or drained yogurt ("yogurt cheese") as a replacement for sour cream.

- Use low-fat cottage cheese.

- Use low-fat or nonfat cheeses.

- When frying in butter, use ½ butter and ½ unsaturated vegetable oil. This will not reduce fat, but will reduce cholesterol.

- When the recipe calls for cooking in oil, substitute chicken stock or water.

- Substitute ground turkey in recipes calling for ground beef.

Garnishes for Dips

strawberries
beets (carved)
berries
onion flowers
gherkins
lettuce
green onions
lemon, lime or grapefruit slices, or baskets
kale
tomatoes
mushrooms (fluted)
grapes (fresh or frosted)
pineapple wedges
cilantro
watercress
parsley

Helpful Hints

- When planning your menu, try to achieve a balance between taste, color, texture and temperature.

- Make some vegetarian and low-fat dishes for health-conscious guests.

- If you have a guest with allergies you are aware of, avoid those ingredients if possible, or make a card listing the ingredients and place it by the food.

- There should be a minimum of 4 different types of appetizers prepared for a party of 20 guests. Allow at least 10 "bites" per person for a 2- to 3-hour party.

- Make sure the garnish is appropriate for the dish.

- Take a little extra time to prepare those finishing touches — presentation really makes a difference.

- Vary the dippers.

- Provide a receptacle to deposit used toothpicks, napkins and other disposables.

Crab Dip

This quick, simple dip goes well with plain crackers or Triscuits.

2 cups fresh crabmeat
1/2 cup mayonnaise
1 can (8 oz.) water chestnuts, drained and finely chopped
1-2 tbs. soy sauce
2 green onions, finely chopped
2 tbs. chopped fresh parsley
lemon juice to taste

Save a few pieces of crabmeat for garnish. Gently mix all ingredients together, taste and adjust quantity of lemon juice and soy sauce to taste.

Tex-Mex Dip

No baking is required for this delicious dish. If you wish to make it totally vegetarian, make sure that the bean dip is made without animal fat. Serve with tortilla chips, or for a change try using blue corn tortilla chips.

3 ripe avocados, peeled and pitted
2 tbs. lemon juice
1/2 tsp. salt
2 cups sour cream
1/2 cup mayonnaise
1 pkg. (2.25 oz.) taco seasoning
2 cans (10 oz. each) bean dip
1 bunch green onions, chopped
1-2 tomatoes, diced
2 cans (6 oz.) olives, drained and chopped
8 oz. sharp cheddar cheese, shredded

With a food processor, blender or mixer, mix avocados with lemon juice and salt until smooth. Layer this on the bottom of a shallow serving dish. Stir sour cream, mayonnaise and taco seasoning mix together and gently spread sour cream mixture over avocado mixture. Mix bean dip, green onions, tomatoes and olives together and spread this over sour cream mixture. Sprinkle with cheddar cheese and serve.

Hummus Dip

Makes 3 cups

This is a version of a garbanzo bean dip that originated in the Middle East. It's quick to put together and is ideally served with fresh or toasted pita bread. If you use canned garbanzos, rinse them with cold water and drain them well. Tahini is sesame seed paste, which greatly enhances the flavor but adds fat to the recipe.

1 tbs. olive oil
1 small onion, chopped
2-3 cloves garlic, minced
2 cups cooked garbanzo beans (chickpeas)
½ tsp. turmeric
2 tbs. chopped fresh parsley
1-2 tbs. lemon juice, to taste
2-3 tbs. tahini, optional

Heat olive oil in a skillet and sauté onion and garlic until soft and transparent. Place all ingredients in a blender container or food processor workbowl and puree until the consistency resembles that of mayonnaise.

Mango Chutney Dip

Makes 10-12 servings

This can be used as a dip or a spread. If you want a spread, do not add chutney to the recipe. Oil and fill a 3-cup mold, chill the mixture for several hours, unmold and drizzle chutney over the top.

12 oz. cream cheese, softened
3 tbs. mayonnaise
3 tbs. chopped peanuts
3-4 tbs. raisins
1 tbs. chopped green onions
3-4 slices bacon, fried crisp and crumbled
2 tsp. curry powder
½ cup shredded coconut
1 cup chopped mango chutney

With a food processor or blender, combine cream cheese and mayonnaise until smooth. Add remaining ingredients, adjusting the quantity of curry powder to your personal taste. If desired, reserve coconut to garnish top of dip.

Guacamole

Save the avocado pit and embed it in the center of the mixture until ready to serve — this will help to keep the dip from becoming dark. Serve with tortilla chips, corn chips or plain tortillas.

4 large ripe avocados, peeled and pitted
juice of 2 limes
½ cup shredded cheddar cheese
½ cup chopped tomatoes
½ cup chopped Bermuda onion
dash salt
1 jalapeño pepper, chopped, optional
1 tbs. chopped cilantro, optional
chopped tomatoes or chopped cilantro for garnish

With a food processor or blender, blend avocados until smooth. Add remaining ingredients, taste and adjust seasonings to personal taste.

Salmon Dip

This deliciously simple recipe will get rave reviews. Serve with crackers, bread rounds or fresh vegetables for dipping.

8 oz. cream cheese, softened
1 can (1 lb.) salmon
2 tsp. minced onion
1 tbs. lemon juice
1 tbs. horseradish
¼ tsp. salt
¼ tsp. Liquid Smoke
1 tbs. chopped fresh parsley
milk to thin mixture, optional
chopped toasted pecans for garnish

With a mixer, beat cream cheese until smooth. Add salmon, onion, lemon juice, horseradish, salt, liquid smoke and parsley. If mixture appears too thick, add enough milk to thin mixture for easy dipping. Sprinkle top with toasted pecans.

Dill Dip

This delicious dip goes well with a vegetable tray or potato chips. Beau Monde seasoning is a blend of salt, sugar, onion and celery seed, and is available wherever spices and herbs are sold.

1 cup sour cream (can use nonfat)
⅓ cup mayonnaise
1 tbs. chopped green onion
1 tbs. chopped fresh parsley
1 tsp. dill weed
1 tsp. Beau Monde seasoning

Mix all ingredients together in a bowl and refrigerate for 2 to 3 hours before serving.

Three Cheese Dip

For cheese lovers, this is a must. Serve with breadsticks or small rounds of rye bread.

½ cup butter, softened
¼ lb. Edam cheese
¼ lb. Parmesan cheese
¼ lb. Danish blue cheese, finely crumbled
1 ½ tsp. paprika
½ tsp. salt
⅓ cup sour cream (can use nonfat)

With a mixer, beat butter until smooth. Finely grate Edam cheese and add to butter with Parmesan, blue cheese, paprika and salt, mixing well. Gently stir in sour cream and serve.

Avocado Dip

This is another simple dip that goes well with all types of chips. You can also use this as a spread for sandwiches. If you plan to store this dip, save the avocado pit and mix it in with the dip until ready to serve. This will help to keep the mixture from turning dark.

2 large ripe avocados, peeled and pitted
4 tsp. lemon juice
2 tsp. grated onion
½ cup sour cream or mayonnaise
dash Tabasco Sauce
salt and pepper

Place all ingredients in a food processor or blender and beat until smooth. Taste and adjust seasonings.

Pimiento Cream Cheese Dip

You can enhance this recipe with a little smoked salmon. It makes an extraordinary sandwich.

16 oz. cream cheese, softened
¼ cup minced onion
4 tsp. lemon juice
4 chicken bouillon cubes
⅔ cup hot water
2 tbs. chopped pimiento
⅛ tsp. dill seed, optional

With a mixer, beat cream cheese until smooth. Beat in onion and lemon juice. Dissolve chicken bouillon cubes in hot water and beat into cream cheese mixture. Gently beat in pimiento and dill, if desired. Do not overmix.

Olive Appetizer Dip

This quick dip goes well with French bread, breadsticks or vegetable trays. Or spread it on rounds of French bread, sprinkle them with grated Swiss cheese and broil until bubbly. Add the celery for crunch, if you like.

1 avocado, peeled and pitted
1 tsp. lemon juice
1 cup finely chopped black olives
¼ cup finely chopped red or green bell peppers
¼ cup finely chopped tomatoes
1 tbs. finely chopped fresh parsley
8 oz. cream cheese, softened
¼ cup finely chopped celery, optional

Mash avocado with lemon juice. Using a mixer or stirring by hand, blend in remaining ingredients, making sure not to overmix so that vegetables remain somewhat intact. Chill until ready to serve.

Veggie Dip

This vegetable dip is similar to a very creamy vinaigrette.

1 tbs. Dijon mustard
1 ½ tbs. vinegar (prefer balsamic)
1 ½ tbs. lemon juice
1 tsp. salt
pepper
pinch sugar
½ cup olive oil
1 large ripe avocado, peeled and pitted
8 oz. cream cheese
1-2 cloves garlic, minced
2-3 tbs. minced green onion
2 tbs. minced fresh parsley

Place Dijon mustard, vinegar, lemon juice, salt, pepper and sugar in a blender or food processor and process until well mixed. Slowly pour olive oil in a fine stream into mustard mixture, allowing it to emulsify. Add remaining ingredients, taste and adjust seasonings.

Pecan Cheese Dip

This somewhat strange combination is especially a favorite of men. Great with crackers, bread or even as a dip for meats.

8 oz. cream cheese
1 cup chopped toasted pecans
2 tbs. steak sauce
1 clove garlic, minced
few drops Tabasco Sauce
enough milk to thin mixture

Place all ingredients except milk in a food processor workbowl or blender container and process until just mixed. Add milk a few tablespoons at a time to thin to the consistency you desire.

Curry Veggie Dip

This dip can be used with vegetable trays and also for dipping cooked meats like chicken and beef strips. Serve it in a hollowed-out green vegetable, such as a large zucchini, for a beautiful contrast.

3 cups mayonnaise
2 tbs. finely chopped onion
2 tsp. curry powder, or to taste
1 tsp. dry mustard
few drops Tabasco Sauce
1 tsp. salt
pepper

Place all ingredients in a food processor workbowl or blender container and process until smooth. Taste and adjust seasonings. Refrigerate until ready to use.

Cottage Clam Dip

Makes 1 1/2 cups

This is a relatively low-fat dip that goes well with hearty crackers or chips.

1 cup creamed cottage cheese (low-fat can be used)
6 drops Tabasco Sauce, or to taste
1/2 tsp. Worcestershire sauce
1/2 tsp. onion salt
1/4 tsp. salt
1 tbs. clam juice
1 can (6 oz.) minced clams, drained, liquid reserved

Place cottage cheese, Tabasco, Worcestershire, onion salt, salt and reserved clam juice in a food processor workbowl or blender container and process until smooth. Add more clam juice if you prefer a thinner consistency. Stir in clams and refrigerate until ready to serve.

Deviled Ham Dip

Makes 2 3/4 cups

This dip makes a little change from the ordinary with the addition of apple. Serve with toasted bread rounds.

1 cup cooked ham
1 green bell pepper, minced
1 large tart apple, chopped
1/4 cup diced sweet pickle
1/2 cup mayonnaise
1/2 tsp. dry mustard
1/4 tsp. salt
dash Tabasco Sauce or cayenne pepper

Place ham, green pepper, apple and pickle in a food processor workbowl or blender container and process until finely minced. Add remaining ingredients and process until just mixed. Add more mayonnaise if you desire a thinner consistency. Taste and adjust seasonings. Refrigerate until ready to use.

Avocado Crab Dip

This creamy, delicate dip is ideally served with plain crackers or melba toast.

2 ripe avocados, peeled and pitted
¼ cup lemon juice
8 oz. cream cheese, softened
2 tsp. minced onion
salt and pepper
milk to thin mixture
2 cans (6 oz. each) crabmeat

Place avocados and lemon juice in a food processor or blender and process until avocados are pureed. Add cream cheese, onion, salt and pepper to avocado mixture and blend until smooth. Add milk a few tablespoons at a time until you reach the desired consistency. Gently stir in crabmeat. Taste and adjust seasonings. Refrigerate until ready to use.

Chutney and Shrimp Dip

This dip is best with crackers, but also good with crunchy fresh vegetable dippers. Garnish the top with a sprinkling of chopped fresh parsley.

8 oz. cream cheese, softened
2 tsp. curry powder
½ tsp. crushed garlic
¼ cup mango chutney
⅓ tsp. salt
1 cup chopped cooked shrimp
½ cup sour cream
chopped fresh parsley for garnish

Beat cream cheese, curry powder, garlic, chutney and salt together until well mixed. Fold in shrimp and sour cream. Garnish with parsley. Refrigerate until ready to serve.

Ginger Sesame Dip

Try this great dip with skewered meat, especially chicken.

2 cups sour cream
2½ tbs. soy sauce
4 tsp. Worcestershire sauce
1 tsp. ground ginger
2 tbs. toasted sesame seeds

Stir all ingredients together. Taste and adjust seasonings. Refrigerate for several hours before serving.

Sun-Dried Tomato and Bean Dip

Makes 2 cups

This easy no-bake bean dip with an Italian flair is best served with breadsticks. If your sun-dried tomatoes are dry-packed, rather than packed in a jar in oil, reconstitute them in water before draining and chopping.

2 cans (15 oz. each) white beans
⅓ cup drained chopped sun-dried tomatoes
2 tbs. chopped fresh basil
2 tbs. olive oil
2 tsp. minced garlic
¼ tsp. salt, or more to taste
⅛ tsp. pepper

Drain beans and rinse. Place all ingredients in a food processor workbowl or blender container and process until well mixed but not completely mashed. Taste and adjust seasonings. Cover and refrigerate until ready to use.

Roasted Red Pepper Dip

Makes 2 ½ cups

Here is another excellent dip to serve with fresh vegetables. Cut the top off a red bell pepper, remove the seeds and fill it with this mixture to serve.

1 jar (15 oz.) roasted red bell peppers, drained
2 green onions, cut into fine pieces
1-2 tbs. lemon juice
1 cup whipped cream cheese

Place all ingredients in a food processor workbowl or blender container and process into a coarse puree. Chill before serving.

Sweet Potato and Carrot Dip

Makes 4 cups

Dip into this piquant yet sweet vegetable dip with vegetables or pita bread. For a healthy alternative, rather than boiling the vegetables, steam them until tender and add a sprinkling of salt for flavor.

1 lb. sweet potatoes or yams
1 lb. carrots
water to cover
1 tsp. salt
3 cloves garlic
1 tsp. ground cumin
1 tsp. cinnamon
3-4 tbs. olive oil
3 tbs. vinegar (prefer balsamic)
pinch cayenne pepper, or more to taste

Peel sweet potatoes and carrots and cut into pieces. Place in a saucepan, cover with water, add salt and boil until vegetables are soft. Drain. Puree cooked vegetables in a food processor workbowl or blender container until smooth. Add remaining ingredients and puree until blended. Taste and adjust seasonings to your personal preference.

Mixed Cheese Dip

Makes 5 cups

Quick, simple and delicious!

8 oz. cream cheese, softened
½ lb. butter, softened
2 jars (5 oz. each) pimiento cheese spread
1 jar (5 oz.) Roquefort cheese spread
1 jar (5 oz.) Old English cheese spread
1 cup grated cheddar cheese
dash salt
dash Worcestershire sauce
few drops Tabasco Sauce
⅓-½ cup cream or milk

Place all ingredients in a food processor workbowl or blender container and process until smooth. Add enough cream or milk to make a good dipping consistency. Taste and adjust seasonings to your personal preference.

Eggplant Caviar

This great, all-vegetable dip is even better served in a hollowed-out eggplant.

2 eggplants
1 tbs. olive oil
2 cloves garlic
1 small onion
1 red bell pepper, seeded
1 green bell pepper, seeded
1 tomato, peeled and seeded
2 tsp. capers
1 tbs. fresh lemon juice
1/8 tsp. Tabasco Sauce
1 tsp. salt
1/4 tsp. pepper
3 tbs. vinegar (prefer balsamic)
1 tsp. basil
1/4 cup olive oil
1/2 cup chopped black olives
1/2 cup chopped green olives

Brush eggplants with olive oil and bake in a 350° oven for 30 minutes (or until they begin to soften). Remove from oven, cut in half and scoop out flesh. Save the eggplant shell if you wish to serve the dip in it.

In a food processor workbowl or blender container, chop garlic. Add onion and bell peppers. Pulse on and off to coarsely chop vegetables. Remove chopped vegetables and set aside. Add tomato, eggplant pulp, capers, lemon juice, Tabasco, salt, pepper, vinegar, basil and oil to processor or blender and process until well mixed. Add coarsely chopped vegetables and process just until mixed.

Transfer vegetables to a heavy saucepan and cook over medium heat for 20 minutes. Add chopped olives, taste and adjust seasonings, and chill. Serve in a hollowed-out eggplant shell or colorful dish.

Tapenade (Olive Dip)

Makes 3 cups

This is a perfect dip to take to a party. Cut little baguettes into small rounds for dipping, or use breadsticks.

2 cans (6 oz. each) pitted black olives
3 tbs. capers
1/2 cup minced onion
1 tsp. minced garlic
2 tbs. chopped fresh parsley
1/4 cup grated Parmesan cheese
2 tbs. olive oil
2 tbs. vinegar (prefer balsamic)
1/2 tsp. salt
1/2 tsp. pepper
1/4 cup chopped red bell pepper

With a food processor or blender, just barely chop olives; remove and set aside. Put remaining ingredients into processor except 2 tbs. red bell pepper. Chop into a fine blend and stir this mixture into olives. Taste and adjust seasonings. Sprinkle remaining chopped red pepper on top for garnish.

Spinach Dip

Makes 5 cups

This is an old favorite. If you use nonfat sour cream and mayonnaise, it's perfect for serving to health-conscious guests who also like delicious food. This recipe will keep for about 2 days.

1 pint sour cream (can use nonfat)
1 cup mayonnaise (can use low-fat or nonfat)
3/4 pkg. (1.8 oz.) dried leek soup mix
1 pkg. (10 oz.) frozen spinach
1/2 cup chopped fresh parsley
1/2 cup chopped green onion
1 tsp. dill
1 tsp. dry Italian salad seasoning mix

In a bowl, stir sour cream, mayonnaise and leek soup mix together. Defrost spinach and squeeze out all excess liquid. Add spinach to sour cream mixture and stir well. Add remaining ingredients and stir. Refrigerate for several hours to allow flavors to mellow.

Salsa

It's a must to serve salsa with tortilla chips (freshly made if you've got the time). It's also good with bean dishes, vegetable salads and chicken.

1 medium sweet onion
3 cloves garlic, crushed
½ green bell pepper, chopped
½ red bell pepper, chopped
½ cup chopped cilantro
2 tbs. lemon juice
2 tsp. sugar
1 can (15 oz.) Mexican-style stewed tomatoes
salt and pepper
chopped fresh jalapeño chiles, optional

Place all ingredients in a food processor workbowl or blender container. Process with pulsing action until blended. Taste and adjust seasoning .

Asparagus Mayo Dip

This recipe makes a good alternative dip for vegetable trays or as a dipping sauce for artichokes. Use it as a dressing for vegetable pasta salad that has chopped asparagus as one of the ingredients. If you wish to avoid the use of raw eggs, you can mix asparagus with commercially prepared mayonnaise for a reasonable alternative. Thin with a little vegetable oil if it seems too thick.

1 cup finely chopped asparagus
4 egg yolks
1 tbs. dry mustard
salt and pepper
1 tbs. vinegar
1 ½ cups vegetable oil

Steam asparagus until tender and process in a blender or food processor to a smooth puree. You should have about ½ cup puree. Transfer puree to a bowl and cool. Process egg yolks, mustard, salt, pepper and vinegar to mix thoroughly. Add oil in a thin stream while food processor or blender is running, until it has all been added and mixture is smooth and thick. Add asparagus puree to mixture and blend until well mixed. Refrigerate until ready to use.

Apricot Chutney Dip

Makes 1 ½ cups

Put this dip on your buffet table surrounded by bite-sized chunks of fresh fruit on picks. This somewhat sweet dip can also be served with crackers. It is delicious as a sauce over chopped fruit.

8 oz. cream cheese
4-5 tbs. apricot chutney
¾ tsp. curry powder
½ cup toasted coconut
milk to thin mixture

Place cream cheese, chutney, curry powder and coconut in a food processor workbowl or blender container and process until blended. Add milk a few tablespoons at a time until you reach a dipping consistency.

Creamy Pecan Dip

Makes 7-8 cups

This is an incredible dip that uses a unique combination of creamy ingredients finished off with toasted pecans. It is appreciated by adults and children both. Serve it with a fruit tray. It also makes a really wonderful dressing for fruit salads.

8 oz. cream cheese, softened
1 jar (7 oz.) marshmallow creme
1 container (8 oz.) Cool Whip
2 cups vanilla yogurt
1 cup chopped toasted pecans

With a mixer, whip cream cheese until soft. Add marshmallow creme and blend until smooth. Gently fold in Cool Whip and vanilla yogurt until mixed. Chill until ready to use. Just before serving, stir in toasted pecans.

Fruit Custard Dip

This is another favorite dip for fruits or to use as a dressing on fruit salads. This can be stored for days.

1 cup orange juice
2 cups pineapple juice
1 cup sugar
1/3 cup cornstarch
enough cold water to make a paste
2 tbs. butter

Place orange juice, pineapple juice and sugar in a saucepan and bring to a boil. Mix cornstarch with enough water to make a paste and stir this into hot juice mixture. Continue to stir until mixture thickens. Watch carefully that you do not scorch. Remove from heat, add butter and stir until butter melts. Cool completely before using.

Pineapple-Orange Yogurt Dip

You can't go wrong with the combination of pineapple and orange. It makes a great dip for fruit, fruit salad dressing and even spooned on top of granola. If you aren't crazy about coconut, use chopped toasted almonds.

1 can (8¼ oz.) crushed pineapple, drained
8 oz. orange yogurt
4 oz. whipped cream cheese
¼ cup toasted coconut
2 tbs. brown sugar, or to taste
milk to thin mixture, optional

Mix all ingredients together with a mixer. If desired, add a little milk to thin mixture. Chill for several hours before serving.

Creamy Berry Dip

This is a great dessert dip that utilizes frozen berries, so it can be made any time of year. It goes particularly well with cake cubes. This is especially good if you use the liqueur to match the type of berries you use — such as framboise with frozen raspberries.

1 lb. cream cheese, softened
¼ cup berry liqueur or brandy
2 pkg. (10 oz. each) frozen berries, thawed
sugar, optional

In a heavy saucepan, mix cream cheese and liqueur together and melt over low heat. Add berries to saucepan, stirring until berries are heated through. Taste and determine whether or not you wish to add sugar. Stir gently until sugar is dissolved. Refrigerate until ready to serve.

Strawberry Ginger Dipping Sauce

Makes 2 cups

This creamy fruit sauce goes well with fruit such as bananas, strawberries and grapes. It is best to chill overnight so the flavor can develop. Pour this sauce over chopped fruit and serve as a breakfast fruit or a fruit dessert.

2 tbs. chopped crystallized ginger
1 cup sour cream
½ cup strawberries
1 medium banana
1 tbs. light brown sugar
1 tbs. rum

In a food processor workbowl or blender container, process crystallized ginger until finely chopped. Add remaining ingredients and blend until smooth. Chill for at least 3 hours before serving.

Hot Nachos Dip

This delicious Mexican-type dish is perfect to take to parties. It is easy to prepare and there is never any left. Serve it with tortilla chips.

½ lb. lean ground beef
½ lb. sausage (chorizo or hot Italian variety)
1 large onion, chopped
salt
1 can (1 lb.) refried beans
1 can (4 oz.) chopped green chiles (mild or hot)
2-3 cups shredded cheddar cheese
¾ cup taco sauce (mild or hot)
1 cup sour cream
1 can (6 oz.) frozen avocado dip, thawed
1 cup chopped black olives
¼ cup chopped green onions

In a skillet, crumble ground beef and sausage and cook until just brown. Drain off fat. Add onion and cook until wilted. Add salt to taste. Spread refried beans in a large, low-sided baking dish and cover with cooked meat mixture. Sprinkle with chopped green chiles, top with shredded cheese and drizzle with taco sauce. Bake uncovered in a 400° oven for 20 to 25 minutes. Remove from oven and spread with sour cream. Mound avocado dip in the center (or gently spread over sour cream). Sprinkle with olives and green onions. Serve hot.

Hot Artichoke Dip

This incredibly rich hot dip is best served with thin crackers or French bread rounds.

2 cans (8½ oz. each) artichoke hearts
1 cup mayonnaise
1 cup sour cream
2 cups grated Parmesan cheese
1 cup chopped water chestnuts
1-2 green onions, finely chopped

Cut artichoke hearts into small pieces. Combine with remaining ingredients, mix well and place in a baking dish. Bake at 350° for 35 minutes. Keep warm while serving.

Hot Clam Dip

Makes 3 cups

Instead of the common onion dip, consider using clam dip with a little tang of hot pepper sauce. Serve with crackers or French bread rounds.

8 oz. cream cheese, softened
1 cup grated mild cheddar cheese
1 tbs. lemon juice, or more to taste
1 tsp. Worcestershire sauce
2 cloves garlic, minced
1/2 tsp. hot pepper sauce
1/2 tsp. salt

1/2 cup minced onion
3 tbs. minced parsley
2 cans (7 oz. each) minced clams,
   drained, juice reserved
3 tbs. clam juice, or more if necessary
grated cheddar cheese for garnish
chopped fresh parsley for garnish

Combine cream cheese, cheddar cheese, lemon juice, Worcestershire, garlic, hot pepper sauce and salt. Stir minced onion and parsley into cream cheese mixture. Add clams and 3 tbs. clam juice and stir. Add more clam juice if a thinner consistency is desired. Just barely heat in a casserole dish or chafing dish and serve. Garnish with a little grated cheddar cheese and sprinkle with chopped parsley.

Hot Crab Dip

Makes 4 cups

An expensive dip, this can be reserved for special occasions. Although you can use canned crab, fresh is better. Stand 3 leg pieces in a cluster of parsley for a beautiful garnish. Serve with Triscuits, other crackers or vegetables for dipping.

16 oz. cream cheese
1/4 cup finely chopped onions
2-3 tbs. milk
1 tsp. horseradish
1/2 tsp. salt
dash white pepper
1 lb. fresh or canned crabmeat
crab legs (if available) for garnish
fresh parsley or toasted slivered almonds for garnish

Mix all ingredients together except crabmeat and garnishes. Mixture should be smooth. Heat mixture gently in a chafing dish or fondue pot. Just before serving, gently stir in crabmeat, trying not to break up crabmeat too much. Garnish with crab legs if possible, and parsley or a sprinkling of toasted almonds.

South-of-the-Border Dip

You can make this dip a vegetarian one by eliminating the ground beef and using vegetarian refried beans. Serve with tortillas or corn chips. Or consider making your own chips by cutting corn tortillas into wedges, deep frying until crisp and draining on paper towels.

1 lb. lean ground beef
2 cans (16 oz. each) refried beans
1 pkg. (2.25 oz.) taco seasoning mix
2 cups shredded cheddar or Jack cheese
½ cup finely chopped onions
4-6 drops Tabasco Sauce
enough milk or water to thin mixture, optional
chopped green onions for garnish

In a large skillet, cook meat until brown and drain off any excess fat. Add remaining ingredients and stir until well mixed. If mixture appears too thick, add a little milk or water to thin. Serve in a chafing dish, fondue pot or slow cooking pot to keep warm and sprinkle top with a small amount of chopped green onions.

Creamy Hot Crab Dip

Here is another version of a crab dip, creamy, old-fashioned and wonderful. The paprika adds color. Serve with French bread or plain crackers.

2 tbs. butter
2 oz. mushrooms, sliced
½ tsp. lemon juice
3 egg yolks
1 cup cream
¼ cup sweet sherry
salt and pepper
dash cayenne pepper
paprika
1 lb. fresh crabmeat

In a saucepan, melt butter and sauté mushrooms until tender, adding lemon juice to help prevent mushrooms from darkening. Beat egg yolks together, add cream and stir. Add sherry, salt, pepper, cayenne and paprika; stir until smooth. Add crabmeat just before serving. Serve warm.

Sweet and Sour Dipping Sauce

Makes 2 cups

This sauce can be used with all kinds of meat for dipping, such as cooked chicken, rumaki, barbecued pork, fried prawns and even cooked pork.

1½ tbs. cornstarch
¾ cup pineapple juice
½ cup brown sugar
1 tsp. salt
½ cup cider vinegar
4 tsp. ketchup
1 cup drained crushed pineapple
2 drops red food coloring, optional

Mix cornstarch with pineapple juice and bring to a boil. Add brown sugar, salt, vinegar, ketchup, crushed pineapple and red food coloring (if desired). Stir until thickened. Serve warm.

Seafood Cheddar Dip

Makes 4 cups

Like many dips, this one is extremely simple and quick to prepare. Serve with mild crackers or thinly sliced French bread.

12 oz. cream cheese, softened
8 oz. sour cream
onion or garlic salt
white pepper
1 cup cooked shrimp or crabmeat
1 cup shredded cheddar cheese

In a bowl, mix together cream cheese, sour cream, onion or garlic salt and pepper until mixture is smooth. Gently fold in shrimp or crabmeat. Place mixture in a small, shallow baking dish. Sprinkle with cheddar cheese. Bake in a 350° oven for 20 minutes.

Creamy Hamburger Dip

Here's a dip for those times when you need a protein-rich appetizer and want an alternative to chicken wings. Serve with hearty crackers, chips, toasted bread fingers or cooked new potatoes. Sugar is added to remove the slight bitterness that garlic and tomatoes may impart.

1 lb. extra lean ground beef, or ground turkey
½ cup chopped onions
garlic salt
¼ cup ketchup
1 can (8 oz.) tomato sauce
8 oz. cream cheese
⅓-¼ cup grated Parmesan cheese
¾ tsp. dried oregano
1 tsp. sugar

Cook hamburger, onions and garlic salt in a skillet until onions are wilted. Add remaining ingredients and cook on low for ½ hour. Serve hot in a chafing dish.

Jalapeño Bean Dip

Makes 2 ¾ cups

The quantity of jalapeños will determine the heat, so be careful or go wild! Serve with chips or toast triangles.

2½ cups cooked pinto beans, or canned, rinsed and drained
1-6 jalapeño chiles
1 tbs. olive oil
½ tsp. salt, or to taste
½ tsp. dried oregano
¼ tsp. garlic powder

Mash pinto beans well and place in a saucepan. Cut tops off jalapeños, leaving them whole with seeds inside. Add remaining ingredients and simmer over low heat for 15 minutes. If mixture appears too thick, add water until the proper consistency is reached. Remove jalapeños and cool before serving.

Chili Con Queso

Makes 3 cups

This creamy, piquant dip deserves the extra effort of making homemade tortilla chips. Also good as a sauce for chicken, eggs, fish or pasta.

1 small onion, minced
2 tbs. butter
1 cup drained canned tomatoes
1 can (4 oz.) chopped mild green chiles
4 oz. cheddar cheese, grated
4 oz. Monterey Jack cheese, grated
1 cup cream
salt and pepper

In a saucepan, sauté onion in butter until soft. Chop tomatoes and add to saucepan with chiles. Simmer for 15 minutes. Add grated cheeses and stir until cheese melts. Gradually stir in cream until mixture is smooth. Season to taste. Serve hot in a chafing dish.

Pork and Bean Dip

Makes 3 ½ cups

A slightly different version of a bean dip, this one hints of barbecued beans. Good with crisp pita triangles, chips or breadsticks.

1 can (16 oz.) pork and beans
1 can (8 oz.) tomato sauce
½ cup grated sharp cheddar cheese
1 tsp. garlic salt
½ tsp. salt
1 tsp. chili powder
2 tsp. vinegar
2 tsp. Worcestershire sauce
¼-½ tsp. Liquid Smoke
dash Tabasco Sauce, or cayenne pepper
½ cup crumbled fried bacon for garnish

Place all ingredients in a heavy saucepan and warm until cheese is melted. Leave texture as is, or place all ingredients, except bacon, in a food processor or blender and process until smooth. Sprinkle bacon pieces on top for garnish.

Hot Pimiento Cheese Dip

A simple dip, this can be expanded into many variations with the addition of "texture crunchies."

1 lb. cheddar cheese, grated
1 can (12 oz.) evaporated milk
1 jar (4 oz.) chopped pimientos, drained
½ cup finely chopped raw vegetables
½ cup chopped black or green olives
½ cup crisp bacon bits
¼ cup chopped green onions

In a heavy saucepan or double boiler, melt cheese and evaporated milk together over low heat, stirring until smooth. Add pimiento and, if desired, any "crunchy" of choice. Serve in a chafing dish.

Cheesy Bean Dip

This dish is quick and always a hit because it is so flavorful. Serve with taco chips or bread rounds.

8 oz. cream cheese, softened
1 can (10 oz.) bean dip
1 cup sour cream
10-20 drops Tabasco Sauce
¼ cup chopped green onions, or more to taste
½ pkg. (2.25 oz.) taco seasoning mix
4 oz. Jack cheese, shredded
4 oz. cheddar cheese, shredded

Mix all ingredients together except shredded cheeses. Place in a shallow casserole dish. Finish by covering with shredded cheeses. Bake in a 350° oven for 20 minutes. Serve hot.

Chili Dip

This quick, easy-to-fix dish goes best with chips, breadsticks or celery sticks.

8 oz. cream cheese, softened
1 can (8 oz.) no-bean canned chili
1 can (4 oz.) chopped green chiles
1 cup grated cheddar cheese

Spread cream cheese on the bottom of a pie plate. Cover with chili and sprinkle with green chiles. Cover with cheddar cheese and bake 325° for 15 to 20 minutes.

Hot Mango Sauce

Mango has an exotic flavor that complements meat beautifully. Serve this with chunks of pork, beef, fish or chicken.

3 mangoes, peeled and seeded
1 tbs. Madeira wine
⅓ cup butter, melted
2-3 green chile peppers, seeded and finely diced
salt and pepper
1 tsp. caraway seeds, optional
water to thin sauce, optional

Place mangoes in a food processor workbowl or blender container and puree until smooth. Add Madeira and mix well. Place all ingredients except caraway in a saucepan and simmer for 10 minutes. Taste and add caraway seeds if desired. If mixture appears too thick, thin with a little water.

Savory Cherry Dipping Sauce

Dip pork or more exotic meats, such as duck or barbecued pork, into this sauce.

1 ½ cups drained canned pitted cherries
¾ cup corn syrup
½ cup vinegar
¼ tsp. cinnamon
⅛ tsp. nutmeg
pinch ground cloves
salt
pepper

Place all ingredients in a saucepan and bring to a boil. Reduce heat and simmer for about 5 minutes. Depending on the texture that appeals to you, keep cherries whole, partially grind in a food processor workbowl to leave some chunks for texture, or thoroughly puree and sieve for a fine sauce. Taste and adjust seasonings.

Creamy Tuna Dip

Serve this dip warm from a chafing dish. If you use cayenne pepper for garnish, you will add a little heat to the dish; paprika only adds color. It's good with chips or bread rounds.

8 oz. cream cheese
2 tbs. bottled chili sauce
1 jar (5 oz.) sharp processed cheese spread
2-3 tbs. chopped green onions
1 can (6 ½ oz.) tuna, drained
milk to thin mixture
cayenne pepper or paprika for garnish

Place cream cheese, chili sauce and processed cheese in a saucepan over low heat and stir until melted and smooth. Add green onions, tuna and enough milk to thin. Stir until mixed. Garnish with cayenne pepper or paprika. Serve warm.

Hot Anchovy Dip

Makes 2 cups

This Italian favorite is commonly known as bagna cauda, and is served barely warm. Traditional dippers are raw vegetables and bread.

1 ½ cups olive oil
6 tbs. butter
1 ½ tbs. minced garlic
18 flat anchovy fillets, chopped
1 tsp. salt, or to taste
dash Tabasco Sauce

Heat olive oil and butter together in a saucepan until they just begin to foam. Immediately toss in minced garlic and sauté very briefly (don't let it brown). Reduce heat and add anchovies to "wilted" garlic, stirring until anchovies dissolve into a paste. Add salt and Tabasco, if desired, and transfer mixture to a warming dish.

Hearty Italian Dipping Sauce

Makes 5 cups

This is very fast and easy to make. You can always experiment with herbs like oregano and basil for subtle changes. Serve with breadsticks or bread cubes for dipping.

½ lb. lean ground beef
2 cups spaghetti sauce
1 ½ cups grated cheddar cheese
1 ½ cups shredded mozzarella cheese
½ cup dry red wine, or more to thin mixture

In a skillet, brown ground beef. Drain off excess fat. Stir in spaghetti sauce and cheeses until thoroughly melted. Add wine and transfer mixture to a chafing dish to serve.

Hot Fudge Dipping Sauce

This is a great sauce for dipping pieces of pound cake, angel food cake or fruits like bananas, pears and apples.

4 oz. unsweetened chocolate
¼ cup butter
¼ cup light corn syrup
2 cups cream
2 cups sugar
4 tsp. vanilla extract
¼ tsp. salt

Grate chocolate into a heavy saucepan and melt with butter and corn syrup, stirring constantly over low heat. When chocolate is melted, add cream and sugar and cook until sugar is dissolved. Bring to a boil over moderate heat and boil without stirring for 8 minutes. Remove pan from heat and stir in vanilla and salt.

Jelly Fruit Dip

Makes 1 quart

This can be served warm like a fondue for dipping fruits such as bananas, pineapple, melons or dried fruits. It can also be chilled and used as a dip for a fruit tray, in which case you may want to thin with additional orange juice.

¼ cup cornstarch
6 tbs. sugar
1 ½ cups cold water
1 cup currant jelly
½ cup sweet sherry
½ cup orange juice
6-7 tbs. lemon juice, or to taste

Place cornstarch, sugar and water in a saucepan and bring to a boil. Cook until mixture is thickened and sugar is dissolved. Add remaining ingredients and stir until smooth.

Caramel Dipping Sauce

Makes 2 cups

This popular flavor makes a delicious sauce for dipping fruits or cake pieces. Keep warm in a chafing dish.

1 cup sugar
½ cup water
⅓ cup heavy cream
¼ cup butter, optional

Combine sugar and water in a small saucepan. Wash down any crystals on the sides of the pan with a pastry brush dipped in water, and bring to a boil. Cook gently without stirring until liquid is a deep golden brown. Remove pan from heat and carefully whisk in cream, a little at a time. If you want an even richer sauce, add butter and whisk until butter melts and mixture is smooth.

Lemon Dessert Dipping Sauce

Makes 1 ½ cups

Here's a delicious sauce for dipping fruits, pound cake, angel food cake, sponge cake or even lemon tea bread.

6 tbs. butter
1 cup sugar
1 tbs. grated lemon zest
¼ cup lemon juice
1 egg, beaten

Melt butter in a saucepan and gradually stir in remaining ingredients. Cook over medium heat until just before it begins to boil. Immediately remove from heat. Serve warm.

English Dessert Sauce

Serve this rich, thick vanilla dessert sauce with chunks of cake or fruit. Create other sauce flavors from this base recipe by substituting flavored liqueurs in the place of vanilla extract.

8 egg yolks
1 cup sugar
1 ½ cups cream
1 cup milk
1-2 tsp. vanilla extract, to taste

With a mixer, beat egg yolks and sugar together until mixture is thick and pale yellow. Add cream and milk; mix until smooth. Pour into a heavy-bottomed saucepan and cook over medium heat, stirring constantly, until mixture thickens and coats the back of a spoon. Remove from heat and stir in vanilla extract or liqueur of choice. (A whisk produces a smoother sauce.) If desired, strain through a sieve. Serve either warm or cooled.

Hot Raspberry Liqueur Cream

Serve this flavorful sauce with fresh berries, pound cake, chocolate cake or crisp cookies for dipping.

8 egg yolks
1 ¾ cups raspberry liqueur
¼ cup sugar, or more to taste

Beat all ingredients together and place in a heavy-bottomed saucepan or double boiler. Continually whisk over medium heat until mixture becomes very thick, about 20 minutes. Serve warm.

The Best 50
Salsas

Christie and Thomas Katona

Tips for Making and Serving Salsas

Salsas are the newest culinary rage. For the first time in history, salsas are outselling ketchup at the grocery store and people everywhere are whipping up their own renditions at home. Salsas are easy to prepare and the ingredients vary from common to unusual. The only tool necessary is a sharp knife or a food processor.

A salsa is a spicy sauce made with vegetables or fruits. Although the traditional salsa is made with tomatoes, onions and peppers, people have discovered that other vegetables can be used to make delicious salsas, and spicy fruit salsas are wonderful accompaniments to many foods. Cooks can be as innovative as they wish, experimenting with different fresh or dried chiles, exotic fruits, fresh tomatillos or various kinds of avocados.

Salsas are also low in fat and calories while adding a great amount of flavor to your food.

Most salsas keep well in the refrigerator for a few days. Their flavors are enhanced by serving them at room temperature, so plan on removing them from the refrigerator an hour or so before serving.

Favorite Ways to Enjoy Salsas

- As a dip or spread with chips, crackers, bread rounds
- As a topping for bruschetta (Italian-style toasts)
- Over a brick of cream cheese as an appetizer with crackers
- On crackers spread with cream cheese
- Combined with sour cream or plain yogurt as a dip for chips
- Stirred into cheese sauce as a "fondue" for tortilla chips
- As a topping for individual or large pizzas
- In grilled sandwiches
- On cottage cheese
- In burgers or sandwiches
- With seviche
- On hot dogs
- With any and all Mexican food
- On baked potatoes

- As a topping for rice
- In or on meat loaf or stuffed peppers
- In soups or stews
- As a topping for cheese soufflés or frittatas
- As a sauce for grilled poultry, fish, seafood, pork or other meat
- On scrambled eggs or omelets
- As a topping for cheese and garlic grits or polenta

Some Ingredients for Salsas

avocado: a native fruit of America that is high in vitamins and adds a delicious buttery richness. Avocados darken when exposed to air, so brush them with lemon juice or add just at the last minute. The dark, pebbly-skinned Hass avocado has the best flavor.

cilantro: the fresh, young, leafy plantlets of the herb coriander. Cilantro packs a flavor wallop. It is used in salads and various dishes as a flavoring and garnish and is sometimes called Chinese parsley. Chop the leaves along with the stems to add wonderful flavor to salsas.

chile peppers: there are more than 140 varieties of chiles grown in Mexico. Many are fiery hot and others are sweet and mild. The hotness of the chile is in the ribs or veins, and the seeds are hot due to their proximity to the veins. When the chile is cut in half, yellow or orange veins are an indication that the chile will be a potent one. The oil in the chile, capsaicin, can cause severe burns, so never touch your face or eyes when handling hot chiles. Some people with sensitive skin wear rubber gloves. It also helps to handle chiles under running water. A small, sharp knife or serrated grapefruit spoon works well to remove ribs, veins and seeds from chiles. If by chance you eat a chile that's far too hot for your comfort, milk is a great soother.

Anaheim: a long (4 to 7 inches), light green chile with a mild flavor. They are sold fresh or in cans, whole or diced.

ancho: the most widely used dried chile in Mexico. It is reddish brown in color and very wrinkled. It is mild and sweet in flavor.

arbol: a small dried red chile, with the smallest being the hottest.

bell pepper: the most frequently used pepper in the United States. Most familiar in green and red, they are also available in deep dark purple, yellow and orange. Their sweet, mild flavor and crisp, firm texture make them a favorite for snacks, salads, stir-fry, pizza and Mexican dishes.

caribe: a crushed, dried red chile, often seen in pizza parlors. The flavor improves when heated.

cascabel: a round, rust-brown chile, about 1 ½ to 2 inches in diameter. It has a nutty, sweet flavor and loose seeds. It is often available dried.

chipotle: often sold canned as "chipotle en adobo." It is used as a condiment, much like Tabasco.

fresno: about 2 inches long and 1 inch in diameter, these bright green chiles change in color to orange and red when fully mature. They are often canned or bottled and labeled as "hot chile peppers."

habanero: the hottest chile of all, one thousand times hotter than a jalapeño. Used in Caribbean cuisine where it is referred to as a "Scotch bonnet." Due to its extreme heat, it is not readily available.

jalapeño: the most popular hot chile in the United States. Sold fresh in most produce sections at the local grocery store, jalapeños are dark green in color and 2 to 3 inches in length. They are also sold pickled and sliced.

pasilla: can be as long as 12 inches and 1 inch in diameter. They are dark green and turn to dark brown as they mature. Often dried, this chile is particularly good in salsas for fish and in moles.

pimiento: available canned in the United States, these chiles are heart-shaped, softer and sweeter than the common red bell pepper.

poblano: mild to fairly pungent, wedge-shaped, dark green pepper with a thick, leathery skin. This chile is highly regarded for its flavor complexity.

serrano: slightly smaller than a jalapeño (1 ½ to 3 inches long), this light green chile is very hot but has excellent flavor. Remove the stems and seeds inside to reduce the heat.

tomatillo: related to the gooseberry family, tomatillos are sold fresh and in cans. They are light green in color with a papery brown husk. Remove the husk and rinse the tomatillo thoroughly before using. They have a tart flavor and are used both fresh and cooked.

Freezer Salsa

When your garden is overflowing with tomatoes, make some of this delicious salsa for the freezer. Most salsas don't freeze well, but this one was created for the freezer.

7 lb. fresh tomatoes
3 cups seeded, chopped chile peppers, such as Anaheim or poblano
1/2 cup seeded, finely chopped jalapeño or serrano chiles
2 cups chopped onion
5 cloves garlic, minced
1/2 cup chopped fresh cilantro
1/2 cup vinegar
1 tbs. sugar
1 tsp. salt
1 tsp. pepper

Peel, seed and coarsely chop tomatoes. Place tomatoes in a large colander and drain for 30 minutes. Place drained tomatoes in a large kettle and bring to a boil. Reduce heat and simmer, uncovered, for 45 minutes or until thickened. Add remaining ingredients and bring to a boil. Remove from heat and place kettle in a sink filled with ice water to cool quickly. When cool, spoon into freezer containers, leaving 1/2-inch head space. Freeze for up to 6 months.

Artichoke Salsa

Makes 2 cups

Especially tasty with grilled chicken. If you don't find fresh tomatillos, look for them in cans in the Mexican foods section of your supermarket.

6 tomatillos, husked and chopped
2 jars (4 oz. each) marinated artichokes, drained and chopped
1/4 cup sliced green onions
2 cloves garlic, minced
3 tbs. chopped fresh cilantro
grated zest and juice of 1 lime
1 jalapeño chile, seeded and finely chopped
1/2 tsp. salt

Combine all ingredients. Cover and chill.

Garbanzo Salsa

This hearty salsa is excellent with Mexican food. It's great on cheddar cheese omelets for Sunday brunch. Serve with chorizo sausage, fresh fruit and corn muffins to round out your menu.

1 can (19 oz.) garbanzo beans, drained and pureed
3 cups chopped celery
1 can (28 oz.) peeled tomatoes with juice
1 cucumber, peeled, seeded and diced
1 cup chopped fresh cilantro
1 can (4 oz.) chopped green chiles
1/2 cup sliced green onions
2 cloves garlic, minced
2 tbs. lemon juice
1 tbs. red wine vinegar
1 tbs. lime juice
1 tbs. crumbled dried oregano
1 tbs. Tabasco Sauce, or to taste
1 tsp. ground cumin
1 tsp. sugar

Combine ingredients with a food processor. Process just to mix, leaving salsa chunky.

Horseradish Salsa

This salsa has plenty of bite, and is particularly good with barbecued steak off the grill.

1 can (28 oz.) whole peeled tomatoes
1 can (4 oz.) diced green chiles
1 clove garlic, minced
1/2 cup chopped onion
1-3 tsp. drained bottled horseradish
few drops Tabasco Sauce
pepper

Drain tomatoes, discard liquid and chop coarsely. Add remaining ingredients, seasoning to taste.

Zucchini Salsa

Makes 3 quarts

Just the thing to make when your garden is over-zealous with the zucchini crop.

10 cups finely chopped zucchini
3 cups finely chopped onion
3½ cups finely chopped Anaheim chiles (about 25)
5 tbs. salt

Combine zucchini, onion, peppers and salt in a large bowl and refrigerate overnight. The next day, rinse thoroughly in a large colander. Squeeze dry in a large dish towel to remove excess moisture.

Add:
5 cups chopped fresh tomatoes
2 cups cider vinegar
1 cup brown sugar
1 tbs. cornstarch
1 tbs. crushed red pepper flakes
1 tbs. ground cumin
2 tsp. dry mustard
1 tsp. pepper
1 tsp. turmeric
1 tsp. garlic powder
1 tsp. nutmeg

Combine ingredients until well mixed. Place in a large kettle (or 2!). Bring to a boil and reduce heat. Cook gently for 30 minutes. Pour into jars and refrigerate.

Fresh Herb Salsa

Makes 1 ½ cups

Use the ripest tomatoes available and serve over freshly grilled tuna.

4 tomatoes, seeded and chopped
¼ cup chopped fresh basil
2 tbs. chopped fresh marjoram
1 shallot, minced
2 tbs. balsamic vinegar
1 tbs. olive oil
salt and freshly ground pepper

Combine ingredients, cover and stand at room temperature 1 hour before serving.

Tomatillo Apple Salsa

This spicy salsa is excellent with grilled salmon.

5 fresh tomatillos, husked and chopped
1 green bell pepper, seeded and chopped
1 Red Delicious apple, cored and chopped
1/2 cup chopped red onion
3 tbs. chopped fresh cilantro
2 tbs. olive oil
1 tbs. fresh lemon juice
1 jalapeño chile, seeded and finely chopped
1/2 tsp. salt

Combine all ingredients. Cover and chill.

Roasted Corn and Red Pepper Salsa

Makes 2 cups

Plan on roasting the corn and peppers when you already have your grill going, the night before you intend to serve this salsa. This salsa has a particular affinity for pork. If you prefer, you can use commercially prepared roasted red bell peppers.

3 ears corn, shucked, silk removed
3 red bell peppers
1 tbs. vegetable oil
salt and pepper
1/4 cup thinly sliced green onion
1/4 cup chopped fresh cilantro
2 tsp. minced garlic
1/4 cup fresh lemon juice

Grill corn and peppers until charred and tender, brushing with oil and sprinkling with salt and pepper. It will take about 5 minutes for the peppers and 10 for the corn. Turn frequently using tongs. Cool. Remove kernels from cob with a very sharp knife. Remove charred skin from peppers, halve, and remove ribs and seeds. Chop coarsely. Combine corn, peppers and remaining ingredients. Cover and chill.

Corn and Black Bean Salsa

Makes 3 cups

Try this salsa on refried beans, Mexican rice or as a topping for enchiladas. It's great on baked potatoes with sour cream and sliced green onions.

1 cup drained canned corn
1 cup canned black beans, rinsed
1 green bell pepper, seeded and diced
2 tomatoes, seeded and diced
1 avocado, seeded, peeled and diced
2 jalapeño chiles, seeded and finely diced
2 tbs. minced fresh cilantro
1/4 cup diced red onion
1 tbs. lime juice
1 tsp. ground cumin
1/4 tsp. salt

Combine all ingredients. Cover and chill.

Sweet Onion Salsa

Makes 2 cups

Sweet onions, such as Maui, Walla Walla, Texas Sweet 100's or Vidalia varieties, are gaining in popularity. Their availability is limited and because of their high liquid and sugar content, they do not keep well. Whenever you see them, be sure to get some to enjoy with burgers and sandwiches, in salads or in this tasty salsa.

1 cup chopped sweet onion
3/4 cup chopped tomatoes
3 tbs. sliced ripe olives
1 can (4 oz.) chopped green chiles
2 tbs. chopped fresh cilantro
2 tbs. white wine vinegar
1/4 tsp. salt
1/4 tsp. pepper
1/4 tsp. ground cumin
1/4 tsp. Worcestershire sauce
1/4 tsp. Tabasco Sauce

Combine all ingredients. Cover and chill.

Roasted Tomatillo Salsa

Makes 2 cups

Roasting the vegetables gives them a smoky depth of flavor that's hard to duplicate. This is a recipe to try when you have some spare time and want to impress your guests with authentic Mexican flavor.

¾ lb. tomatillos
¼ lb. small onions, about 1 inch with skins on
2 fresh Anaheim chiles
½ cup chopped fresh cilantro
3 tbs. lime juice
1 tsp. salt

To roast tomatillos, remove paper husks. Set 1 tomatillo aside to add later. Place tomatillos, onions and chiles in a cast iron skillet or other very heavy skillet. Over high heat, roast vegetables, shaking the pan frequently to prevent burning. When vegetables are charred all over, about 15 minutes, remove from pan and cool. Peel onions. Remove charred skin from chiles, cut in half, and remove stems and seeds. Place all ingredients, including the 1 fresh tomatillo, in the workbowl of a food processor. Combine until coarsely chopped. Season to taste with lime juice and salt. Cover and chill for up to 4 days or serve immediately.

Tomato and Avocado Salsa

Makes 4 cups

Avocados are rich in vitamins and their creamy flavor is wonderful with spicy salsas. Several varieties are available, but the most flavorful is the pebbly dark-skinned Hass. To prevent avocados from turning black when exposed to air, sprinkle with lemon or lime juice. Wrap cut surfaces tightly with plastic wrap to seal.

3 cups chopped tomatoes
1 cup finely diced avocado
¼ cup chopped red onion
1 jalapeño chile, seeded and minced
¼ cup lime juice
1 tbs. chopped fresh cilantro
1 clove garlic, minced
¼ tsp. salt

Combine all ingredients. Cover and chill.

Roasted Garlic Salsa

Makes 2 cups

Baking the garlic softens and mellows the flavor. Try this with blue corn nachos — sprinkle blue corn chips with cheddar and Monterey Jack cheeses. Top with sliced green onions, black olives, chopped tomatoes and pickled jalapeño slices. Wow!

3 large heads garlic
3 tbs. olive oil
2 cups chopped tomatoes
½ cup chopped onion
1 jalapeño chile, seeded and minced
2 tbs. chopped fresh cilantro
1 tsp. salt
½ tsp. Tabasco Sauce

Remove most of papery skin from garlic. Slice off tops, place in a shallow baking dish and drizzle with olive oil. Heat oven to 300° and roast garlic for 1 hour or until softened. Cool. Squeeze garlic cloves from skin and chop finely. Combine with remaining ingredients. Cover and chill.

Salsa Verde

Makes 2 ½ cups

This is an all-purpose green salsa. It's excellent with chicken enchiladas, grilled fish and of course, served with chips.

10 tomatillos, husks removed
2 serrano chiles, finely chopped, including seeds
1 clove garlic, minced
¼ cup chopped white onion
¼ cup chopped fresh cilantro
salt
water to thin mixture to desired consistency

Place tomatillos in a saucepan and cover with water. Simmer until tender, drain and cool. Combine ingredients. You may wish to chop using a food processor. Add salt to taste and enough water to thin to desired consistency. Serve at room temperature or cover and chill.

Pico de Gallo

Pico de Gallo means "beak of the rooster" in Spanish. The "bits" of ingredients resemble the way the rooster pecks his food.

3 tomatoes, seeded and coarsely chopped
1 cup chopped white onion
1 can (4 oz.) chopped green chiles
⅓ cup chopped fresh cilantro
2 jalapeño chiles, seeded and minced
3 tbs. fresh lime juice
¾ tsp. salt

Combine all ingredients. Cover and chill.

Salsa Cruda

Makes 3 cups

Salsa Cruda is an all-purpose salsa, similar to Salsa Fresca and others. Experiment with different combinations of ingredients to develop your own "signature" salsa.

2 cups chopped fresh tomatoes
1 cup canned crushed tomatoes with added puree
¼ cup chopped yellow onion
2 green onions, thinly sliced
1 tbs. canned chopped jalapeño chiles
2 fresh serrano chiles, seeded and minced
2 tsp. fresh lime juice
¼ cup chopped fresh cilantro
¼ tsp. ground cumin
¼ tsp. crumbled dried oregano
¼ tsp. salt

Combine all ingredients. Cover and chill.

Salsa Picante

Makes 1 ½ cups

To peel a tomato, immerse it in boiling water for several seconds. Make a slit in the skin with a sharp knife and it will slip off easily.

4 medium tomatoes, peeled and seeded
8 green onions, thinly sliced
5 pickled jalapeño chiles, minced
4 cloves garlic, minced
2 tbs. olive oil
¼ cup chopped fresh cilantro
½ tsp. salt

Coarsely chop all ingredients by hand or with a food processor. Cover and chill.

Jicama Salsa

Makes 2 cups

Jicama is a root vegetable from South America that is gaining in popularity throughout the country. Its crunchy texture is very appealing in this salsa. Try this with quesadillas.

½ lb. tomatillos, husks removed
½ lb. jicama, peeled
1 fresh jalapeño chile, seeded and finely minced
⅓ cup lime juice
½ tsp. salt
dash cayenne pepper

Remove cores from tomatillos. Chop tomatillos and jicama until fine. Add remaining ingredients and season to taste. Serve immediately or cover and refrigerate.

Tequila Salsa

Makes 3 cups

This quick and easy salsa is delicious with fajitas or chips. The serrano chiles are very hot, so adjust the amount if you wish.

1 can (28 oz.) tomatoes
3 serrano chiles, seeded and minced
½ cup chopped red onion
¼ cup tequila
grated zest and juice of 1 lime
¼ cup chopped fresh cilantro
1 tsp. salt
½ tsp. pepper

By hand or with a food processor, coarsely chop ingredients and combine. Cover and refrigerate.

Pico de Gallo with Mexican Beer

Makes 2 ½ cups

The Mexican beer adds interesting flavor, but tequila, vodka or regular beer would work as well. This is an all-purpose salsa that's good with chips or with tacos.

2 cups chopped fresh tomatoes
2 serrano chiles, seeded and finely chopped
¼ cup chopped sweet white onion
2 tbs. chopped fresh cilantro
¼ cup Mexican beer
1 tsp. sugar
1 tsp. salt
juice of 1 lime

Combine all ingredients and chill for 30 minutes.

Watermelon and Avocado Salsa

Makes 1 ½ cups

Prepare this salsa at the last moment. The watermelon becomes too juicy if it is held longer than an hour. This is very tasty with teriyaki chicken.

1 cup diced watermelon
1 avocado, peeled, seeded and diced
¼ cup diced red onion
2 tbs. chopped fresh cilantro
grated zest and juice of 1 lime

Gently combine all ingredients. Serve immediately.

Three Berry Salsa

Makes 4 cups

Serve this salsa on a bed of bright green spinach leaves topped with grilled chicken breast for a colorful presentation. Try it with chips or Jack cheese quesadillas.

1 cup blueberries
1 cup stemmed, quartered strawberries
1 cup raspberries
1 cup diced tomatoes
¼ cup chopped red onion
¼ cup chopped fresh cilantro
grated zest and juice of 1 orange
grated zest and juice of 1 lime
2 tsp. sugar
½ tsp. salt

Combine all ingredients. Cover and chill.

Orange Ginger Salsa

Store fresh ginger in vodka in a jar in your refrigerator and it will last until you've used it all. Fresh ginger also can be frozen. It adds a wonderful fresh tang to many foods.

2 cups diced fresh oranges, peeled, seeded, membrane removed
1 cup seeded, diced plum tomatoes
1/2 cup diced red onion
2 tsp. finely minced fresh ginger
2 tbs. fresh lime juice
2 tbs. olive oil
2 tbs. finely chopped fresh cilantro
1 tsp. salt
1 tsp. sugar
1/2 tsp. ground coriander

Combine all ingredients. Cover and chill.

Mixed Fruit Salsa

Eliminate the jalapeño and red onion, and you can serve this on frozen yogurt for a fresh and delicious dessert. In its spicy state, it is wonderful with grilled fish.

2 bananas, peeled and diced into 1/2-inch pieces
1/2 cup diced fresh or frozen peaches (1/2-inch pieces)
1/2 cup fresh or frozen raspberries
2 kiwis, peeled and diced into 1/2-inch pieces
1/2 cup diced fresh strawberries (1/2-inch pieces)
1 jalapeño chile, minced
1/4 cup minced red onion
sugar or Equal to taste
1 tbs. tequila

Gently stir all ingredients together. Cover and chill.

Pineapple and Date Salsa

Makes 2 cups

This is excellent on a turkey sandwich with cream cheese. Try it with poultry or pork.

1 cup finely diced fresh pineapple
½ cup chopped fresh cranberries
⅓ cup chopped dried dates
¼ cup finely chopped red onion
1 tbs. honey
1 tsp. lemon juice
1 tsp. finely minced fresh ginger
¼ tsp. cayenne pepper

Combine all ingredients. Cover and chill.

Summer Salsa

Makes 2 ½ cups

Serve this colorful, tasty salsa with roasted Cornish game hens or grilled chicken for a change of pace.

2 cups diced strawberries
½ cup chopped red onion
½ cup chopped fresh cilantro
1 jalapeño chile, finely chopped
¼ cup finely chopped fresh mint
2 tbs. olive oil
¼ cup balsamic vinegar
salt and white pepper

Combine all ingredients. Cover and chill.

Grape Salsa

Makes 2 ½ cups

This salsa is unusual and colorful. Serve it with grilled chicken.

2 cups halved seedless red grapes
¼ cup diced red onion
1 jalapeño chile, seeded and minced
2 tbs. chopped fresh cilantro
1 clove garlic, minced
1 tbs. lemon juice
1 tbs. rice vinegar
¼ cup slivered almonds, lightly toasted
½ tsp. salt
dash cayenne pepper

Combine all ingredients. Cover and chill.

Peach and Ginger Salsa

Makes 3 cups

This is a favorite with grilled lamb chops.

2 cups peeled, diced peaches
½ cup chopped red bell pepper
½ cup chopped red onion
1 serrano chile, minced
¼ cup chopped fresh mint
1 ½ tbs. lime juice
2 tsp. grated fresh ginger
2 tsp. olive oil
salt

Combine ingredients and chill for 30 minutes.

Melon, Cucumber and Mint Salsa

Makes 4 cups

This very refreshing salsa is delicious with grilled fish.

2 cups diced honeydew melon
2 tomatoes, seeded and diced
½ cup peeled, seeded, diced cucumber
2 tbs. red wine vinegar
1 tbs. vegetable oil
1 tbs. chopped fresh parsley
2 tsp. thinly sliced fresh chives
2 tsp. chopped fresh mint
2 tsp. sugar
1 tsp. salt
½ tsp. white pepper

Combine all ingredients. Cover and chill.

Papaya and Watermelon Salsa

Makes 2 cups

This is another salsa that does not keep well because the watermelon is so juicy. Be sure to prepare it just before serving.

1 cup peeled, seeded, diced papaya
½ cup seeded, diced watermelon (½-inch pieces)
¼ cup peeled, seeded, diced cucumber
¼ cup diced red onion
grated zest and juice of 1 lime
2 tbs. chopped fresh cilantro
2 tsp. olive oil
1 tsp. minced jalapeño chile
salt and pepper

Combine all ingredients. Cover and chill.

Pineapple and Mango Salsa

Makes 3 cups

Fresh fruit salsa is delicious with grilled chicken, and goes well with grilled fish, too. Use Thai fish sauce if you can find it, or substitute soy sauce.

1 cup diced fresh pineapple
1 cup peeled, diced fresh mango
1 cup diced tomatoes
1/4 cup thinly sliced green onions
2 tbs. vegetable oil
1 tbs. chopped fresh cilantro
1 tbs. soy sauce
1 tbs. fish sauce
2 tsp. finely minced fresh ginger
1 jalapeño chile, finely chopped
2 tsp. rice vinegar
1 tsp. minced garlic
1 tsp. honey

Combine all ingredients. Cover and chill.

Cantaloupe Lime Salsa

Makes 1 1/2 cups

Try this with grilled fish such as halibut or swordfish. It's also delightful with grilled prawns.

1 cup diced cantaloupe
1/4 cup chopped red onion
1 tbs. diced green chiles
2 tbs. chopped fresh cilantro
grated zest and juice of 1 lime
1/2 tsp. white pepper

Combine all ingredients. Cover and chill.

Spicy Tropical Salsa

Makes 4 cups

This fruity, spicy salsa is excellent with grilled fish or chicken.

1 cup diced mango
1 cup diced papaya
1 cup diced pineapple
2 kiwis, peeled and diced
1 tsp. crushed red pepper flakes
1/4 cup seasoned rice wine vinegar
3 tbs. chopped fresh cilantro

Combine all ingredients. Cover and chill.

Tangerine Salsa

Makes 2 cups

Refreshing and colorful with citrus tang, this salsa could also be prepared with fresh oranges. It is excellent with firm-textured fish such as halibut, sturgeon or swordfish.

4 tangerines, peeled, membrane and seeds removed, sectioned
4 plum tomatoes, seeded and diced
1/3 cup diced red onion
1/3 cup diced red bell pepper
1/4 cup diced poblano chile
1 tbs. fresh lime juice
1 tbs. peanut oil or other light oil
1 tsp. ground coriander
1/2 tsp. pepper
1/4 tsp. salt
2 tbs. chopped fresh cilantro

Combine all ingredients. Cover and chill.

Mango and Sun-Dried Tomato Salsa

Makes 2 cups

Sun-dried tomatoes originally come from Italy and Americans have fallen in love with their intense flavor and interesting, chewy texture. You'll find them packaged dry or packed in jars in herb-infused oil.

1 ripe mango, peeled and diced
1/4 cup chopped sun-dried tomatoes
1/4 cup chopped red onion
1/4 cup chopped green onions
2 tbs. minced fresh cilantro leaves
1 jalapeño chile, seeded and minced
2 tbs. olive oil
2 tbs. fresh lime juice
1/4 tsp. salt

Combine all ingredients. Cover and chill.

Grapefruit Salsa

Makes 2 cups

Here's another salsa that's great with grilled fish. To seed and devein fresh chiles, cut them in half lengthwise and remove veins and seeds with a small sharp knife or a serrated grapefruit spoon.

6 pink grapefruits, peeled, membrane removed, chopped
4 serrano chiles, diced
1/4 cup chopped red onion
1/4 cup chopped fresh cilantro
1/4 tsp. salt

Combine all ingredients. Cover and chill.

Orange and Black Bean Salsa

Makes 2 cups

This salsa makes an excellent vegetarian meal spooned over rice. Top with shredded Jack or cheddar cheese if you like.

1 can (15 oz.) black beans, rinsed and drained
2 oranges, peeled and diced
1 jalapeño chile, seeded and finely chopped
¼ cup chopped fresh cilantro
¼ cup chopped green onions
3 tsp. vegetable oil
1 tsp. lemon juice
¼ tsp. salt
¼ tsp. ground cumin

Combine all ingredients. Cover and chill.

Mango and Tangerine Salsa

Makes 1 cup

People with sensitive skin should wear rubber gloves when peeling chiles and hold them under cool running water. Never touch your eyes when handling chiles!

1 mango, peeled and chopped
2 tangerines, peeled and chopped
¼ cup diced red bell pepper
¼ cup sliced green onions
1 jalapeño chile, seeded and finely chopped
2 tsp. orange juice
¼ tsp. ground coriander
¼ tsp. salt

Combine all ingredients. Cover and chill.

Mango and Corn Salsa

Makes 1 ½ cups

Fresh mangoes are becoming a popular item in the produce stand. Select a mango that is just beginning to yield to pressure. Mangoes can be stored at room temperature to ripen.

1 mango, peeled and diced
½ cup whole kernel corn
½ cup diced green bell pepper
¼ cup diced red onion
2 tbs. chopped fresh cilantro
1 tsp. lime juice
1 tsp. vegetable oil
¼ tsp. salt

Combine all ingredients. Cover and chill.

Mixed Fruit Salsa with Ginger

Makes 2 ½ cups

Frozen peach slices are almost indistinguishable from fresh in the off-season, and are easy to keep on hand.

1 peach, peeled and chopped
1 cup diced honeydew melon
1 cup halved red flame grapes
2 tbs. chopped fresh cilantro
2 green onions, chopped
½ tsp. crushed red pepper flakes
1 tsp. grated fresh ginger
1 tsp. honey
dash salt

Combine all ingredients. Cover and chill.

Raspberry Salsa

Try this with Cornish game hens or roast duck. To use frozen berries, thaw and drain off as much juice or syrup as possible.

2 cups fresh raspberries
2 jalapeño chiles, seeded and finely chopped
¼ cup chopped red onion
2 tbs. minced fresh cilantro
2 tbs. raspberry vinegar
¼ tsp. salt

Gently stir ingredients together. Cover and chill for 30 minutes to blend flavors.

Pineapple Salsa

Crushed pineapple packed in its own juice can also be used in this recipe. It's great on soft chicken tacos.

2 cups diced fresh pineapple
4 kiwis, peeled and diced
¼ cup chopped red onion
2 jalapeño chiles, seeded and finely chopped
2 tbs. chopped fresh cilantro
1 tbs. lime juice
¼ tsp. salt

Combine all ingredients. Cover and chill.

Peach Salsa

Cover a brick of cream cheese with Peach Salsa and serve it with crackers as an appetizer. You can use this idea with almost any salsa.

1 ½ cups chopped peeled peaches
¾ cup chopped red bell pepper
¾ cup seeded chopped cucumber
¼ cup sliced green onion
2 jalapeño chiles, seeded and finely chopped
2 tbs. honey
2 tbs. lime juice
1 tbs. chopped fresh cilantro

Combine all ingredients. Cover and chill.

Apricot Salsa

Stir a cup of this salsa into sour cream or unflavored yogurt and use it as a sauce with pork or chicken.

1 ½ cups chopped fresh apricots
¾ cup chopped green bell pepper
1¾ cups seeded chopped cucumber
¼ cup sliced green onion
1 jalapeño chile, seeded and finely chopped
2 tbs. honey
2 tbs. lime juice
1 tbs. finely chopped fresh cilantro

Combine all ingredients. Cover and chill.

Pineapple and Papaya Salsa

Makes 3 cups

A papaya is a tropical fruit with orange pulp and yellow rind when ripe. You can eat it like melon or bake it and serve it as a side dish. Slices of papaya are wonderful on a fruit platter or grilled and brushed with curry or ginger butter. If you haven't done so already, try it! It will become one of your favorites.

2 cups finely diced fresh pineapple
1 cup finely diced fresh papaya
½ cup finely diced red bell pepper
½ cup finely diced sweet onion
1 clove garlic, minced
1 serrano chile, seeded and finely minced
2 tbs. snipped fresh mint leaves

Combine all ingredients. Cover and chill overnight.

Pepper and Papaya Salsa

Makes 4 cups

Be sure to wear rubber gloves when you seed and chop the poblano chile.

3 cups peeled, seeded, diced papaya
½ cup finely chopped red bell pepper
½ cup finely chopped green bell pepper
½ cup finely chopped fresh pineapple
¼ cup finely chopped red onion
¼ cup finely chopped fresh cilantro
½ fresh poblano chile, seeded and finely chopped
2 tbs. lime juice
1 tbs. lemon juice

Combine all ingredients. Cover and chill.

Kiwi Salsa

If you can't find fresh tomatillos, they are available canned in the Mexican foods section of your grocery store. Fresh kiwi will keep for weeks in the refrigerator.

1 cup peeled chopped kiwis (about 5-6)
1/3 cup sliced green onions
1/3 cup chopped tomatillos
1 jalapeño chile, seeded and minced
2 tbs. chopped fresh cilantro
1/4 cup rice wine vinegar
1 tbs. unsweetened pineapple juice
1 tsp. sugar

Combine all ingredients. Cover and chill.

Bing Cherry Salsa

This salsa should be served immediately. Try it with pork, chicken or on top of cream cheese.

1 cup pitted fresh Bing cherries
1 tbs. minced green bell pepper
2 tbs. chopped fresh basil
grated zest and juice of 1 lemon
1/4 tsp. Worcestershire sauce
dash Tabasco Sauce
salt

Chop ingredients to medium coarseness and combine. Season to taste and serve immediately.

Pear Salsa

This makes a nice accompaniment to pork or chicken.

2 pears, peeled, cored and diced
2 dried pear halves, finely chopped
¼ cup chopped red onion
¼ cup chopped fresh cilantro
grated zest and juice of 1 lime
1 tbs. minced fresh ginger
1 jalapeño chile, seeded and minced
½ tsp. salt
¼ tsp. crushed red pepper flakes

Combine all ingredients. Cover and chill.

Cranberry Salsa

Cranberries are always a good accompaniment to poultry. This salsa is good on turkey sandwiches, and gives a delicious flavor burst to Brie quesadillas.

1 ½ cups fresh or frozen cranberries
⅓ cup sugar
¼ cup thinly sliced green onions
¼ cup chopped fresh cilantro
grated zest and juice of 1 lime
1 jalapeño chile, seeded and minced
2 tsp. finely chopped fresh ginger
¼ tsp. salt

Coarsely chop cranberries. Combine with remaining ingredients, cover and chill. Or, coarsely chop all ingredients in a food processor, cover and chill.

The Best 50 Bruschetta Recipes

Dona Z. Meilach

A Study of Bruschetta

The word bruschetta, (pronounced either broo-SKEH-tah or broo-SHEH-tah) is derived from the Latin verb "bruscare," meaning "to toast" or "to roast." Bruschetta is probably as old as Rome itself, but it has become part of the modern vernacular in Italian cuisine. Bruschetta traditionally was a slice of thick bread that was toasted on a grill or over a fire, rubbed with garlic, drizzled with a high-quality olive oil and sprinkled with coarse salt. Making bruschetta gave farmers the opportunity to demonstrate the quality of the season's new olive oils.

When people began to add chopped tomatoes, basil and olives, purists considered it heresy; they claimed that nothing should compete with the delicate flavor of the olive oil. However, these items, plentiful in the Italian countryside, soon became standard additions to bruschetta. Bruschetta was served as a mid-afternoon treat to satisfy hungry people who customarily ate a late dinner.

Today, bruschetta can be served hot or cold as appetizers, snacks, main courses, and, with a little ingenuity, desserts. Usually, the topping is spooned onto a full slice of thick, hearty bread that has been toasted so that it is crisp on the outside and soft on the inside. Bruschetta can be served on plate and eaten with a knife and fork, or the topping can be served in a bowl and scooped up with the garlic and oil-flavored bread.

Bruschetta can also be served as hors d'oeuvres or canapés. The toppings are placed on small rounds or squares of toast to be eaten with the fingers.

Seasonal tomatoes and olives were the choice toppings in old-world Italy, but contemporary chefs also use mushrooms, cheese, fish, peppers, meat, chicken and more. A variety of sauces can flavor today's bruschetta, such as pesto, salsa, Alfredo and others. Flavorings such as basil, dill, oregano, thyme salt and pepper are often used. Goat, Romano, feta, Parmesan, and mozzarella cheese can be added along with a touch of balsamic or other flavored vinegars. Creative chefs are taking bruschetta to new levels, assembling combinations culled from various ethnic cuisines. Dessert bruschetta has become popular, too.

A Bushel of Breads

In Italy, hearty country breads indigenous to an area are used for bruschetta. These breads are made only with flour, water, yeast and salt; and without seeds, sugar or fat. Generally, they have a nonporous texture that can withstand a drizzle of oil.

Italian, French, Greek or American country breads that have a good crust are ideal choices for making bruschetta. Look for breads with names such as:

- pane filone
- pugliese
- levain
- batarde
- baguette
- sflatino

Sliced rolls, English muffins and focaccia also make fine bruschetta. Sweet breads such as raisin and egg bread twists are perfect for building dessert bruschette. Avoid using thinly sliced soft white bread, as it does not provide the proper texture and density for bruschetta.

The type of the bread you select will depend on its texture, size and how you plan to serve it. Usually, the bread is sliced about ½- to ¾-inch thick, but a 1-inch slice can be used. Rolls and baguettes can be sliced horizontally for longer bruschetta. For canapés and hors d'oeuvres, the slices can be ⅜- to ½-inch thick so they can be easily eaten with one or two bites.

Toasting Bread

Ideally, the bread for bruschetta should be toasted on a grill, but toasting in an oven, toaster oven or toaster will suffice. A small round stovetop grill will also work. The toast should be crisp on the outside, its texture firm enough to withstand a rub-down from a cut clove of garlic, a drizzle of olive oil and a good helping of your choice of topping. One can also omit either the oil or garlic if a topping already has a good amount of these ingredients.

Basic Bruschetta

True bruschetta is made from thick slices of densely textured bread. Bruschetta can be served with simple accompaniments. both savory and sweet. Figs, prosciutto or cheese are good choices.

8 slices crusty white bread, ½- to ¾-inch thick
1 clove garlic, cut in half
3-4 tbs. extra virgin olive oil
freshly ground black pepper, optional

Toast bread and rub one side of each bread slice with cut side of garlic clove and drizzle with olive oil. Season with pepper. Makes 8.

Stewed Tomato Bruschetta

With a can of stewed Italian tomatoes on your pantry shelf, you can quickly create this delicious appetizer for an elegant dinner or for last-minute guests.

6 slices crusty white bread, ½- to ¾-inch thick
1 clove garlic, cut in half, or ¼ tsp. garlic salt
2 tbs. extra virgin olive oil
1 can (11.5 oz.) Italian-style stewed tomatoes

Toast bread, rub one side of each bread slice with cut side of garlic, and drizzle with olive oil. Top bread with stewed tomatoes. Serve at room temperature or heat in a microwave on HIGH for 1½ minutes. Makes 6.

Fresh Tomato Bruschetta

A simple bruschetta topping is, most often, the best. Savor fresh, slightly sweet tomatoes on this bruschetta.

3 ripe tomatoes, peeled, seeded and diced
1/2 tsp. salt
1/4 tsp. freshly ground black pepper
1/4 cup chopped onion
1 tbs. chopped fresh basil
4 cloves garlic, cut in half
8 slices Vienna bread, 1/2- to 3/4-inch thick
1/3 cup extra virgin olive oil

In a small bowl, combine tomatoes with salt and freshly ground black pepper, onion and basil and mix well. Toast bread, rub one side of each bread slice with cut side of garlic clove and drizzle with olive oil. Top bread with tomato mixture. Serve immediately. Makes 8.

To peel and seed tomatoes: Drop tomatoes into boiling water for 15 to 60 seconds, depending on ripeness. Plunge tomatoes into ice water to cool completely. With a paring knife, remove peels. Cut tomatoes in half crosswise. Squeeze tomato halves over a bowl and use the tip of a spoon to remove seeds.

Tuscan Tomato-Cheese Bruschetta

In Italy, bruschetta toppings and the types of bread used differ, reflecting the foods of the region.

1 cup chopped drained oil-packed sun-dried tomatoes
1/2 cup minced green onions
1 clove garlic, minced
1/2 cup pine nuts, toasted and coarsely chopped
3 oz. Asiago or Parmesan cheese, grated
8 oz. provolone cheese, shredded
8-10 slices Italian bread, 1/2- to 3/4-inch thick
1/4 cup extra virgin olive oil

In a bowl, mix tomatoes, green onions, garlic, nuts and cheeses. Toast bread and drizzle with olive oil. Top bread with tomato mixture. Makes 8-10.

Tomato-Eggplant Bruschetta

Serve the eggplant topping in a bowl with a platter of toasted bread and let your guests spoon the topping over the toast.

1 large eggplant, about 1 lb.
1 cup finely chopped onion
2 tbs. extra virgin olive oil
1 tomato, finely chopped
salt and freshly ground black pepper to taste
12-15 slices French bread, ½- to ¾-inch thick

Roast eggplant on a medium-hot grill, turning eggplant occasionally until limp, about 10 minutes. Cool and peel eggplant. Cut in half lengthwise, scrape flesh into a bowl and set aside. In a large skillet over medium heat, brown onion in olive oil. Add eggplant flesh and tomato and cook until mixture is heated through. Season with salt and pepper. Toast bread slices. Top bread with eggplant mixture. Makes 12 to 15.

Tomato, Basil and Cheese Bruschetta

This is a perfect appetizer to serve on summer evenings.

1 lb. plum tomatoes, peeled, seeded and diced
2 tbs. extra virgin olive oil
2 cloves garlic, minced
½ tsp. salt
½ tsp. freshly ground black pepper, plus more to taste
3 tbs. finely chopped fresh basil
1 tbs. finely chopped fresh Italian parsley, plus more for garnish if desired
¼ lb. fresh mozzarella cheese, cut into ½-inch cubes
4 slices French bread, ½- to ¾-inch thick
1 clove garlic, cut in half
2 tbs. extra virgin olive oil

Combine tomatoes, 2 tbs. olive oil, garlic, salt, pepper, basil, parsley and mozzarella in a small bowl and mix well. Toast bread, rub one side of each toast slice with cut side of garlic clove and top with tomato mixture. Drizzle remaining oil on top and sprinkle with additional pepper or parsley, if desired. Makes 4.

Sun-Dried Tomato Bruschetta

This combination has a hearty, tangy taste and visual appeal.

4 dry-packed sun-dried tomatoes
1 cup boiling water
3 medium tomatoes, peeled, seeded and diced
3 tbs. minced red onion
3 tsp. capers
3 cloves garlic, minced
2 tsp. balsamic or white wine vinegar
1 tbs. chopped fresh oregano
½ tsp. salt
1 tsp. freshly ground black pepper
24 slices Italian bread, ⅜- to ½-inch thick
¼ cup grated Parmesan cheese

Soak sun-dried tomatoes in boiling water until water cools. Drain tomatoes and chop finely. In a bowl, combine sun-dried tomatoes, fresh tomatoes, onion, capers, garlic, vinegar, oregano, salt and pepper. Let stand at room temperature for about 1 hour.

Heat oven to 350°. Toast bread and top with tomato mixture. Bake bruschetta for about 5 minutes, or until tomato mixture is slightly bubbly. Sprinkle with Parmesan cheese and serve warm. Makes about 24.

Tomato, Olive and Basil Bruschetta

Garnish the serving platter with extra olives and basil leaves.

3 large tomatoes, diced
8 green or black olives, minced
½ red onion, diced
4 cloves garlic, minced
½ cup white wine vinegar
⅓ cup virgin olive oil
2 tsp. chopped fresh basil, or ½ tsp. dried
salt and freshly ground black pepper to taste
6 slices French bread, ½- to ¾-inch thick

In a bowl, combine tomatoes, olives, onion and minced garlic and mix well. In a separate bowl, combine vinegar, olive oil and basil and add to tomato mixture; mix well. Season with salt and pepper. Toast bread and top with tomato mixture. Makes 6.

Tomato, Feta and Mushroom Bruschetta

Peel tomatoes easily by parboiling them in boiling water until skins split, 2 to 3 minutes. Cool slightly; skins should just slip off, or peel with a knife.

4 Italian plum tomatoes, peeled and coarsely chopped
2 teaspoons minced fresh basil
1 clove garlic, minced
salt and freshly ground black pepper to taste
8 slices Vienna bread, 1/2- to 3/4-inch thick
1 large clove garlic, cut in half
1/3 cup extra virgin olive oil
1/2 cup crumbled feta cheese
8 large white mushrooms, stems removed

Combine tomatoes, basil, garlic, salt and pepper in a medium bowl and mix well. Toast bread, rub one side of each toast slice with cut side of garlic clove and drizzle with 1/2 of the olive oil. Top bread with tomato mixture, sprinkle with feta cheese and top each piece with 1 large mushroom cap. Brush remaining olive oil over mushrooms. Serve cold, or heat for about 5 minutes in a 350° oven and serve warm. Makes 8.

Tomatoes and Portobello Mushroom Bruschetta

Portobello mushrooms are known for their rich, earthy flavor, meaty texture and giant size.

3 medium tomatoes diced
1 yellow or red bell pepper, finely chopped
1 tsp. balsamic or red wine vinegar
salt and freshly ground black pepper to taste
1/4 cup extra virgin olive oil
4 portobello mushroom caps (about 1 1/2-lb.), cut into 1/4-inch slices
3 cloves garlic, minced
8 slices Italian bread, 1/2- to 3/4-inch thick
1/4 cup crumbled feta cheese

In a bowl, mix tomatoes, bell pepper, vinegar, salt and pepper. Heat 2 tbs. of the olive oil in a large skillet over moderate heat and sauté mushrooms and garlic until mushroom liquid evaporates, about 5 minutes. Remove skillet from heat and toss mushrooms with remaining 2 tbs. oil. Toast bread and top with tomato and mushroom mixture. Sprinkle with crumbled feta cheese. Makes 8.

Tomato and Wine Bruschetta

Serve these accompanied by a cool glass of white wine.

2 tomatoes, peeled, seeded and chopped
2 tbs. coarsely chopped sun-dried tomatoes
1 tsp. minced garlic
½ cup dry white wine
3 tbs. extra virgin olive oil
6 tbs. unsalted butter
6 slices Italian bread, ½- to ¾-inch thick

Combine fresh tomatoes, sun-dried tomatoes, garlic, wine and olive oil in a small saucepan over medium heat. Cook, uncovered, for 5 minutes or until wine evaporates and mixture begins to thicken slightly. Remove from heat and stir in butter. Transfer to a blender container or food processor workbowl and pulse-blend on low speed until well mixed, but still slightly chunky. Toast bread and top with tomato mixture. Makes 6.

Greek-Style Tomato Bruschetta

These Greek salad ingredients make a festive appetizer.

3 large firm tomatoes, diced
2 cloves garlic, minced
6 Greek black or green olives, pitted and sliced
½ red onion , minced
¼ cup seeded, minced cucumber
⅓ cup olive oil
¼ cup balsamic vinegar
½ tsp. dried basil
salt and freshly ground black pepper
3 French baguette rolls, cut in half lengthwise
3 tbs. crumbled feta cheese

In a bowl, toss tomatoes, garlic, olives, onions and cucumber. Mix oil, vinegar and basil in a small bowl and add to tomato mixture. Season with salt and pepper, mix well and chill for at least ½ hour. Toast bread and top with tomato mixture. Sprinkle with crumbled feta cheese. Makes 6.

Tomato and Arugula Bruschetta

Use thin slices of bread for appetizer bruschetta. Thicker slices are key for a heavier luncheon dish.

4 ripe tomatoes, peeled, seeded and diced, juice reserved
1 bunch arugula, washed and cut into ¼-inch pieces
¼ cup minced onion
2 cloves garlic, minced
1 tbs. drained capers
1½ tbs. balsamic or red wine vinegar
1½ tbs. extra virgin olive oil
salt and freshly ground black pepper to taste
24-36 slices Italian bread, ½- to ¾-inch thick
1 clove garlic, cut in half

In a medium bowl, combine tomatoes, arugula, onion, garlic, capers, vinegar, oil and just enough tomato juice to make the mixture moist but not wet. Season with salt and pepper. Toast bread and rub one side of each toast slice with cut side of garlic clove. Top with tomato-arugula mixtures. Makes 24 to 36.

Tomato Bruschetta, Dijon-Style

Use any flavored mustard to add a subtle twist to this bruschetta.

¼ cup red wine vinegar
2 tbs. Dijon-Style mustard
¼ cup extra virgin olive oil
4 large tomatoes, peeled, seeded and chopped
½ cup sliced black olives
½ cup sliced green onions
18-24 slices French baguette, ⅜- to ½-inch thick
1 clove garlic, cut in half
2 tbs. extra virgin olive oil

In a bowl, blend vinegar and mustard and slowly whisk in ¼ cup oil. Add tomatoes, green onions and olives, tossing to coat well. Refrigerate mixture for 30 minutes to blend flavors. Toast bread, rub one side of each bread slice with cut side of garlic clove and drizzle with olive oil. Top bread with tomato mixture. Makes 18 to 24.

Tomato and Cheese Pizza Bruschetta

These mini pizzas work well when you need appetizers for a large crowd.

one 16-inch Italian-style flatbread, focaccia or pizza round
1 clove garlic, cut in half
1 medium tomato, chopped
1 clove garlic, minced
1 red or green bell pepper, coarsely chopped
5 tsp. minced fresh basil, or 2 tsp. dried
1½ cups shredded mozzarella cheese

Heat oven to 425°. Rub both sides of bread with cut side of garlic clove. In a bowl, combine tomato, minced garlic, bell pepper and basil; mix well. Spread tomato mixture over flatbread. Sprinkle with mozzarella. Bake for 15 minutes, or until cheese melts. Cut into wedges. Makes 12.

Artichoke and Feta Bruschetta

A fruity red wine is a fine complement to the sharp feta.

1 jar (8½ oz.) marinated artichoke hearts
⅓ cup crumbled feta cheese
¼ cup low-fat mayonnaise
¼ cup plain yogurt
8 slices Italian or French bread, ½- to ¾-inch thick
1 clove garlic, cut in half
¼ cup extra virgin olive oil
paprika

Heat oven to 350°. Drain and rinse artichoke hearts and cut into quarters. Mix artichoke hearts with feta, mayonnaise and yogurt and spoon into a small casserole. Bake for about 25 minutes or until mixture bubbles. Toast bread, rub one side of each toast slice with cut side of garlic clove and drizzle with olive oil. Top bread with hot artichoke mixture. Sprinkle with paprika. Makes 8.

Pesto and Mozzarella Bruschetta

When you can't find ripe tomatoes, opt to make pesto, instead.

2 cups coarsely chopped fresh basil, loosely packed
3 cloves garlic, coarsely chopped
½ cup pine nuts, toasted
½ tsp. salt
¼ tsp. freshly ground black pepper
¾ cup extra virgin olive oil
1 tbs. freshly grated Parmesan cheese
1 tbs. freshly grated pecorino Romano cheese
5 slices mozzarella cheese
8-10 slices Italian bread or French baguette, ½- to ¾-inch thick

Heat oven to 350°. Combine basil, garlic and pine nuts in a blender container or food processor workbowl and process on low for about 1 minute. Add salt, pepper and about ½ of the olive oil and process until blended, about 30 seconds. Add cheeses and blend until mixed but still coarse in texture. Transfer from blender to a small bowl. Beat in remaining oil, a little at a time, until it is the desired consistency for spooning. Toast bread and top with pesto. Place ½ slice of mozzarella on each piece of bread and bake until cheese melts, about 2 to 3 minutes. Serve warm. Makes 8 to 10.

Ricotta-Mushroom-Anchovy Bruschetta

The anchovies add zest to the delicate bruschetta flavors.

1 cup thick tomato sauce
¾ cup ricotta cheese
¼ cup sliced fresh mushrooms, broken into small pieces
2 tbs. chopped red onion
1 tbs. chopped fresh basil, or 1 tsp. dried
8 slices Italian or French bread, ½- to ¾-inch thick
3 tbs. extra virgin olive oil
8 anchovy fillets, cut in half

In a glass bowl, mix tomato sauce, ricotta, mushrooms, onion and basil and warm for about 2 minutes in the microwave on MEDIUM-HIGH. Toast bread, drizzle with olive oil and top with sauce. Arrange crosswise over the top of each bruschetta. Makes 8.

Goat Cheese and Black Olive Bruschetta

This recipe will taste best with high-quality brine-cured olives. They have more flavor than canned California ripe olives.

4 slices Italian bread, ½- to ¾-inch thick
1 clove garlic, cut in half
2 tbs. extra virgin olive oil
½ cup olive paste or pureed black olives
4 oz. soft fresh goat cheese, crumbled
3 oz. light cream cheese
2 tsp. lemon juice
1 tsp. minced fresh oregano, or ¼ tsp. dried
¼ cup coarsely chopped black olives

Toast bread, rub one side of each bread slice with cut side of garlic clove and drizzle with olive oil. Spread bread with olive paste and top with crumbled cheese. Makes 4.

Bruschetta with Red Pesto Sauce

Red pesto, made with fresh tomatoes, is a favorite bruschetta topping in southern Italy.

2 lb. ripe plum tomatoes, peeled, seeded and diced
2 cups chopped fresh basil leaves, loosely packed
3 cloves garlic, coarsely chopped
1/2 tsp. salt
3 dashes Tabasco Sauce
2 tbs. extra virgin olive oil
2 tbs. capers, rinsed and drained
8-10 sliced Italian or French bread, 1/2- to 3/4-inch thick
1 tbs. freshly grated Parmesan cheese
1 tbs. freshly grated Asiago or Romano cheese, optional

In a blender container, combine tomatoes, basil, garlic, salt, Tabasco and olive oil and blend at low speed. Add capers and pulse-blend just enough to mix, but retain a chunky texture. Toast bread and top bread slices with tomato mixture. Sprinkle with grated cheese. Makes 8 to 10.

Bruschetta Provençal with Goat Cheese

French bread slices covered with lightly browned goat cheese are a perfect prelude to a true French Provençal menu. Herbes de Provence is a traditional French blend of basil, rosemary, thyme, summer savory and lavender.

6 oz. soft fresh goat cheese
1/4 cup whipping cream
2 tbs. herbes de Provence
4 slices French bread, 1/2- to 3/4-inch thick
1 clove garlic cut in half
2 tbs. extra virgin olive oil
2 tsp. chopped fresh parsley

Heat broiler. In a bowl, mix goat cheese, whipping cream and herbes de Provence; leave mixture slightly lumpy. Toast bread, rub both sides of bread slices with cut side of garlic clove and drizzle with olive oil. Spread about 1 tbs. of the cheese mixture on one side of each bread slice. Broil 5 inches from heat source until lightly browned, 3 to 4 minutes, watching carefully so bread does not burn. Garnish with chopped parsley and serve slightly warm. Makes 4.

Goat Cheese and Roasted Pepper Bruschetta

Look for roasted peppers marinated in olive oil or vinegar.

4 slices Italian bread, ½- to ¾-inch thick
1 clove garlic, cut in half
2 tbs. extra virgin olive oil
4 oz. soft fresh goat cheese, crumbled
1 jar (6½ oz.) roasted red, yellow or orange bell pepper strips

Toast bread, rub one side of each bread slice with cut side of garlic clove and drizzle with olive oil. Top bread with goat cheese and strips of roasted peppers. Makes 4.

Stir-Fry Vegetable Bruschetta

This make-ahead stir-fry recipe will save you time during a busy work week.

1 tbs. extra virgin olive oil
1 onion, finely chopped
2 cloves garlic, minced
1 carrot, peeled and diced
1/2 cup finely chopped red and green bell pepper
1/4 cup chopped celery
1/4 cup balsamic or white wine vinegar
1/4 cup chopped fresh basil
1/4 cup crumbled feta cheese
4 slices Italian bread, 1/2- to 3/4-inch thick
2 tbs. extra virgin olive oil

In a skillet, heat 1 tbs. oil over medium heat and sauté onion, garlic, carrot, peppers and celery for about 3 minutes. Remove from heat, add vinegar, basil, feta cheese and 2 tbs. olive oil; mix. Refrigerate for 4 hours. Toast bread and spoon over bread slices. Makes 4.

Eggplant-Onion Bruschetta with Feta

Eggplant and onions melt together and make a hearty winter bruschetta.

6 tbs. extra virgin olive oil
1 medium-sized red onion, diced
2 cloves garlic, minced
1 medium eggplant (about 1 lb.), diced or 3 Japanese eggplants,
   sliced crosswise
1/4 cup finely chopped fresh parsley or dill
salt and freshly ground black pepper to taste
8 slices Italian bread, 1/2- to 3/4-inch thick
2 cloves garlic, cut in half
1/2 cup coarsely crumbled feta cheese
balsamic or white wine vinegar to taste

In a skillet, heat oil over medium heat and add onion. Sauté onion for 4 minutes, stirring gently, until soft. Add garlic and cook another 2 minutes. Add eggplant and cook for 15 to 20 minutes, stirring frequently, until eggplant is golden-brown and soft. Remove skillet from heat, mix in parsley and season with salt and pepper. Toast bread and rub one side of bread slices with cut side of garlic clove. Top bread slices with eggplant mixture. Sprinkle with feta cheese and balsamic vinegar. Makes 8.

Grilled Vegetable Bruschetta

Grill the vegetables on an outdoor grill or use the broiler in your oven.

½ cup prepared Italian dressing
1 clove garlic, minced
¼ cup chopped fresh basil, or 1 ½ tbs. dried
1 small eggplant (about ¾ pound) cut into ½-inch slices
1 zucchini, cut into ½-inch slices
1 yellow, red or green bell pepper, quartered and seeded
1 large tomato, cut into ½-inch slices
8 slices Italian bread, ½- to ¾-inch thick
2 tsp. garlic salt
2 tsp. extra virgin olive oil
1 cup shredded mozzarella cheese

Prepare a medium-hot barbecue fire. In a bowl, combine Italian dressing, garlic and basil and brush over vegetables. Grill vegetables, turning once until softened: about 10 minutes for eggplant, 5 minutes for zucchini and bell pepper and 2 minutes for tomato. Grill one side of each bread slice until lightly toasted, about 1 minute.

Place bread toasted-side up on a baking pan and apply sprinkle with garlic salt. Drizzle bread with olive oil, top with grilled vegetables and sprinkle with cheese. Transfer bruschetta from pan to grill with a wide spatula. Close grill cover and cook bruschetta until cheese melts and the bottom sides of bread are lightly toasted, about 1 minute. Makes 8.

Spicy Avocado and Salsa Bruschetta

Avocado and salsa makes an appealing topping for a light bruschetta.

2 ripe avocados, mashed
1 tbs. lemon juice
salt and freshly ground black pepper to taste
2 tbs. jalapeño salsa or other flavored salsa
4 slices country bread, ½- to ¾-inch thick
1 clove garlic, cut in half
¼ cup extra virgin olive oil, plus more for drizzling
4 slices white onion, separated into rings

In a bowl, combine mashed avocados, lemon juice, salt, pepper and salsa and mix well. Toast bread, rub one side of each bread slice with cut side of garlic clove and drizzle with olive oil. Spread avocado mixture on bread slices and top with onion rings. Drizzle extra olive oil over onion. Makes 4.

Curried Olive and Cheese Bruschetta

Curry powder adds an exotic element to this flavorful mixture.

1 can (6 oz.) pitted ripe black olives, chopped
½ cup shredded mozzarella cheese
½ cup shredded cheddar cheese
2 green onions, chopped
1 clove garlic, minced
½ cup mayonnaise
1 tsp. curry powder
salt and freshly ground black pepper to taste
10 slices country bread, ½- to ¾-inch thick, or 5 English muffins, split
2 tbs. extra virgin olive oil, plus more for dipping, optional
1 medium-sized red bell pepper, cut into strips

Heat oven to 375°. In a medium bowl, mix olives, cheeses, onions, garlic, mayonnaise, curry, salt and pepper until blended. Toast bread and drizzle with olive oil. Top bread slices with olive and cheese mixture and place a strip of red pepper on each slice. Place bruschetta on a baking pan and bake for about 7 minutes or until cheese browns, taking care not to burn bread. Serve with extra olive oil in a dish for dipping, if desired. Makes 10.

Avocado-Green Onion Bruschetta

Green onions and arugula add pepper to this creamy topping.

2 ripe avocados, coarsely mashed
1 tbs. lemon juice
salt and freshly ground black pepper to taste
4 slices country bread, ½- to ¾-inch thick
1 clove garlic, cut in half
2 green onions, sliced
¼ cup extra virgin olive oil
1 cup chopped arugula, coarse stems removed

In a bowl, combine avocados with lemon juice, salt and pepper. Toast bread, rub one side of each bread slice with cut side of garlic clove and drizzle with olive oil. Spread avocado mixture on bread slices and sprinkle with sliced onions. Drizzle a few drops of olive oil over onions and top with arugula. Makes 4.

Roasted Garlic Salsa Bruschetta

Roasted garlic adds a smooth touch to this peppy salsa.

1 bulb garlic
2 cups diced tomatoes
½ cup diced green bell pepper
½ cup diced zucchini
½ cup shredded carrot
⅓ cup diced red onion
2 tbs. chopped fresh cilantro
2 tbs. lemon juice
1 tbs. extra virgin olive oil
½-1 tsp. Tabasco Sauce
20-24 slices French baguette, ⅜- to ½-inch

Heat oven to 350°. Remove papery outer skin from garlic bulb, leaving bulb intact. Place garlic in a small ovenproof custard dish, cover and bake for 35 to 40 minutes, or until soft enough for a knife to be easily inserted; cool. Remove garlic pulp from casings and chop. In a bowl, combine chopped garlic, tomatoes, pepper, zucchini, carrot, red onion, cilantro, lemon juice, olive oil, and hot pepper sauce. Cover and chill for at least 30 minutes to blend flavors. Toast bread and top with salsa. Makes 20 to 24.

Roasted Shallot Salsa Bruschetta

Roasted shallots have a sweet, unique flavor all their own.

8 shallots
¼ cup extra virgin olive oil
1 tsp. minced garlic
½ red onion, finely diced
1 ripe tomato, finely diced
¼ cup chopped fresh cilantro
8 drops Tabasco Sauce, or more to taste
salt and freshly ground black pepper to taste
8 slices Italian bread, ½- to ¾-inch thick
2 tbs. extra virgin olive oil

Heat oven to 250°. Place the shallots and ¼ cup olive oil in a small baking dish or ovenproof sauté pan and roast until soft, about 40 minutes. Cool and cut into quarters. Place shallots in a bowl with garlic, onion, tomato, cilantro, Tabasco, salt and pepper and mix well. Toast bread and drizzle with olive oil. Top bread slices with salsa. Makes 8.

Southwestern Bean Bruschetta

Almost any type of beans can become a quick bruschetta topping with the addition of a favorite cheese.

1 can (15.5 oz.) black beans, rinsed and drained
1 medium tomato, chopped
½ cup chopped green bell pepper
1 tbs. finely chopped onion
1 tbs. chopped fresh cilantro
½ cup extra virgin olive oil
1 tbs. lime juice
½ tsp. salt
¼ tsp. ground cumin
½ tsp. dried oregano
1 tsp. minced garlic
4 English muffins, split
1 cup shredded Monterey Jack cheese

Heat broiler. In a bowl, combine beans, tomato, green pepper, onion and cilantro. In a small bowl, whisk together 2 tbs. of the olive oil, lime juice, salt, cumin and oregano. Add oil mixture to black bean mixture, toss and set aside.

In small saucepan over medium heat, heat remaining olive oil, add garlic and sauté until golden, about 2 minutes. Toast muffin halves lightly and brush evenly with garlic-oil mixture. Spread bean mixture evenly over 8 muffin halves. Sprinkle evenly with cheese. Place bruschetta in a broiler pan and broil 6 inches from heat until cheese melts, about 3 minutes. Serve immediately. Makes 8.

Recipe courtesy of Bay's English Muffins

Chicken Bruschetta with Pineapple-Ginger Chutney

Chutney, an East Indian condiment, comes in a variety of flavors.

1 lb. boneless, skinless chicken breads, cut into 1-inch strips
½ cup finely chopped green onions
½ cup thinly sliced green bell pepper
⅔ cup pineapple-ginger chutney
3 tbs. extra virgin olive oil
6 slices country bread, ½- to ¾-inch thick
2 cloves garlic, cut in half

Combine chicken, green onions, bell pepper and chutney in a bowl and mix well. In a skillet, heat 1 tbs. of the olive oil over medium heat and quickly stir-fry chicken and vegetables until chicken is tender, about 5 minutes. Toast bread, rub one side of each bread slice with cut side of a garlic clove and drizzle with remaining olive oil. Top bread with chicken mixture. Makes 6.

Eggplant and Turkey Bruschetta

If you like, prosciutto or ham can be substituted for the turkey.

3 tbs. extra virgin olive oil
1 medium-sized red onion, thinly sliced
2 cloves garlic, minced
1 lb. eggplant, cut into ¼-inch cubes
½ lb. fresh mozzarella, cut into ½-inch cubes
3 tbs. red wine vinegar
8 fresh basil leaves, minced
salt and freshly ground black pepper to taste
8 slices Italian bread, ½- to ¾-inch thick
8 slices smoked turkey

In a skillet, heat olive oil over medium-high heat. Add onion and garlic and cook until soft, about 3 minutes. Add eggplant and cook for 15 to 20 minutes stirring until eggplant is soft. Stir in mozzarella, vinegar, basil, salt and pepper. Toast bread and top with eggplant mixture. Place a slice of turkey on each bread slice. Makes 8.

Stir-Fried Chicken Bruschetta

Make this as an appetizer or serve it as a full meal with extra bread on the side for sopping up the savory chicken juices.

2 tbs. extra virgin olive oil
1 lb. boneless, skinless chicken breasts, cut into 1-inch pieces
6 fresh white button mushrooms, sliced
4 cloves garlic, minced
salt and freshly ground black pepper to taste
½ cup chopped red onion
½ cup chopped fresh basil, loosely packed, or 2 tbs. dried
4 medium plum tomatoes, chopped
4 tsp. balsamic vinegar
¼ cup shredded Parmesan cheese
shredded fresh basil leaves for garnish, optional
6 slices Italian or French bread, ½- to ¾-inch thick
1 clove garlic, cut in half
2 tsp. extra virgin olive oil

In a large skillet or wok, heat 2 tbs. oil over medium heat and cook chicken until no longer pink, about 4 minutes. Push to one side of pan. Add mushrooms, minced garlic, salt and pepper and cook until mushrooms are soft, about 3 minutes, stirring occasionally. Add onion, chopped basil, tomatoes and vinegar and cook for about 1 minute or until heated through. Stir in Parmesan.

Toast bread, rub one side of each bread slice with cut side of garlic clove and drizzle with 2 tsp. oil. Top with chicken mixture on toast and serve warm. Garnish with basil leaves, if desired. Makes 6.

Meatball Bruschetta with Chutney

Make these in record time with prepared meatballs and prepared chutney.

24 cooked cocktail-size meatballs
1 jar (11-oz.) mango or mango-ginger chutney
½ cup water
8 slices country bread, ½- to ¾-inch thick
2 tbs. extra virgin olive oil

Place meatballs in a saucepan. Add chutney and water and bring to a boil. Reduce heat to low, cover pan and simmer for about 10 minutes. Toast bread and drizzle with olive oil. Top each bread slice with 3 meatballs and spoon chutney sauce on top. Makes 8.

Chicken Liver Paté Bruschetta

Prepared chicken-liver paté makes an impressive appetizer bruschetta.

4 slices French baguette, ½- to ¾-inch thick
1 clove garlic, cut in half
2 tsp. extra virgin olive oil
¾ lb. chicken-liver paté, cut into 4 slices
⅓ cup low-fat mayonnaise
2 tbs. plain nonfat yogurt or nonfat sour cream
1 tbs. chopped fresh rosemary, optional

Toast bread, rub one side of each bread slice with cut side of garlic clove and drizzle with olive oil. Place a slice of chicken-liver paté on each piece of bread. In a small bowl, mix mayonnaise and yogurt to the consistency of a thin sauce. Stir in rosemary, if using. Serve sauce over paté. Makes 4.

Chicken Liver Bruschetta

Serve these as appetizers for a small dinner party of four.

2 tbs. vegetable oil
1 small onion, thinly sliced
2 large cloves garlic, thinly sliced
½ lb. chicken livers, trimmed and cut in half
1 tsp. freshly ground black pepper
1 tsp. salt
2 large fresh sage leaves, minced, or 1 tsp. dried
8 slices Italian bread, ½- to ¾-inch thick
3 tbs. extra virgin olive oil

In a skillet, heat oil over medium heat and sauté onion until golden. Transfer onions to a paper towel to drain. Add garlic and chicken livers to skillet and cook for 1½ to 2 minutes. Add pepper, salt and sage. Transfer mixture to a food processor workbowl and process until coarsely puréed. Toast bread, drizzle with olive oil and top with chicken liver mixture. Top with onions and serve. Makes 8.

Sweet and Sour Meatball Bruschetta

You can also use prepared meatballs with this favorite flavor combination.

2 lb. lean ground beef
2 slices soft white bread, soaked in cold water for 3 minutes and squeezed dry
1 egg, lightly beaten
1 tsp. salt
½ tsp. freshly ground black pepper
2 tbs. grated onion
1 jar (4 oz.) grape jelly
¾ cup ketchup
¼ cup water
1 tbs. brown sugar
¼ cup lemon juice
½ cup raisins
48 slices Italian bread, ½- to ¾-inch thick

In a large skillet, brown ground beef and pour off any fat. In a bowl, mix beef, bread, eggs, salt, pepper and onion and shape into small balls. Add jelly, ketchup, water, brown sugar and lemon juice. Simmer mixture over low heat for 2 hours. Add raisins during last half hour. (If using prepared meatballs, simmer for only about ½ hour and add raisins during last 15 minutes.) Makes 48.

Alfredo Bruschetta

Assemble these ingredients for a cosmopolitan appetizer.

8 slices Italian bread, ½- to ¾-inch thick
1 clove garlic, cut in half
¼ cup extra virgin olive oil
½ cup prepared Alfredo sauce
1 cup frozen chopped spinach, thawed and squeezed dry
1 cup sliced fresh mushrooms
1 tbs. olive oil or vegetable oil
8 oz. prosciutto, thinly sliced
⅓ cup grated Romano cheese

Heat oven to 350°. Toast bread, rub one side of each bread slice with cut side of garlic clove and drizzle with olive oil. Spread bread generously with Alfredo sauce. Top with spinach, pressing down lightly. Top with prosciutto, place bruschetta on a baking sheet and warm in oven for 10 minutes. Sprinkle with Romano cheese. Makes 8.

Smoked Salmon Bruschetta

This variation on bagel, lox and cream cheese can be served as a morning delicacy or for brunch.

4 diagonal slices Italian bread, ½- to ¾-inch thick
1 clove garlic, cut in half
4 tsp. extra virgin olive oil
8 thin slices smoked salmon or lox
8 slices white or purple onion
¼ cup cream cheese, softened

Toast bread and rub one side of each bread slice with cut side of garlic clove. Drizzle with olive oil. Arrange smoked salmon and onion slices on bread and top with a dollop of cream cheese. Makes 4.

Anchovy, Olive and Goat Cheese Bruschetta

The olive spread in this recipe has the appearance and texture of caviar. The anchovy flavor lends a terrific bite to this bruschetta.

1 cup pitted black olives
1 clove garlic, chopped
2 anchovy fillets
¾ cup pine nuts or walnuts, toasted
½ teaspoon freshly ground black pepper
½ cup extra virgin olive oil
8 slices French baguette, ½- to ¾-inch thick
1 clove garlic, cut in half
4 oz. soft white goat cheese
1 red bell pepper, roasted, peeled, seeded and cut into strips

Combine olives and garlic in a food processor workbowl and pulse briefly to chop. Add anchovies, pine nuts, pepper and oil. Process until mixture is slightly coarse.

Toast bread and rub one side of each bread slice with cut side of garlic clove. Spread a thin layer of goat cheese on bread and top with olive paste. Top bruschetta with red pepper strips and serve. Makes 8-10.

Mixed Seafood Bruschetta

Mild fish flavors and plum tomatoes make this bruschetta reminiscent of cioppino.

1 tbs. extra virgin olive oil
1 tbs. lemon or lime juice
1 tbs. snipped fresh chives
1 tbs. minced fresh basil
1 tsp. minced garlic
6 oz. frozen or canned crabmeat, rinsed, drained and flaked
8 oz. cooked medium shrimp, peeled, deveined and coarsely chopped
1 cup chopped plum tomatoes
1/2 cup finely chopped onion
36 slices French baguette, 1/2- to 3/4-inch thick
2 tsp. extra virgin olive oil

In a large bowl, stir together 1 tbs. olive oil, lemon juice, chives, basil and garlic. Add crabmeat, shrimp, plum tomatoes and onion and toss until coated. Toast bread and drizzle with olive oil. Top bread with seafood mixture. Serve immediately. Makes 36.

Grilled Shrimp and Mango Salsa Bruschetta

Pair mango with shrimp for a bright bruschetta topping.

2 French rolls, each cut into six 1/2-inch-thick slices
1/4 cup extra virgin olive oil
2 tsp. minced garlic
1 tbs. chopped fresh basil, thyme or rosemary
24 medium shrimp, cooked, peeled, deveined and tails removed
3/4 cup mango salsa or chutney
chopped fresh basil for garnish

Toast bread. In a bowl, combine olive oil, garlic, and herbs and drizzle over each bread slice. Grill shrimp for about 1 minute on each side or until cooked through. Arrange toast on a platter and place 2 shrimp on each bread slice. Top with salsa and garnish with chopped basil. Makes 12.

Caviar Bruschetta

This will set just the right tone for a memorable candlelight dinner. Assemble the ingredients just before you serve.

4 slices French baguette, 3/8- to 1/2-inch thick
1 clove garlic, cut in half
2 tsp. extra virgin olive oil
1 can (4 oz.) black caviar
1 tsp. chopped onion
1 tsp. chopped hard-cooked egg yolk
1 tsp. chopped fresh chives

Toast bread, rub one side of each bread slice with garlic clove and drizzle with olive oil. Top bread with caviar and sprinkle with onion, egg yolk and chives. Makes 4.

Chopped Herring Bruschetta

Buy prepared herring in sour cream for a fast, refreshing appetizer. This Scandinavian delicacy is one you will serve often.

6 slices Italian bread, 1/2- to 3/4-inch thick
1 clove garlic, cut in half
2 tbs. extra virgin olive oil
1/2 purple onion, thinly sliced
1 cup coarsely chopped prepared herring fillets in sour cream
1/2 cup coarsely diced roasted red pepper

Toast bread, rub one side of each bread slice with cut side of garlic clove and drizzle with olive oil. Top bread with a thin slice of onion, chopped herring and diced red pepper. Makes 6.

Greek Breakfast Bruschetta

This bruschetta makes a nourishing morning meal.

6 slices day-old raisin or soft egg bread, ½- to ¾-inch thick
3 tbs. butter, melted
2 tsp. sugar
1 tsp. cinnamon
2 cups chopped fresh plums, peaches or other seasonal fruit
1 cup corn flakes or similar breakfast cereal
1 cup plain yogurt
2 tbs. honey

Heat oven to 350°. Brush bread with butter and toast in oven until bread is golden brown. In a bowl, mix sugar and cinnamon and sprinkle over bread. Return to oven for about 3 minutes to warm. Arrange bread on plates and top with fruit, corn flakes and yogurt. Drizzle with honey. Makes 6.

Mixed Fresh Fruit Bruschetta

Your bruschetta will win raves when served for breakfast or dessert. Substitute any fruits in season for those in the recipe.

8 slices raisin bread, ½- to ¾-inch thick
2 tbs. butter or margarine, melted
1 tbs. sugar
2 tsp. cinnamon
1 fresh pear, peach or other fruit in season, diced
1 banana, diced
8 large strawberries sliced, or ½ cup blueberries
½ cup plain or fruit-flavored yogurt
¼ cup honey
½ cup shredded coconut, toasted, optional, for garnish

Heat oven to 375°. Arrange bread slices in one layer in a shallow baking pan and toast in oven until golden, about 5 minutes. Heat broiler. Brush butter on one side of each bread slice. In a small bowl, stir together ½ tbs. of the sugar and the cinnamon and sprinkle evenly over buttered side of each toast slice. Broil toast about 5 inches from heat for 30 seconds, or until tops bubble. Remove bread from oven and place on a serving platter. In a bowl, mix together fruit and remaining ½ tbs. sugar. Top bread with fruit and yogurt and drizzle with honey. Garnish with coconut, if using. Makes 8.

Berry Good Bruschetta

Sweet bread and prepared pie filling make a smashing dessert bruschetta.

8-10 slices day-old egg challah or other sweet bread, 1/2- to 3/4-inch thick
2 tbs. unsalted butter, melted
1/2 cup nonfat sour cream
1 tsp. vanilla extract
1/4 cup sugar
1 can (16 oz.) blueberry pie filling
1/3 cup coconut, toasted

Heat broiler. Toast bread under broiler until lightly browned on both sides and drizzle one side with melted butter. In a small bowl, mix sour cream, vanilla and sugar. Top with sour cream mixture and blueberry pie filling. Sprinkle with toasted coconut. Makes 8-10.

Broiled Fruit Bruschetta

Fruit broiled on lightly toasted bread is a fashionable summer treat. You can also use seasonal berries for this bruschetta.

4 slices day-old country bread or sweet bread, 1/2- to 3/4-inch thick
4 tsp. butter, softened
1 tsp. sugar, plus more to taste
sliced peaches, pears, plums, apples or other seasonal fruit
3 tablespoons lemon or lime juice
whipped cream

Heat broiler. Toast bread slices on one side under broiler until brown. Spread bread with softened butter and sprinkle with 1 tsp. of the sugar. In a bowl, combine fruit with extra sugar. Arrange fruit on bread slices and brush with lemon juice. Broil for about 4 minutes or until the fruit softens. Cool. Top with a dollop of whipped cream. Makes 4.

Strawberry-Cinnamon Bruschetta

Use fresh or frozen strawberries for a rewarding dessert.

1½ cups sliced strawberries
2 tbs. honey
2 tbs. chopped fresh mint leaves, or ¼ tsp. mint extract
⅛ tsp. cinnamon
1 tbs. lime juice
2 tbs. butter, softened
4 slices day-old country bread, ½- to ¾-inch thick
1 tsp. cinnamon
1 tsp. sugar
plain yogurt or sour cream

In a bowl, combine strawberries, honey, mint, ⅛ tsp. cinnamon and lime juice and toss gently. Chill. Toast bread until lightly browned. Spread with butter and sprinkle with 1 tsp. cinnamon and sugar. Top bread with strawberry mixture. Serve with a dollop of yogurt or sour cream. Makes 4.

The Best 50
Sushi Rolls

Carol M. Newman

Sushi – Refined, Simple and Fresh

The Japanese lifestyle is admired for its minimalist, streamlined simplicity. This living structure is, no doubt, carried over into Japanese culinary formalities. On the surface, the well-designed sushi one orders or visualizes appears to be complex. And at first glance, these tightly-wrapped petite structures may appear intimidating. But elegant does not always mean complex. Rather, it is the natural result when one emphasizes refined, simple and fresh.

Generally, there are very few ingredients in a given Japanese sushi item. But what gives these special pieces their character is that the ingredients are incredibly fresh and pleasing to the eye, mind and palate. For the Japanese, refinement in all things — taste, size, smell, or texture — outweighs a melange of mismatched traits.

Unfortunately, narrow assumptions often box in Japanese cuisine. Sushi is misunderstood as being "too expensive" and/or "all about fish." Whereas *sashimi* purely defines raw fish, the definition for *sushi* is a little more slippery. Sushi refers to rolls made with or without fish and with vegetables or other fillings. Rice, however, must be included in the roll in order to be called sushi.

You can have the roll inside-out, or *maki,* a cone-shaped hand roll that is the size of an ice cream cone. Maki is usually served in six slices and is made with seaweed. *Nigiri,* or hand-made sushi, is typically ordered and served in pairs. There is also pressed sushi or oshi, which is cut into small squares. This book focuses on maki, rolled with the rice on the inside or outside of the roll.

About Fish

A rather stiff myth is that eating sushi is a cause for alarm, that raw fish is in some way a danger. This needs explanation. There are some fish that are considered safer to eat raw than others. Saltwater fish, however, such as tuna, halibut, salmon and shellfish are safe to eat raw if caught in nonpolluted waters. *Sashimi-grade* fish is of a higher quality and is more expensive. The higher the fat content of a fish, the more flavor it will have. So, keep this in mind when you shop for tuna or salmon. If you are still hesitant about eating raw fish, double check with your fish purveyor. Let him or her know you are planning to make sushi and seek their advice on quality and freshness. The general rule for freshness is this: make sure the fish smells like the ocean, rather than ammonia. You'll want to make sure the eyes are clear (if buying a whole fish), rather than dull, that the flesh bounces back when poked and that there are no signs of browning. Freshwater fish from lakes and streams should never be used for sushi. If you plan to use a freshwater fish, cooking it thoroughly is resistance against parasites. If you are still squeamish, use the recipes in this book that call for cooked fish, canned fish or produce.

Learn a New Skill

Learn to roll sushi and you will not only add a culinary skill to your repertoire, but you will be able to share in a Japanese custom from the nineteenth century. For hundreds of years, the Japanese preserved their fish with salt and pressed it in layers until the fish was fermented. In the early 1800s, a Japanese entrepreneur decided to put raw seafood on pads of rice. The new trend emerged and quickly caught on.

Equipment

A quick word about equipment. You can do a lot with very little. There are no fancy gadgets involved. If you have the basics and some skill, you are on the way to becoming a sushi aficionado. When you do reach that level, think about investing in some sake cups, your own special chopsticks and some real Japanese dish-ware. In the meantime, pick up these few items:

- A bamboo mat or hot pad, called a *sushimaki sudare* or a *makisu*. This is used to roll the sushi.
- A wooden rice paddle, or a *shamoj*. This is used to "cut" the rice after cooking and spread it on the nori.
- A very sharp knife is a must. The classic sushi knife is called a *bento* knife.
- Chopsticks are called *hashi;* learn to use them like a pro.

Rolling Method

Lay your sushi mat flat on the counter and cover with plastic wrap. Take a piece of sushi nori and lay it glossy-side down. Wet your hands and scoop ½ cup cooked rice out of the bowl. Make a thin, loose "line" of rice across the seaweed. Wet hands again and gently massage rice so that you distribute rice into a thin sheet. The grains should be kept intact. Fill your roll in layers, trying to use long pieces of whatever filling you are going to roll. Using the bam-boo mat to guide you, take the edge nearest you and curl it over (as you would a sleeping bag), tuck the edge in as tightly as you can and begin to roll. You may have to use your finger to keep the filling from popping out. DO NOT ROLL THE BAMBOO MAT INTO YOUR ROLL. Seal with a swipe of water. Finally, using a very sharp, clean knife, cut the ends to make them even. When slicing the roll, cut straight through very quickly. Next, cut the roll in half and put the two identical shorter rolls next to each other. Cut these pieces until there are six equal pieces of sushi.

Inside-Out

You can also wrap your rolls inside-out. Flip the nori sheet over after you massage the rice, and place the fillings on the other side of the nori, layering them as you would with the regular roll. Follow the same rolling procedure as on previous page. Cut into six equal slices with a clean, sharp knife.

Inside the Sushi Kitchen

avocado: make sure it is ripe and dark-skinned.

daikon: radish

gari or shoga: sliced, pickled ginger, a condiment used to reset the palate and tastebuds.

imitation crab: look for this if you can't find (or your budget won't handle) the real thing .

kappa: cucumber. European cucumbers are recommended because there is less waste.

kuro goma: sesame seeds, available in black or white

nori: toasted seaweed sheets. Look for the dark green color with a high glossy finish.

shoyu: the fermented soy bean sauce or soy sauce comes in different styles. Japanese soy has a relatively sweet flavor and is less salty than Chinese or American varieties.

su or awaze-zu: sushi vinegar. Fermented rice wine or rice vinegar.

sushi rice: look for Kokuho Rose or Nishiki brands. Do not use sweet rice. The grains of sushi rice are small and fat. The rice tends to be starchy; rinse it well.

plum sauce: a thick sauce made from apricots, chiles, vinegar and sugar

wasabi: green horseradish paste that either comes in dry form or in small cans. It comes in varying degrees of "heat." Wasabi is a perennial plant and, as it ages, a rhizome forms. That is the most valued part of the plant. Fresh wasabi is premium, and if you can find it, use it. Unfortunately, many restaurants and food markets carry green food-colored horseradish.

A Few Polite Japanese Phrases May Help Your Popularity When You Visit a Sushi Bar

arigato: thank you. Be nice; use it often.

arigato gozaimashita: Final thank you at the end of the meal.

itamae-san: the sushi chef. These chefs "conduct" the sushi bar as a conductor conducts an orchestra. By just glancing at your plate, a good itamae san will pin your sushi tastes down. He may make suggestions. A sushi chef is involved in every detail of the preparation, from haggling with fish and produce purveyors, to preparing the sushi and being the master showman behind the sushi bar. Show plenty of respect for your itamae-san.

kanapi: the Japanese equivalent of "cheers," used when drinking.

konbonwa: good evening.

o kadasai: please give me. First, say the type of sushi you want, and then, "o kadasai." Example: "Terka-maki o kodasai" means, "Please give me a tuna roll."

oma ka se: chef's choice. This is a magic word with your itamae-san. It tells the chef to make whatever he wants. It is considered a great honor. Use it to your advantage (you may receive extra sushi, gratis).

oshibori: hot towel to wipe your face and hands before you eat.

oyasumi nasai: good night.

Do's and Don'ts at the Sushi Bar

Here are a few words of etiquette to keep in mind. Know the Japanese traditions and try them. But within the restraints of common law and courtesy, enjoy your meal however you like!

1. Use the hot towel that is given to you at the sushi bar to clean your hands and your face before a meal.

2. Avoid drinking sake with sushi. Because sake is made with rice, it is redundant for the Japanese to have both in the same sitting. Example: Serving baked potatoes with a side of French fries.

3. Avoid using wasabi (even though they give it to you) with your sushi. The itamae-san sometimes puts wasabi in your sushi, between the rice and fish. To add wasabi is to tell the itamae-san he did not season the sushi properly. (Example: Adding salt to a plate you have not tasted yet with the cook sitting beside you).

4. It's okay to eat sushi with your fingers. When you dip your sushi in soy sauce, try not to let any grains fall into the soy and be careful about how much you get on your rice; the sushi roll could fall apart. If the roll is too big for one bite, bite it in half, but NEVER PUT IT BACK YOUR PLATE, HALF-EATEN; this is not appropriate.

5. If you decide to sample sushi from a friend's plate with your chopsticks, turn them around and use the back end.

6. If your sushi chef is doing a nice job for you, offer to buy him a drink, maybe a sake or beer. This is a nice thing to do and it may help build your relationship.

7. Like Mom used to say, finish your food! In Japan, it is an insult to leave food on your plate.

8. When you are finished eating, align your chopsticks neatly on the edge of your plate. Do not haphazardly lie them down in the soy sauce or on your placemat.

Sushi Rice

This is the recipe you will use to make all of the sushi recipes in this book. The recipe makes 4 sushi rolls or 24 pieces of maki. The rice tastes best when it is a little crunchy; this will help keep the grains intact.

2 cups short-grain rice (Kokuho Rose or Nishiki)
2 cups water
¼ cup rice vinegar
3 tbs. sugar
1 tsp. salt

Wash rice until water runs clear; drain in a colander. Transfer rice to a pot or electric rice cooker and add water. Bring water to a boil. Simmer over low heat, allowing rice to steam for 15 minutes with the lid on at all times. Remove from heat and keep covered, steaming for 15 minutes. Mix rice vinegar, sugar and salt. With a wooden spoon, fold vinegar mixture into rice; avoid smashing grains. Spread rice on a baking pan to cool. Makes 4 cups.

Shrimp Tempura Roll

Tempura means battered and lightly fried. It a favorite Japanese cooking method, and popular with the less daring sushi fanatics.

¼ cup all-purpose flour, plus more for dredging
½ tsp. cornstarch
1 egg
½ cup ice water
6 black tiger shrimp, peeled and deveined
canola oil, for deep frying
2 sheets sushi nori
1 cup cooked sushi rice, page 314
2 green onions, ends trimmed

In a small bowl, mix flour, cornstarch, egg and ice water. Sprinkle extra flour on a plate. Score shrimp across backs and press down to elongate. Heat oil over high heat, checking temperature by dropping a spoonful of batter in oil. The temperature is right if the piece drops halfway and then floats back to the surface. Batter shrimp, dredge in flour and fry until golden brown. Drain on paper towels.

Heat nori in a 350° oven to soften slightly, about 3 to 4 minutes. Working with one sheet of nori at a time, with shiny side facing down and with long side facing you, spread ½ cup of the rice in an even layer on each sheet, leaving a ½-inch border on long sides. Arrange shrimp in a line across rice. Arrange a green onion on top of shrimp. Follow rolling procedure on page 311 and cut each roll into 6 equal slices. Makes 12 slices.

Variation: Vegetable Tempura Roll

Batter and fry assorted chopped vegetables, such as broccoli.

The California Roll

A Western tradition, this little gem has made its way onto virtually every sushi menu, East and West.

2 sheets sushi nori
½ avocado, pitted, peeled and sliced
1 tbs. fresh lemon juice
1 cup cooked sushi rice, page 314
½ cucumber, peeled, seeded and sliced
¼ lb. fresh crabmeat
wasabi as an accompaniment
soy sauce as an accompaniment
pickled ginger as an accompaniment
black sesame seeds for garnish

Heat nori in a 350° oven to soften slightly, about 3 to 4 minutes. Rub avocado with lemon juice. Working with one sheet of nori at a time, with shiny side facing down and with a long side facing you, spread about ½ cup of the rice in an even layer on each sheet, leaving a ½-inch border on the long sides. Arrange some avocado strips horizontally across middle of rice, followed by a layer of cucumber and crab. Dab crabmeat with wasabi. Follow rolling procedure on page 311. Cut into 6 equal slices and sprinkle generously with sesame seeds. Makes 12 slices.

English Cucumber Roll (Kappa)

A staple vegetarian item, this roll is always a must when ordering from the sushi bar. English cucumbers work best because their size allows for long, manageable strips.

2 pieces sushi nori
1 cup cooked sushi rice, page 314
¼ cup plum paste
½ cucumber, peeled and cut into ½-inch strips

Heat nori in a 350° oven to soften slightly, about 3 to 4 minutes. Working with one sheet of nori at a time, with shiny side facing down and with long side facing you, spread ½ cup of the rice in an even layer on each sheet, leaving a ½-inch border on long sides. Spread a thin layer of plum paste across rice. Arrange a line of cucumber across middle of rice. Follow rolling procedure on page 311 and cut into 6 equal slices. Makes 12 slices.

Spicy Tuna Roll (Teka Maki)

Tuna rolls are the ultimate in sushi rolls. This one is kicked up a notch with some hot chili sauce.

2 pieces sushi nori
1 cup cooked sushi rice, page 314
1/4 lb. fresh ahi tuna, cut into 1/2-inch-wide strips
1 tbs. chili sauce
1 tbs. white sesame seeds, plus more for sprinkling
2 green onions, ends trimmed

Heat nori in a 350° oven to soften. Working with one sheet of nori at a time, with shiny side facing down and with long side facing you, spread 1/2 cup of the rice in an even layer on each sheet, leaving a 1/2-inch border on long sides. Arrange a line of tuna across middle of rice. Brush with chili sauce and sprinkle with sesame seeds. Place green onion on top of tuna. Follow rolling procedure on page 311 and cut each roll into 6 equal slices. Sprinkle with sesame seeds. Makes 12 slices.

Eggs McSushi Roll (Tamago)

For those on-the-go fast-food eaters, "have this your way" on the way to work. There won't be a wait at the drive-through, either.

1 tbs. canola cooking oil
1/2 carrot, peeled and cut into 1/2-inch strips
1 clove garlic, mashed
1 slice fresh ginger, mashed
1 tsp. rice vinegar
1 tbs. soy sauce
2 eggs
2 pieces sushi nori
1 cup cooked sushi rice, page 314
2 tbs. plum paste
2 green onions, ends trimmed

In a small skillet over medium-high heat, heat oil. Sauté carrot, garlic and ginger for about 2 minutes, or until carrots are tender-crisp. In a small bowl, whisk rice vinegar, soy sauce and eggs. Add to skillet and cook until eggs are firm. Cut omelet into 1/2-inch-wide strips. Heat nori. Working with one sheet of nori at a time, with shiny side facing down and with long side facing you, spread 1/2 cup of the rice in an even layer on each sheet, leaving a 1/2-inch border on long sides. Brush middle of rice with plum paste. Place omelet strips in a line across middle of rice. Follow rolling procedure on page 311 and cut each roll into 6 equal slices. Makes 12 slices.

Portobello Roll

Portobello mushrooms are thick, rich in taste and a beautiful deep brown color. You might think you are eating eel.

2 pieces sushi nori
1 tbs. butter
2 medium portobello mushrooms, wiped clean, stems removed and coarsely
  chopped
1 cup cooked sushi rice, page 314

Heat nori in a 350° oven to soften, about 3 to 4 minutes. In a sauté pan over medium-high heat, heat butter. Sauté mushrooms until tender, about 3 to 4 minutes. Working with one sheet of nori at a time, with shiny side facing down and with long side facing you, spread ½ cup of the rice in an even layer on each sheet, leaving a ½-inch border on long sides. Spoon equal amounts of mushrooms in a line across middle of rice. Follow rolling procedure on page 311 and cut each roll into 6 equal slices. Makes 2 rolls.

Salmon Sushi (Shake Maki)

The ideal time to make this sushi is when the salmon just start their spring run in mid-May.

1 small salmon fillet (¼ lb.)
1 cup water
¼ cup vinegar
2 tbs. salt
2 sheets sushi nori
1 cup cooked sushi rice, page 314
2 green onions, ends trimmed

Place salmon fillet in a dish and and add water, vinegar and salt; cover with plastic wrap. Marinate until cured, about 3 hours; discard marinade. Break salmon into small chunks. Working with one sheet of nori at a time, with shiny side facing down and with long side facing you, spread ½ cup of the rice in a layer on each sheet, leaving a ½-inch border on long sides. Place salmon strips in a line across middle of rice. Place green onions on top of salmon. Follow rolling procedure on page 311. Cut into 6 equal slices. Makes 12 slices.

Poached Salmon Sushi

For those who love salmon, but may be too timid to eat it uncooked, poaching preserves its subtle texture.

2 cups water
2 tbs. salt
2 tbs. vinegar
1 small salmon fillet (1/4 lb.)
salt and pepper to taste
2 sheets sushi nori
1 cup cooked sushi rice, page 314
2 green onions, ends trimmed

In a shallow pan, bring water, salt and vinegar to a boil. Reduce heat to a simmer. Add salmon and cook for about 4 minutes. Remove from water and break into chunks; cool and season with salt and pepper. Heat nori. Working with one sheet of nori at a time, with shiny side facing down and with long side facing you, spread 1/2 cup of the rice in an even layer on each sheet, leaving a 1/2-inch border on long sides. Place salmon in a line across middle of rice. Place a green onion in each roll. Follow rolling procedure on page 311 and cut each roll into 6 equal slices. Makes 12 slices.

Eel Roll (Unagi)

Pick up barbecued eel at a local Japanese market or buy a few pieces from the local sushi bar. The time you save is worth the small price.

2 sheets sushi nori
1 cup cooked sushi rice, page 314
1/4 lb. barbecued eel
1/2 avocado, pitted, peeled and cut into 1/2-inch slices

Heat nori. Working with one sheet of nori at a time, with shiny- side facing down and with long side facing you, spread 1/2 cup of the rice in an even layer on each sheet, leaving a 1/2-inch border on the long sides. Place eel in a horizontal line across middle of rice. Place avocado strips in a layer on top of eel. Follow rolling procedure on page 311 and cut each roll into 6 equal slices. Makes 12 slices.

Crab and Edamame Bean Roll

Edamame beans are fresh green Japanese soy beans.

2 sheets sushi nori
1 cup cooked sushi rice, page 314
4 oz. fresh crabmeat
½ cup boiled, shelled edamame beans

Heat nori. Working with one sheet of nori at a time, with shiny side facing down and with long side facing you, spread rice in an even layer on each sheet, leaving, a ½-inch border on long sides. Line equal amounts of crabmeat in center of each roll. Top with a layer of edamame beans. Follow rolling procedure on page 311 and cut each roll into 6 equal slices. Makes 12 slices.

Variations

Crab, Edamame Bean and Mayo Roll. Add ¼ cup mayonnaise on top of crab layer.

Seafood and Edamame Bean Roll. Add cooked baby shrimp on top of crab layer.

Crab, Edamame Bean and Cheese Roll: Spread 2 oz. whipped cream cheese on rice; top with crab.

Tobiko Roll

Tobiko, or flying fish roe, are fish eggs. This specialty is commonly found in Japanese markets. Make this an inside-out roll and dab with enough tobiko to cover.

2 sheets sushi nori
1 cup cooked sushi rice, page 314
¼ lb. salmon skin
¼ cup tobiko

Heat nori. Working with one sheet of nori at a time, with shiny side facing down and with long side facing you, spread rice in an even layer on each sheet, leaving a ½-inch border on long sides. Line equal amounts of salmon skin in center of each roll. Follow inside-out rolling procedure on page 312 and cut each roll into 6 equal pieces. Dab with tobiko. Makes 12 slices.

The Midtown Roll (The New York Roll)

New Yorkers will forever be bonded to lox and cream cheese. Midtown Manhattan is teeming with delis and bagel shops. This roll was created for those devotees.

2 sheets sushi nori
1 cup cooked sushi rice, page 314
½ cucumber, peeled, seeded and cut into ½-inch slices
¼ cup whipped cream cheese
¼ lb. smoked salmon

Heat nori. Working with one sheet of nori, with shiny side facing down and with long side facing you, spread ½ cup rice in an even layer on each sheet, leaving a ½-inch border on long sides. Place cucumber in a horizontal line across middle of rice. Spread cream cheese on top of cucumber strips in a thin layer. Place smoked salmon on top of cream cheese. Follow rolling procedure on page 311 and cut each roll into 12 equal slices.

Plantain and Shrimp Roll

Plantains are staple ingredients in Caribbean cooking.

1 ripe plantain, peeled and cut into ½-inch slices
2 tbs. canola oil
6 large tiger shrimp, peeled and deveined
2 sheets sushi nori
1 cup cooked sushi rice, page 314

Heat oven to 375°. Arrange plantain on a baking sheet and bake for 10 minutes, or until very soft. Set aside to cool.

In a small skillet over medium heat, heat oil and add shrimp. Toss until shrimp turn pink; remove and cool. When cool, chop coarsely. Heat nori. Working with one sheet of nori at a time, with shiny side facing down and with long side facing you, spread ½ cup of the rice in an even layer on each sheet, leaving a ½-inch border on long sides. Layer equal amounts of plantain slices in center of each roll. Arrange shrimp over plantains. Follow rolling procedure on page 311 and cut each roll into 6 equal slices. Makes 12 slices.

Shrimp and Pineapple Roll

If you are one who appreciates the tart, stinging flavor of pineapple, this roll is for you! Forget about putting pineapple on your pizza — try using it here, instead.

2 tbs. canola oil
6 black tiger shrimp, peeled and deveined
½ cup cooked sushi rice, page 314
2 sheets sushi nori
½ cup fresh pineapple chunks

Score shrimp across backs and press down to elongate. In a small skillet over medium-high heat, heat oil. Add shrimp and cook until pink. Remove from heat and cool. Chop coarsely. Heat nori. Working with one sheet of nori at a time with shiny side facing down and with long side facing you, spread ½ cup of the rice in an even layer on each sheet, leaving a ½-inch border on long sides. Spoon equal amounts of shrimp in a line across middle of rice. Top with a layer of pineapple. Follow rolling procedure on page 311 and cut into 6 equal slices. Makes 12 slices.

The Santa Monica Roll

Michael McCarty, a founding father of "California cuisine," is known for his innovative cooking style. This roll pays tribute to the Santa Monica pioneer who started the trend.

2 sheets sushi nori
1 avocado, peeled and pitted
1 tbs. lemon juice
1 cup cooked sushi rice, page 314
1 tbs. plum sauce
1 cup English peas, shelled, cooked in boiling water until tender
　　and refreshed in cold water
1 mango, pitted, peeled and cut into ½-inch wide strips

Heat nori in a 350° oven to soften, about 3 to 4 minutes. Cut avocado into ½-inch strips and rub with lemon juice. Working with one sheet of nori at a time, shiny side facing down and long side facing you, spread ½ cup of the rice in an even layer on each sheet, leaving a ½-inch border on long sides. Brush plum sauce in a line across middle of rice. Arrange equal amounts of English peas and sliced mango on top of plum sauce. Top with a layer of avocado.

Follow rolling procedure on page 311 and cut each roll into 6 equal slices. Makes 12 slices.

Sweet Potato Sushi

The Japanese sometimes grate raw sweet potatoes over their food for garnish. Cooked, the heavy, sweet flesh makes a smooth filling.

2 sheets sushi nori
1 cup cooked sushi rice, page 314
1 small cooked Jersey sweet potato, peeled and sliced into ½-inch strips
¼ cup plum sauce

Heat nori. Working with one sheet of nori at a time, with shiny side facing down and with long side facing you, spread ½ cup of the rice in an even layer on each sheet, leaving a ½-inch border on long sides. Place equal amounts of sweet potato in a line across middle of rice. Brush each with 2 tbs. plum sauce. Follow rolling procedure on page 311 and cut each roll into 6 equal slices. Makes 12 slices.

Anchovy and Sun-Dried Tomato Sushi

Never mind making a trek to the local fish market; pick up a tin of anchovies and roll these up instead!

2 sheets sushi nori
1 cup cooked sushi rice, page 314
1 can (3.5 oz.) anchovies, drained
6 oil-packed sun-dried tomatoes, wiped dry

Heat nori. Working with one sheet of nori at a time, with shiny side facing down and with long side facing you, spread ½ cup of the rice in an even layer on each sheet, leaving a ½-inch border on long sides. Arrange equal amounts of anchovies in a line across middle of rice. Place tomatoes in a layer on top of anchovies. Follow rolling procedure on page 311 and cut each roll into 6 equal slices. Makes 12 slices.

Island Shrimp Sushi Roll

The grated coconut gives these shrimp a taste of the islands. It also offers a little sweetness, waking up the flavor of the shrimp.

6 large black tiger shrimp, peeled and deveined
1 tbs. olive oil
¼ cup grated coconut
¼ tsp. ground ginger
1 tsp. lemon juice
salt and pepper to taste
2 sheets sushi nori
1 cup cooked sushi rice, page 314

Score shrimp across backs and press down to elongate. In a small skillet over medium-high heat, heat oil. Add shrimp, coconut, ginger, lemon juice, salt and pepper and cook until shrimp are pink and other ingredients are heated through. Remove from heat and cool. When cool, chop coarsely. Heat nori. Working with one sheet of nori at a time, with shiny side facing down and with long side facing you, spread ½ cup of the rice in an even layer on each sheet, leaving a ½-inch border on long sides. Arrange equal amounts of shrimp mixture in a line across middle of rice. Follow rolling procedure on page 311 and cut each roll into 6 equal slices. Makes 12 slices.

Goat Cheese, Corn and Basil Roll

These roll ingredients originated from a tamale filling, but they go just as well wrapped tightly in a sushi roll!

2 sheets sushi nori
1 cup cooked sushi rice, page 314
4 oz. fresh goat cheese
½ cup cooked corn kernels
½ cup minced fresh basil leaves

Heat nori. Working with one sheet of nori at a time, with shiny side facing down and with long side facing you, spread ½ cup of the rice in an even layer on each sheet, leaving a ½-inch border on long sides. Spread goat cheese in equal amounts in a line across middle of rice. Layer with corn and basil leaves. Follow rolling method on page 311 and cut each roll into 6 equal slices. Makes 12 slices.

Ginger Scallop Roll

Asian flavors come alive in a refreshing and simple roll.

2 tbs. butter
24 bay scallops
2 tbs. chopped fresh ginger
2 tbs. chopped fresh cilantro
2 sheets sushi nori
1 cup cooked sushi rice, page 314

In a small skillet over medium heat, melt butter. Add scallops, ginger and cilantro and cook for 4 minutes, until scallops are golden brown. Remove from heat and cool. Heat nori. Working with one sheet of nori at a time, with shiny side facing down and with long side facing you, spread ½ cup of the rice in an even layer on each sheet, leaving a ½-inch border on long sides. Place equal amounts of scallops, 12 on each sheet, in a line across middle of rice. Follow rolling procedure on page 311 and cut each roll into 6 equal slices. Makes 12 slices.

Seared Oyster Roll

Oysters are paired with the distinctive flavors of arugula for this special roll.

2 tbs. butter
2 shallots, minced
12 oysters, shucked
pepper to taste
2 sheets sushi nori
1 cup cooked sushi rice, page 314
1 cup torn arugula leaves

In a small skillet over medium heat, heat butter. Add shallots and oysters and sear for 10 seconds on each side. Season with pepper and remove; let cool. Heat nori. Working with one sheet of nori at a time, with shiny side facing down and with long side facing you, spread ½ cup of the rice in an even layer on each sheet leaving a ½-inch border on long sides. Arrange oysters in a line across middle of rice. Top with arugula leaves. Follow rolling procedure on page 311 and cut each roll into 6 equal slices. Makes 12 slices.

Mussel Shoals Sushi Roll

The hazy Southern California coastline is where you can pick up a little mussel — and a little muscle! And if you eat your spinach, you're likely to get some.

2 sheets sushi nori
1 cup cooked sushi rice, page 314
12 cooked green lip mussels, shelled
1 cup baby spinach leaves

Heat nori. Working with one sheet of nori at a time, with shiny side facing down and with long side facing you, spread rice in a layer on each sheet, leaving a ½-inch border on long sides. Place equal amounts of mussels, 6 on each sheet, in a line across middle of rice. Top with spinach leaves. Follow rolling procedure on page 311 and cut each roll into 6 equal slices. Makes 12 slices.

Moroccan Roll

These flavors may inspire a further look into the foods of the continent of Africa.

½ cup shredded zucchini
½ cup shredded red cabbage
1 jalapeño pepper, seeded and
  minced
1 clove garlic, minced
1 tsp. ground cumin

salt and pepper to taste
1 tbs. olive oil
2 sheets sushi nori
1 cup cooked sushi rice, page 314
¼ cup toasted pine nuts

In a large skillet over medium heat, sauté zucchini, cabbage, jalapeño, garlic and spices in oil until vegetables are soft. With a slotted spoon, remove zucchini mixture and transfer to a small bowl; let cool. Heat nori. Working with one sheet of nori at a time, with shiny side facing down and with long side facing you, spread rice in a layer on each sheet, leaving a ½-inch border on long sides. Place equal amounts of zucchini mixture in center of each roll. Sprinkle with pine nuts. Follow rolling procedure on page 311 and cut each roll into 6 equal slices. Makes 12 slices.

Smoked Salmon and Fig Roll

April and May mean open season on salmon and a time when fresh figs are falling from orchard trees.

2 sheets sushi nori
1 cup cooked sushi rice, page 314
4 oz. smoked salmon, broken into small pieces
2 mission figs, thinly sliced

Working with 1 sheet of nori at a time, shiny side facing down and long side facing you, spread rice in an even layer on each nori sheet, leaving a ½-inch border on long sides. Arrange salmon in a line across middle of rice. Top with a layer of figs. Follow rolling procedure on page 311 and cut into 6 equal slices. Makes 12 slices.

Variation: Prosciutto and Fig Roll

Add 2 very thin prosciutto slices on each sheet instead of salmon and top with a layer of figs.

Smoked Salmon and Mango Roll

Sweet fruit flavors are often overlooked as perfectly suitable complements to savory items. Mango, like salmon, is fleshy and a substantial match.

2 sheets sushi nori
1 cup cooked sushi rice, page 314
4 oz. smoked salmon, broken into small pieces
1 mango, pitted, peeled and cut into ½-inch-wide strips

Heat nori. Working with one sheet of nori at a time, shiny side facing down and long side facing you, spread ½ cup of the rice in an even layer on each nori sheet, leaving a ½-inch border on long sides. Arrange equal amounts of salmon in a line across middle of rice. Top with a layer of mango. Follow rolling procedure on page 311 and cut into 6 equal slices. Makes 12 slices.

Tuna Fish Roll

When time is of the essence and you need a quick fix, this roll is an easy out.

2 sheets sushi nori
1 cup cooked sushi rice, page 314
¼ cup mayonnaise
1 can albacore tuna in water, drained
pepper to taste

Heat nori. Working with one sheet of nori at a time, with shiny side facing down and with long side facing you, spread ½ cup of the rice in an even layer on each sheet, leaving a ½-inch border on long sides. Spread mayonnaise in a line across middle of rice. Top with tuna. Season with pepper and follow rolling procedure on page 311. Cut each roll into 6 equal slices. Makes 12 slices.

Variation: Northern Italian Tuna Roll

Add ¼ cup cannellini beans on top of tuna and sprinkle with 1 tbs. rosemary.

Scallop and Avocado Sushi Roll

The light flavor of scallops balances its heavier partner, the avocado.

¼ lb. bay scallops
¼ cup lime juice
2 sheets sushi nori
1 cup cooked sushi rice, page 314
½ avocado, pitted, peeled and cut into ½-inch slices

In a bowl, combine scallops with lime juice. Cover with plastic wrap and set aside for 15 minutes. Heat nori. Working with one sheet of nori at a time, with shiny side facing down and with long side facing you, spread ½ cup of the rice in an even layer on each sheet, leaving a ½-inch border on long sides. Line equal amounts of scallops across middle of rice. Top with a layer of avocado. Follow rolling procedure on page 311 and cut each roll into 6 equal slices. Makes 12 slices.

Variation: Scallop, Calamari and Avocado Sushi Roll

Arrange a layer of cooked calamari on top of avocado.

Prosciutto and Cantaloupe Roll

Prosciutto is the ham of choice to use. If you can't find it, look for a good dry, cured local ham for this roll.

2 sheets sushi nori
1 cup cooked sushi rice, page 314
6 very thin slices prosciutto
½ cup thinly sliced cantaloupe

Heat nori. Working with one sheet of nori at a time, with shiny side facing down and with long side facing you, spread ½ cup rice in an even layer on each sheet, leaving a ½-inch border on long sides. Line each roll with equal amounts of prosciutto, 3 slices, across rice. Lay a layer of cantaloupe slices across middle of rice. Follow rolling procedure on page 311 and cut each roll into 6 equal slices. Makes 12 slices.

A Very "Ducky" Roll

Pick up some barbecued duck from a Chinese market or from the deli counter at a specialty foods store.

2 sheets sushi nori
1 cup cooked sushi rice, page 314
1 cup chopped Chinese barbecue duck
12 basil leaves

Heat nori. Working with one sheet of nori at a time, shiny side facing down and long side facing you, spread ½ cup of the rice in an even layer on each nori sheet, leaving a ½-inch border on long sides. Arrange duck in a line across middle of rice. Top with basil leaves. Follow rolling procedure on page 311 and cut into 6 even slices. Makes 12 slices.

Japanese Eggplant Sushi

This roll has a smooth and rich filling. Eggplant and nori are perfect partners.

1 small Japanese eggplant
salt to taste
1 tbs. canola oil
2 sheets sushi nori
1 cup cooked sushi rice, page 314

Cut eggplant into ½-inch strips. Place in colander and sprinkle with salt. Let stand for 15 minutes. In a small skillet over medium heat, heat oil and cook eggplant strips for 20 minutes, or until completely cooked. Remove from heat and cool. Heat nori. Working with one sheet of nori at a time, with shiny side facing down and with long side facing you, spread ½ cup of the rice in an even layer on each sheet, leaving a ½-inch border on long sides. Place equal amounts of eggplant in a line across middle of rice. Follow rolling procedure on page 311 and cut each roll into 6 equal slices. Makes 12 slices.

The Steak Roll

Thin grilled steak adds flavor to please the meat lover.

¼ lb. boneless sirloin steak, ½-inch thick, trimmed
salt and pepper to taste
2 sheets sushi nori
1 cup cooked sushi rice, page 314
2 green onions, ends trimmed

Prepare a very hot barbecue. Grill steak for 3 to 4 minutes on both sides until browned. Do not overcook; steak is very thin. Season with salt and pepper, let cool and slice into thin strips. Heat nori. Working with one sheet of nori at a time, with shiny side facing down and with long side facing you, spread ½ cup of the rice in an even layer on each sheet, leaving a ½-inch border on long sides. Place equal amounts of steak slices in a line across middle of rice. Top each with a green onion. Follow rolling procedure on page 311 and cut each roll into 6 equal slices. Makes 12 slices.

The Green Roll

Sneak your daily serving of leafy greens into a roll!

½ bunch collard greens or any other dark, green leafy vegetable
2 tbs. olive oil
1 clove garlic, minced
salt and pepper to taste
2 sheets sushi nori
1 cup cooked sushi rice, page 314
black sesame seeds for garnish

In a medium skillet over medium heat, sauté greens and garlic in oil for about 5 minutes, or until bright, but tender. Drain greens well on a layer of paper towels. Season with salt and pepper. Heat nori. Working with one sheet of nori at a time, with shiny side facing down and with long side facing you, spread ½ cup of the rice in a layer on each sheet, leaving a ½-inch border on long sides. Place equal amounts of greens in center of each roll, follow rolling procedure on page 311 and cut roll into 6 equal slices. Sprinkle with black sesame seeds. Makes 12 slices.

Spring Roll

This filling was inspired by Thai rice paper rolls. A cucumber salad or a Thai peanut sauce are perfect accompaniments.

2 sheets sushi nori
1 cup cooked sushi rice, page 314
½ cup snow peas
½ cup shredded carrot
½ cup enoki mushrooms
¼ cup fresh mint leaves
¼ cup fresh Thai basil leaves
¼ cup chili sauce

Heat nori. Working with one sheet of nori at a time, with shiny side facing down and long side facing you, spread ½ cup of the rice in an even layer on each nori sheet, leaving a ½-inch border on long sides. Place equal amounts of snow peas in a line across middle of rice. Add a layer of carrot, mushrooms, mint and basil. Spread 2 tbs. chili sauce on each roll. Follow rolling method on page 311 and cut into 6 equal slices. Makes 12 slices.

Blackened Catfish Roll

A lot of Cajun flavor is packed into this catfish roll for real punch.

2 tbs. butter
¼ lb. freshwater catfish fillet
cayenne pepper to taste
2 sheets sushi nori
1 cup cooked sushi rice, page 314
½ cup red beans

In a small skillet over medium-high heat, melt butter. Add catfish, sprinkle generously with cayenne and cook for 2 to 3 minutes on each side until blackened. Remove from skillet and cool; break into bite-sized pieces. Heat nori. Working with one sheet of nori at a time, with shiny side facing down and with long side facing you, spread ½ cup of the rice in a layer on each sheet, leaving a ½-inch border on long sides. Arrange equal amounts of catfish pieces in a line across middle of rice. Top with a layer of red beans. Follow rolling procedure on page 311 and cut each roll into 6 equal slices. Makes 12 slices.

Tomato and Cucumber Roll

This refreshing roll makes a great palate cleanser.

1 tomato, seeded, diced and strained
½ cup peeled, seeded, diced cucumber
1 tbs. rice wine vinegar
2 tbs. chopped fresh flat-leaf parsley
2 tsp. sugar
salt and pepper to taste
2 sheets sushi nori
1 cup cooked sushi rice, page 314

In a bowl, combine tomato and cucumber with vinegar, parsley, sugar, salt and pepper; mix well. Cover and chill. Heat nori. Working with one sheet of nori at a time, with shiny side facing down and with long side facing you, spread ½ cup of the rice in a layer on each sheet, leaving a ½-inch border on long sides. Place equal amounts of tomato mixture in a line across middle of each roll. Follow rolling procedure on page 311 and cut each roll into 6 equal slices. Makes 12 slices.

Trout Amandine Roll

A classic preparation that defined the cosmopolitan dining era of the late 1960s is resurrected and takes on a new look here. It's often misspelled "almondine."

¼ cup butter
¼ lb. trout fillet
2 tbs. sweet vermouth
salt and pepper to taste
½ cup sliced almonds, toasted
2 sheets sushi nori
1 cup cooked sushi rice, page 314

In a small skillet over medium-high heat, melt butter. Add fillet to skillet, pour in vermouth and cook for 2 to 3 minutes on each side, or until lightly browned. Season with salt and pepper. Remove from skillet, let cool and break into pieces. Heat nori. Working with one sheet of nori at a time, with shiny side facing down and with long side facing you, spread ½ cup of the rice in an even layer on each sheet, leaving a ½-inch border on long sides. Place trout in a line across middle of rice. Top with almonds. Follow rolling procedure on page 311 and cut each roll into 6 equal slices. Makes 12 slices.

Bacon, Lettuce and Tomato Roll

All of the lunchbox sandwich elements are present and accounted for, except for the bread. The sushi rice provides the perfect holder for this addicting combination.

2 sheets sushi nori
1 cup cooked sushi rice, page 314
1/4 cup mayonnaise
4 slices cooked bacon
2 large iceberg lettuce leaves
1 Roma tomato, thinly sliced

Heat nori. Working with one sheet of nori at a time, with shiny side facing down and with long side facing you, spread 1/2 cup of the rice in a layer on each sheet, leaving a 1/2-inch border on long sides. Spread each sheet with a layer of mayonnaise. Top with a layer of lettuce. Place equal amounts of bacon, 2 slices per sheet, across middle of rice and top with a layer of tomato. Follow rolling procedure on page 311 and cut each roll into 6 equal slices. Makes 12 slices.

Grilled Fig Roll

The intense fig flavors are captured. This can be served as an appetizer or a dessert.

6 small fresh mission figs, sliced
2 tbs. port
2 tbs. sugar
2 sheets sushi nori
1 cup cooked sushi rice, page 314

Heat broiler. Place figs on a baking sheet, flesh side up. Brush figs with port and sprinkle with sugar. Broil for 2 to 3 minutes, or until figs are golden. Remove from oven and let cool. Heat nori. Working with one sheet of nori at a time, with shiny side facing down and with long side facing you, spread 1/2 cup of the rice in a layer on each sheet, leaving a 1/2-inch border on long sides. Place equal amounts of fig slices in a line across middle of rice. Follow rolling procedure on page 311 and cut each roll into 6 equal slices. Makes 12 slices.

Nectarine Roll

For this roll, use nectarines that are firm. Overly ripe fruit makes the roll difficult to handle.

2 sheets sushi nori
1 cup cooked sushi rice, page 314
2 small nectarines, pitted and thinly sliced
½ cup torn arugula leaves

Heat nori. Working with one sheet of nori at a time, with shiny side facing down and with long side facing you, spread ½ cup of the rice in a layer on each sheet, leaving a ½-inch border on long sides. Place equal amounts of nectarine slices in a line across middle of rice. Top with arugula leaves. Follow rolling procedure on page 311 and cut each roll into 6 equal slices. Makes 12 slices.

Apricot and Almond Roll

If you don't have Sauternes in the pantry, sherry or port will do.

6 small apricots, pitted, peeled and sliced
2 tbs. Sauternes or other sweet dessert wine
2 tbs. sugar
¼ cup sliced almonds, toasted
2 sheets sushi nori
1 cup cooked sushi rice, page 314

Heat broiler. Place apricots on a baking sheet. Brush with Sauternes and sprinkle with sugar. Broil for 1 to 2 minutes, or until sugar dissolves. Remove from oven and let cool. Heat nori. Working with one sheet of nori at a time, with shiny side facing down and with long side facing you, spread ½ cup of the rice in a layer on each sheet, leaving a ½-inch border on long sides. Place equal amounts of apricots in a line across middle of rice. Top with sliced almonds. Follow rolling procedure on page 311 and cut each roll into 6 equal slices. Makes 12 slices.

The Peanut Butter and Jelly Roll

This one is for the PB and J devotees. Who says you need bread when you've got sushi rice?

2 sheets sushi nori
1 cup cooked sushi rice, page 314
½ cup chunky peanut butter
¼ cup raspberry jam

Heat nori. Working with one sheet of nori at a time, with shiny side facing down and long side facing you, spread ½ cup of the rice in an even layer on each sheet, leaving a ½-inch border on long sides. Spread equal amounts of peanut butter across middle of rice. Wet knife and spread a layer of jam on top of peanut butter. Follow rolling method on page 311 and cut into 6 equal slices. Makes 12 slices.

Variation: Peanut Butter-Banana Roll

Spread layer of peanut butter across rice. Layer with banana slices.

Nutella Roll

Nutella, the chocolate and hazelnut spread, has become increasingly common in the United States. It is often found next to the peanut butter in your supermarket. You may have a little trouble keeping the filling intact, but this roll will disappear so quickly that its appearance will hardly be noticed.

2 sheets sushi nori
1 cup cooked sushi rice, page 314
½ cup Nutella

Heat nori. Working with one sheet of nori at a time, with shiny side facing down and with long side facing you, spread ½ cup of the rice in a layer on each sheet, leaving a ½-inch border on long sides. Spread equal amounts of Nutella in a line across middle of rice. Follow rolling procedure on page 311 and cut each roll into 6 equal slices. Makes 2 slices.

Index

A

Aioli 155, 186
Alfredo bruschetta 302
Almond(s)
    cherry cheese spread 76
    oven-roasted 92
    sauce 156
    sherry sauce 150
Anchovy
    bagna cauda 108
    butter rounds 9
    dip, hot 246
    and fresh pear toasts 95
    olive and goat cheese bruschetta
      303
    sauce 189
    and sun-dried tomato sushi 324
Antipasti, eggplant 46
Antipasto, giardineria 56
Appetizer
    guidelines 2
    pantry 3
    preparing 4
    storage 5
Apple tomatillo salsa 257
Apple walnut and blue cheese
    balls 96
Apricot
    and almond roll 335
    chutney dip 234
    salsa 275
Artichoke(s)
    chicken and oven-dried
      tomatoes 138
    dip, hot 237
    and feta bruschetta 290
    Grecian 551
    marinated 106
    Parmesan dip 74

    salsa 254
Arugula and tomato bruschetta 288
Asparagus
    baked fondue 203
    and ham rolls 107
    mayo dip 233
    mayonnaise 51
Au creme fondue 212
Avocado
    crab dip 228
    and crab molded spread 72
    creamy veggie dip 67
    dip 224
    -green onion bruschetta 296
    guacamole 68, 222
    olive spread 70
    sauce 189
    and salsa bruschetta, spicy 295
    and scallop sushi roll 329
    and tomato salsa 259
    and watermelon salsa 264

B

Baba ghanoush 61
Bacon
    and green onion-stuffed
      mussels 132
    grilled with shrimp 136
    lettuce and tomato roll 334
    scallops with bearnaise 11
    -stuffed cherry tomatoes 25
    sweet and sour pupus 44
Bagna cauda 68
Banderilla
    93
    fresh fig and prosciutto 94
    sherried chicken liver 94
Barbecue sauce, easy 189

Bean
　　black, and corn salsa 258
　　black, and orange salsa 272
　　cheesy dip 243
　　dip, spicy 173
　　edamame and crab roll 320
　　fava, salad cups 111
　　garbanzo salad 107
　　garbanzo salsa 255
　　hummus dip 221
　　jalapeño dip 241
　　lentil and duck salad 144
　　and pork dip 242
　　southwestern bruschetta 298
　　and sun-dried tomato dip 229
Bearnaise sauce, blender 192
Beef
　　anticuchos 145
　　Italian-style meatballs 45
　　mixed grill fondue 182
　　mizutaki 187
　　paté with asparagus mayonnaise 51
　　piroshki 53
　　and potato empanadas 146
　　roast, rolls 147
　　steak roll 331
　　sweet and sour meatballs 28
　　taco snacks 45
Beer in baked fondue 198
Berry
　　dip, creamy 236
　　good bruschetta 307
　　three, salsa 264
Beverages
　　limonada or sangra blanca 164
　　margaritas 165-166
　　sangria 163
　　sherry shrub 164
Black-eyed Susans 35
Blue cheesecake 20

Bread, quick
　　date bread with pineapple cream
　　　cheese 16
　　pumpkin tea sandwiches 17
Bread, yeast
　　red onion foccacia 31
　　sausage in brioche 27
　　taco snacks 45
Brie
　　in aspic 15
　　holiday 8
　　in puff pastry 8
　　with savory stuffing, festive 15
　　wafers 32
Broccoli and carrots, dilled 62
Broccoli, marinated 57
Broth, hot fondue, about 181
Bruschetta
　　Alfredo 302
　　anchovy, olive and goat cheese
　　　303
　　artichoke and feta 290
　　avocado-green onion bruschetta
　　　296
　　basic 282
　　berry good 307
　　breads 281
　　broiled fruit 307
　　caviar 305
　　chicken liver 301
　　chicken liver paté 301
　　chicken with pineapple-ginger
　　　chutney 299
　　chopped herring 305
　　curried olive and cheese 296
　　defined 280
　　eggplant and turkey 299
　　eggplant-onion bruschetta with
　　　feta 294
　　fresh tomato 283
　　goat cheese and black olive 291
　　goat cheese and roasted pepper
　　　293

Bruschetta, continued
  Greek breakfast 306
  Greek-style tomato 287
  grilled shrimp and mango salsa
    304
  grilled vegetable 295
  meatball with chutney 300
  mixed fresh fruit 306
  mixed seafood 304
  pesto and mozzarella 290
  Provençal with goat cheese 292
  ricotta-mushroom-anchovy 291
  roasted garlic salsa 297
  roasted shallot salsa 297
  smoked salmon 303
  southwestern bean 298
  spicy avocado and salsa 295
  stewed tomato 282
  stir-fried chicken 300
  stir-fry vegetable 294
  strawberry-cinnamon 308
  sun-dried tomato 285
  sweet and sour meatball 302
  toasting bread 281
  tomato and arugula 288
  tomato, basil and cheese 284
  tomato and cheese pizza 289
  tomato, dijon-style 288
  tomato-eggplant bruschetta 284
  tomato, feta and mushroom
    bruschetta 286
  tomato, olive and basil 285
  tomatoes and portobello
    mushroom 286
  tomato and wine 287
  Tuscan tomato-cheese 283
  with red pesto sauce 292
Butterscotch fondue 214

C

Calamari cocktail 125
Calamari, fried 123

California roll 316
Canapes 90-91
Cantaloupe lime salsa 269
Cantaloupe and prosciutto roll 329
Caponata (eggplant antipasti) 46
Caramel dipping sauce 248
Caramelized nuts 29
Carrot (s)
  and broccoli, dilled 62
  and chicken with orange sherry
    sauce 140
  and sweet potato dip 61, 230
Catfish, blackened, roll 332
Catsup. spicy 190
Cauliflower, marinated 105
Caviar
  bruschetta 305
  eggplant 60, 231
  potatoes, French 47
Celery, chutney-stuffed 63
Celery, cream of, rarebit 207
Chablis fondue for two 172
Cheddar
  beer fondue, baked 198
  cheese fondue 178
  cheese fondue with apple 215
  cheese seafood dip 240
Cheese
  artichoke Parmesan dip 74
  blue, and apple and walnut 96
  blue cheesecake 20
  Brie in aspic 15
  Brie in puff pastry 8
  Brie wafers 32
  cheddar, baked fondue 196
  cheddar beer baked fondue 198
  cheddar, fondue 178
  cheddar, fondue with apple 215
  cheesy bean dip 243
  cheesy crab toast 9
  cherry almond spread 76
  chili con queso 175, 242
  and chutney spread 71

Cheese, continued
   and corn baked fondue 203
   cottage, clam dip 227
   cream, lattice mold 22
   cream, pimiento dip 224
   cream, pineapple spread 16
   creamy stuffed dates 65
   cucumbers with herbed cream
     cheese 25
   and curried olive bruschetta 296
   easy baked fondue 195
   festive Brie with savory stuffing 15
   feta, and artichoke bruschetta 290
   feta, tomato and mushroom
     bruschetta 286
   gelatin spread 72
   goat, anchovy and olive
     bruschetta 303
   goat, and black olive bruschetta
     291
   goat, corn and basil roll 325
   goat, on Provençal bruschetta 292
   goat, and roasted pepper
     bruschetta 293
   grilled Swiss chard and cheese
     packages 99
   and ham ball, crunchy 73
   holiday Brie 8
   hot goat cheese toasts 97
   hot pepper fondue 179
   hot pimiento dip 243
   marinated goat cheese rounds 97
   marinated manchego 102
   mixed, dip 230
   molded herbed 21
   mozzarella and pesto bruschetta
     290
   pecan dip 226
   pesto Parmesan swirls 12
   portobello and goat cheese
     quesadilla 103
   puffs, Greek 49
   quesadilla ideas 104

   quesadillas 13
   ricotta, mushroom-anchovy
     bruschetta 291
   Roquefort mousse 21
   seafood cheddar dip 240
   squares, fried 54
   straws 30
   terrine with pesto and sun-dried
     tomatoes 20
   three, and walnuts in phyllo 30
   three, dip 223
   tomato and basil bruschetta 284
   tomato bruschetta, Tuscan 283
   and tomato pizza bruschetta 289
Cherry
   almond cheese spread 76
   Bing, salsa 277
   savory dipping sauce 245
Chicken
   artichoke and oven-dried
     tomatoes 138
   baked fondue 201
   breast chunks, velvet 139
   breasts, stuffed with goat cheese,
     eggplant and tomato 141
   bruschetta with pineapple-
     ginger chutney 299
   and carrots with orange sherry
     sauce 140
   empanadas 42
   liver bruschetta 301
   liver paté bruschetta 301
   liver, sherried, banderilla 94
   liver, simple paté 75
   mixed grill fondue 182
   mizutaki 188
   nuggets, wine and garlic 142
   poultry fondue 183
   and rainbow peppers quesadillas
     104
   relish swirls 23
   and rice-stuffed tomatoes 142
   sesame walnut strips 52

Chicken, continued
    skewers teriyaki 48
    stir-fried bruschetta 300
    and vegetable won tons, baked 64
    wings, barbecued 26
    wings, honey 27
    wings, sherried 143
    wings, teriyaki 12
Chile con queso 175, 242
Chives with fondue 176
Chocolate
    fondue au chocolat 213
    hot fudge dipping sauce 247
    rum fondue 214
Chorizo-stuffed mushroom caps 148
Chutney
    and cheese spread 71
    with meatball bruschetta 300
    and shrimp dip 228
    sour cream sauce 192
    -stuffed celery 63
Cider fondue 178
Citrus dipping sauce 187
Clam(s)
    baked 65
    cottage dip 227
    dip 69
    dip, creamy 174
    dip, hot 238
    steamed 124
    stuffed with spinach 125
Cod, salt
    basic preparation 126
    garlicky, topped potato slices 127
    and potato cakes 126
Continental fondue 171
Corn
    and black bean salsa 258
    and cheese baked fondue 203
    goat cheese and basil roll 325
    and mango salsa 273
    roasted, and red pepper salsa 257

Crab
    avocado dip 228
    and avocado molded spread 72
    baked fondue 199
    California roll 316
    dip 220
    dip, creamy hot 239
    dip, hot 238
    and edamame bean roll 320
    fondue 69
    mixed seafood bruschetta 304
    paté 73
    in phyllo 37
    rolls, crispy 38
    spread 74
    stuffed mushrooms 6
    toast, cheesy 9
    turnovers 38
Cranberry salsa 268
Crostini olive spread 46
Cucumber(s)
    dip, low-fat 63
    English, roll 316
    with herbed cream cheese 25
    melon and mint salsa 268
    mint coolers 24
    and smoked salmon tartlets 133
    and tomato roll 333
Curry mayonnaise 191
Curry veggie dip 226

D

Date(s)
    black-eyed Susans 35
    bread with pineapple cream
      cheese 16
    creamy stuffed 65
    and pineapple salsa 266
    walnut wafers, sweet and hot 35
De Berne fondue 174
Dill dip 223

Dips
    apricot chutney 234
    artichoke Parmesan 74
    asparagus mayo 233
    avocado 224
    avocado crab 228
    bagna caoda 108, 185
    cheesy bean 243
    chile con queso 175, 242
    chili 244
    chutney and shrimp 228
    clam 69
    cottage clam 227
    crab 220
    creamy avocado veggie 67
    creamy berry 236
    creamy clam 174
    creamy hamburger 241
    creamy hot crab 239
    creamy pecan 234
    creamy spinach 176
    creamy tuna 245
    curry veggie 226
    deviled ham 227
    dill 223
    eggplant caviar 231
    fruit custard 235
    garnishes 218
    ginger sesame 229
    guacamole 68, 222
    hints for planning, preparing
      and serving 219
    hot anchovy 246
    hot artichoke 237
    hot clam 238
    hot crab 238
    hot nachos 237
    hot pimiento cheese 243
    hummus 221
    jalapeño bean 241
    jelly fruit 247
    low-fat cucumber 63
    mango chutney 221
    mixed cheese 230
    natural containers for 217
    olive appetizer 225
    pecan cheese 226
    pimiento cream cheese 224
    pineapple-orange yogurt 235
    pork and bean 242
    roasted red pepper 229
    salmon 222
    salsa 62, 233
    savory, ideas for dippers 217
    seafood cheddar 240
    south of the border 239
    spicy bean 173
    spinach 232
    sun-dried tomato and bean 229
    sweet, ideas for dippers 218
    sweet potato and carrot 61, 230
    tapenade (olive dip) 232
    taramasalata 55
    Tex-Mex 220
    three cheese 223
    veggie 225
    ways to reduce fat in 218
Duck and lentil salad 144
Duck, a very "ducky" sushi roll 330

E

Eastern-style rarebit 208
Eel roll 319
Egg(s)
    classic tortilla espanola 101
    deviled with capers 100
    deviled with olives 100
    fondue 173
    fondue avec oeufs 180
    marbleized tea 18
    McSushi roll 317
    mini-tortillas 102
    miniature shrimp quiches 37
    and sardine empanadas 133
    and spinach empanada 121

Eggs, continued
    and tuna tartlets 137
Eggplant
    antipasti (caponata) 46
    baba ghanoush 61
    caviar 60, 231
    goat cheese and tomato-stuffed
        chicken breasts 141
    Japanese, sushi 330
    -onion bruschetta with feta 294
    sherry-glazed 110
    -tomato bruschetta 284
    and tomato tartlets 109
    and turkey bruschetta 299
Empanada(s)
    beef and potato 146
    chicken 42
    mushroom 112
    pastry, basic 159
    pastry, easy 160
    sardine and egg 133
    spinach and egg 121
    veal, raisin and pine nut 154
English cucumber roll 316
English dessert sauce 249
Escabeche 129

F

Fava bean salad cups 111
Feta and artichoke bruschetta 290
Fig(s)
    fresh, and prosciutto banderilla 94
    and prosciutto roll 327
    roll, grilled 334
    and salmon roll 327
    and sausage in orange sherry
        sauce 153
Fish
    anchovies in bagna caoda 185
    anchovy butter rounds 9
    anchovy, olive and goat cheese
        bruschetta 303
    anchovy and sun-dried tomato
        sushi 324
    bagna cauda 68, 108
    baked la fondue hestere 200
    baked tuna fondue 197
    basic salt cod preparation 126
    calamari cocktail 125
    catfish, blackened, roll 332
    caviar bruschetta 305
    chopped herring bruschetta 305
    creamy tuna dip 245
    eel roll 319
    escabeche 129
    French caviar potatoes 47
    fried calamari 123
    garlicky salt cod-topped potato
        slices 127
    in sushi 310
    midtown roll 321
    monkfish in tomato almond sauce
        128
    Northern Italian tuna roll 328
    poached salmon sushi 319
    salmon dip 222
    salmon log 23
    salmon mousse 64
    salmon sushi 318
    salt cod and potato cakes 126
    sardine and egg empanadas 133
    sardines and pepper spread 10
    seafood fondue 186
    seafood salad 130
    smoked salmon bruschetta 303
    smoked salmon and cucumber
        tartlets 133
    smoked salmon and fig roll 327
    smoked salmon and mango roll 328
    smoked salmon rolls 13
    smoked salmon treats 24
    smoked trout in endive leaves 136
    spicy tuna roll 317
    taramasalata 55
    Tobiko roll 320

Fish, continued
    trout amandine roll 333
    tuna and egg tartlets 137
    tuna rarebit 211
    tuna roll 328
Foccacia, red onion 31
Fondue
    avec oeufs 180
    bourguignonne, classic 182
    Chablis for two 172
    cider 178
    classic 169
    classic in a microwave 170
    classic variations 169
    continental 171
    crab 69
    de Berne 174
    egg 173
    entertain with 168
    equipment 168
    Greek shrimp 179
    hot pepper cheese 179
    jeune fille 175
    lamb 183
    low calorie 188
    Marseillaise 180
    mixed grill 182
    pesto 172
    pizza 170
    pork or ham 184
    poultry 183
    seafood 186
    simple Simon 177
    Sonoma 171
    types 168
    with chives 176
Fondue, baked
    asparagus 203
    with beer 198
    cheddar beer 198
    cheddar cheese 196
    chicken 201
    corn and cheese 203
    crabmeat 199
    easy cheese 195
    hestere 200
    leek 204
    Maria 196
    New Orleans 200
    Parisian 199
    petite 197
    rice 202
    sausage 202
    spinach 204
    tuna 197
    turkey 201
Fondue, dessert
    butterscotch 214
    cheddar cheese with apple 215
    chocolate rum 214
    dippers 212
    fondue au chocolat 213
    fondue au creme 212
    peanut butter 213
    vanilla 214
Fonduta 176
Frankfurter rarebit 210
French quiche tartlets 54
Fruit
    apple tomatillo salsa 257
    apricot and almond roll 335
    apricot salsa 275
    berry good bruschetta 307
    Bing cherry salsa 277
    broiled, bruschetta 307
    cantaloupe lime salsa 269
    cranberry salsa 278
    custard dip 235
    dip, jelly 247
    grape salsa 267
    grapefruit salsa 271
    grilled fig roll 334
    kabobs 66
    kiwi salsa 277
    mango and corn salsa 273

Fruit, continued
  mango and sun-dried tomato
    salsa 271
  mango and tangerine salsa 272
  melon, cucumber and mint salsa
    268
  mixed fresh, bruschetta 306
  mixed, salsa 265
  mixed, salsa with ginger 273
  nectarine roll 335
  orange and black bean salsa 272
  orange ginger salsa 265
  papaya and watermelon salsa 268
  peach and ginger salsa 267
  peach salsa 275
  pear salsa 278
  pepper and papaya salsa 276
  pineapple and date salsa 266
  pineapple and mango salsa 269
  pineapple and papaya salsa 276
  pineapple salsa 274
  raspberry salsa 274
  Santa Monica roll 323
  spiced melon balls 14
  spicy tropical salsa 270
  strawberry-cinnamon bruschetta
    308
  stuffed strawberries 14
  summer salsa 266
  tangerine salsa 270
  three berry salsa 264
  watermelon and avocado salsa
    264
Fudge dipping sauce, hot 247

G
Garbanzo bean salad 107
Garbanzo salsa 255
Garlic
  roasted, salsa 260
  roasted, salsa bruschetta 297
  shrimp, hot 135

  and wine chicken nuggets 142
Gelatin cheese spread 72
Ginger dipping sauce 187
Ginger sesame dip 229
Goat cheese
  and anchovy bruschetta 303
  and black olive bruschetta 291
  corn and basil roll 325
  eggplant and tomato-stuffed
    chicken breasts 141
  hot toasts 97
  and portobello quesadilla 103
  on Provençal bruschetta 292
  and roasted pepper bruschetta
    293
  rounds, marinated 97
Grape leaves, stuffed 59
Grape salsa 267
Grapefruit salsa 271
Greek
  artichokes 55
  breakfast bruschetta 306
  cheese puffs 49
  shrimp fondue 179
  -style tomato bruschetta 287
Green roll 331
Guacamole 68, 222

H
Ham
  and asparagus rolls 107
  and cheese ball, crunchy 73
  deviled, dip 227
  piquant sauce for 192
  or pork fondue 184
Hamburger dip, creamy 241
Hawaiian mushrooms 44
Herb, fresh, salsa 256
Herbed mushrooms 57
Herring, chopped, bruschetta 305
Hestere baked fondue 200
Hoisin spareribs 49

Honey chicken wings 27
Honey lamb puffs 40
Horseradish
    dipping sauce 187
    salsa 255
    sour cream sauce 190
Hummus dip 221

I

Island shrimp sushi roll 324
Italian dipping sauce, hearty 246
Italian, Northern, tuna roll 328

J

Jalapeño bean dip 241
Japanese eggplant sushi 330
Jelly fruit dip 247
Jelly and peanut butter roll 336
Jeune fille fondue 175
Jicama salsa 262

K

Kiwi salsa 277

L

Lamb
    fondue 183
    meatballs with tomato sauce
      149
    puffs, honey 40
    tangy mint sauce for 193
Leek baked fondue 204
Leek and potato salad, warm 118
Lemon dessert dipping sauce 248
Lemon scallops 134
Lentil and duck salad 144
Lettuce bacon and tomato roll 334
Lime cantaloupe salsa 269
Limonada 164
London rarebit 205

Low calorie fondue 188
Low-fat cucumber dip 63

M

Manchego cheese, marinated 102
Mango
    chutney dip 221
    chutney mold 19
    and corn salsa 273
    and pineapple salsa 269
    salsa and grilled shrimp
      bruschetta 304
    sauce, hot 244
    and smoked salmon roll 328
    spread 17
    and sun-dried tomato salsa 271
    and tangerine salsa 272
Marbleized tea eggs 18
Margaritas 165-166
Mayonnaise
    asparagus 51
    brandied 48
    curry 191
    red pepper 157
Meatball(s)
    in almond sherry sauce 150
    bruschetta with chutney 300
    Italian-style 45
    lamb, with tomato sauce 149
    sweet and sour 28
    sweet and sour bruschetta 302
    turkey 28
Melon balls, spiced 14
Melon, cucumber and mint salsa
    268
Middle Eastern delights 47
Monkfish in tomato almond sauce
    128
Moroccan roll 327
Mozzarella and pesto bruschetta
    290

Mushroom(s)
    caps, chorizo-stuffed 148
    crab-stuffed 6
    empanadas 112
    and goat cheese quesadilla 103
    Hawaiian 44
    herbed 57
    marinated 113
    Middle Eastern delights 47
    pesto 6
    portobello roll 318
    portobello and tomato
        bruschetta 286
    ricotta-anchovy bruschetta 291
    roll 318
    sautéed portobello 113
    spinach-stuffed 58
    strudel tarts 34
    tomato and feta bruschetta 286
Mussel(s)
    bacon and green onion-stuffed
        132
    basic steamed 131
    pesto-topped 133
    shoals sushi roll 326
    steamed, with parsley sauce 131
    stuffed with garlic and bread-
        crumbs 132
Mustard sour cream sauce 191

N

Nachos dip, hot 237
Nectarine roll 335
New Orleans baked fondue 200
Nutella roll 336
Nuts, caramelized 29

O

Oil, hot fondue, about 181
Olive
    anchovy and goat cheese
        bruschetta 303
    appetizer dip 225
    avocado spread 70
    balls, baked 98
    black, and goat cheese
        bruschetta 291
    black, and oranges with scallops
        134
    curried, and cheese bruschetta
        296
    dip (tapenade) 232
    marinated 50
    paté 111
    and prune compote 152
    puffs 34
    spread 70
    swirls 33
    tomato and basil bruschetta 285
    warm marinated 95
Onion(s)
    -eggplant bruschetta with feta
        294
    green, and avocado bruschetta
        296
    marinated blue 7
    red, foccacia 31
    sweet, salsa 258
    sweet and sour 110
Orange
    and black bean salsa 272
    and black olives with scallops 134
    butter 17
    ginger salsa 265
    -pineapple yogurt dip 235
    sherry sauce with chicken and
        carrots 140
    sherry sauce with sausages and
        figs 153

Oriental shrimp toast 50
Oyster, seared, roll 326

P

Papaya and pineapple salsa 276
Papaya and watermelon salsa 268
Parisian baked fondue 199
Parmesan artichoke dip 74
Parsley sauce 156
Pasta, shrimp- and vegetable-filled
    shells 19
Pastry
    baked olive balls 98
    basic empanada 159
    basic tartlet 161
    black-eyed Susans 35
    Brie wafers 32
    cheese straws 30
    easy empanada 160
    olive puffs 34
    olive swirls 33
    piroshki 53
    shrimp puffs 36
    sweet and hot date walnut
        wafers 35
Paté
    with asparagus mayonnaise 51
    chicken liver, bruschetta 301
    crab 73
    olive 111
    simple liver 75
Peach and ginger salsa 267
Peach salsa 275
Peanut butter fondue 213
Peanut butter and jelly roll 336
Peanut sauce, island 190
Pear, fresh, and anchovy toasts 95
Pear salsa 278
Pecan cheese dip 226
Pecan dip, creamy 234
Peperonata 58

Pepper(s)
    and papaya salsa 276
    rainbow 114
    rainbow, and chicken quesadillas
        104
    red, mayonnaise 157
    red, and roasted corn salsa 257
    red, roasted, dip 229
    roasted, and goat cheese
        bruschetta 293
    strips, roasted 114
    three, spread 71
    with tomato and potato stuffing
        115
Pesto
    fondue 172
    and mozzarella bruschetta 290
    mushrooms 6
    Parmesan swirls 12
    sauce 172
    sauce, red bruschetta 292
    -topped mussels 133
Phyllo
    crab in 37
    crispy crab rolls 38
    Greek cheese puffs 49
    Middle Eastern delights 47
    mushroom strudel tarts 34
    spanakopitas 32
    spinach and walnut triangles 33
    with three cheeses and walnuts 30
Pico de gallo 261
Pico de gallo with Mexican beer 263
Pimiento cheese dip, hot 243
Pimiento cream cheese dip 224
Pineapple
    and date salsa 266
    -ginger chutney with chicken
        bruschetta 299
    and mango salsa 269
    -orange yogurt dip 235
    and papaya salsa 276
    salsa 274

Pineapple, continued
    and shrimp roll 322
Piquant sauce for ham 192
Pizza fondue 170
Pizzettes with vegetable toppings 122
Plantain and shrimp roll 322
Plum sauce 41
Pork
    in almond sherry sauce 150
    and bean dip 242
    chorizo-stuffed mushroom caps 148
    chunks, savory 152
    or ham fondue 184
    hoisin spareribs 49
    mixed grill fondue 182
    oven-roasted baby back ribs 151
    paté with asparagus mayonnaise
        51
    pot stickers 43
    satay with plum sauce 41
    swirls, puff pastry 39
    tenderloins, roasted 147
Portobello
    and goat cheese quesadilla 103
    mushrooms, sautéed 113
    roll 318
Pot stickers 43
Potato(es)
    and beef empanadas 146
    French caviar 47
    and leek salad, warm 118
    mini-stuffed 116
    oven-roasted baby with garlic 117
    and salt cod cakes 126
    slices, crisp 116
    slices topped with garlicky salt
        cod 127
    and tomato stuffing in peppers
        115
    wedges, spicy baked 117
Prosciutto
    and cantaloupe roll 329

and fig roll 327
and fresh fig banderilla 94
Prune and olive compote 152
Puff pastry
    Brie in 8
    crab turnovers 38
    honey lamb puffs 40
    pork swirls 39
    sausage roll 39
Pumpkin tea sandwiches 17

Q

Quesadilla(s)
    13
    chicken and rainbow peppers 104
    ideas 104
    portobello and goat cheese 103
Quiche, miniature shrimp 37
Quiche tartlets, French 54

R

Rarebit
    cream of celery 207
    Eastern-style 208
    frankfurter 210
    London 205
    quick Welsh 205
    red and green 209
    rosy 207
    sherry 206
    shrimp 210
    Spanish 206
    spicy 209
    tuna 211
    Western 208
Raspberry liqueur cream, hot 249
Raspberry salsa 275
Red and green rarebit 209
Rice
    baked fondue 202
    and chicken-stuffed tomatoes 142

Rice, continued
    stuffed grape leaves 59
    sushi 314
 Ricotta-mushroom-anchovy
    bruschetta 291
Roast beef rolls 147
Romesco sauce 157
Roquefort butter 191
Roquefort mousse 21
Rosy rarebit 207
Russian-style vegetable salad 119

S

Salad
    cups, fava bean 111
    garbanzo bean 107
    lentil and duck 144
    mixed grilled vegetable 120
    Russian-style vegetable 119
    seafood 130
    warm potato and leek 118
Salmon
    dip 222
    log 23
    midtown roll 321
    mousse 64
    poached sushi 319
    rolls, smoked 13
    smoked, bruschetta 303
    smoked, and cucumber tartlets 133
    smoked, and fig roll 327
    smoked, and mango roll 328
    smoked, treats 24
    sushi 318
Salsa
    62, 233
    apricot 276
    artichoke 254
    and avocado bruschetta, spicy 295
    Bing cherry 277
    cantaloupe lime 269
    corn and black bean 258

cranberry 278
cruda 261
favorite ways to enjoy 251
freezer 254
fresh herb 256
garbanzo 255
grape 267
grapefruit 271
horseradish 255
ingredients 252-253
jicama 262
kiwi 277
mango and corn 273
mango and sun-dried tomato 271
mango and tangerine 272
melon, cucumber and mint 268
mixed fruit 265
mixed fruit with ginger 273
orange and black bean 272
orange ginger 265
papaya and watermelon 268
peach 275
peach and ginger 267
pear 278
pepper and papaya 276
picante 262
pico de gallo 261
pico de gallo with Mexican beef
  263
pineapple 274
pineapple and date 266
pineapple and mango 269
pineapple and papaya 276
raspberry 274
roasted corn and red pepper 257
roasted garlic 260
roasted garlic bruschetta 297
roasted shallot bruschetta 297
roasted tomatillo 259
spicy tropical 270
summer 266
sweet onion 258
tangerine 270

Salsa, continued
 tequila 263
 three berry 264
 tomatillo apple 257
 tomato and avocado 259
 verde 260
 watermelon and avocado 264
 zucchini 256
Salt cod
 and potato cakes 126
 preparation, basic 126
 -topped potato slices, garlicky
  127
Salt, seasoned 92
Sandwiches, pumpkin tea 17
Sangra blanca 164
Sangria 163
Santa Monica roll 323
Sardine and egg empanadas 133
Sardines and pepper spread 10
Sauce
 aioli 155, 186
 almond 156
 almond sherry 150
 anchovy 189
 asparagus mayonnaise 51
 avocado 189
 blender bearnaise 192
 brandied mayonnaise 48
 caramel dipping 248
 citrus dipping 187
 curry mayonnaise 191
 easy barbecue 189
 English dessert 249
 ginger dipping 187
 hearty Italian dipping 246
 horseradish dipping 187
 hot fudge dipping 247
 hot mango 244
 hot raspberry liqueur cream 249
 island peanut 190
 lemon dessert dipping 248
 parsley 156

 pesto 172
 piquant, for ham 192
 plum 41
 red pepper mayonnaise 157
 romesco 157
 Roquefort butter 191
 savory cherry dipping 245
 seafood cocktail 158
 sherry vinegar and shallot 158
 sour cream chutney 192
 sour cream horseradish 190
 sour cream mustard 191
 spicy catsup 190
 spicy tomato 158
 strawberry ginger dipping 236
 sweet and sour 52, 194
 sweet and sour dipping 240
 tangy mint for lamb 193
 tartar 193
 teriyaki 193
 tomato 149
Sausage
 baked fondue 202
 in brioche 27
 chunks, sherry-glazed 153
 and figs in orange sherry sauce
  153
 roll 39
Scallop(s)
 and avocado sushi roll 329
 bacon, with bearnaise 11
 ginger roll 325
 lemon 134
 with oranges and black olives
  134
Seafood
 cheddar dip 240
 cocktail sauce 158
 fondue 186
Seasoned salt 92
Sesame chicken walnut strips 52
Shellfish: see specific kind

Sherry
    rarebit 206
    shrub 164
    vinegar and shallot sauce 158
Shrimp
    and chutney dip 228
    fondue, Greek 179
    grilled with bacon 136
    grilled, and mango salsa
      bruschetta 304
    grilled marinated prawns 10
    hot garlic 135
    a la plancha 135
    mixed seafood bruschetta 304
    and pineapple roll 322
    and plantain roll 322
    puffs 36
    quiches, miniature 37
    rarebit 210
    sushi roll, island 324
    tempura roll 315
    toast, Oriental 50
    and vegetable-filled pasta shells
      19
Simple Simon fondue 177
Skewers, teriyaki chicken 48
Sonoma fondue 171
Sour cream
    chutney sauce 192
    horseradish sauce 190
    mustard sauce 191
South of the border dip 239
Spanakopitas 32
Spanish rarebit 206
Spinach
    baked fondue 204
    dip 232
    dip, creamy 177
    and egg empanada 121
    spanakopitas 32
    stuffed in clams 125
    -stuffed mushrooms 58
    and walnut triangles 33

Spreads
    apple, walnut and blue cheese
      balls 96
    avocado olive 70
    blue cheesecake 20
    cheese terrine with pesto and
      sun-dried tomatoes 20
    cherry almond cheese 76
    chutney and cheese 71
    crab and avocado molded 72
    crabmeat 74
    crab paté 73
    crostini olive 46
    crunchy ham and cheese ball 73
    gelatin cheese 72
    lattice cream cheese mold 22
    mango 17
    mango chutney mold 19
    molded herbed cheese 21
    olive 70
    olive paté 111
    orange butter 17
    paté with asparagus mayonnaise
      51
    pineapple cream cheese 16
    Roquefort mousse 21
    salmon log 23
    salmon mousse 64
    sardines and pepper 10
    simple liver paté 75
    three pepper 71
Spring roll 332
Steak roll 331
Strawberries
    -cinnamon bruschetta 308
    ginger dipping sauce 236
    stuffed 14
Summer salsa 266
Sushi
    anchovy and sun-dried tomato
      324
    apricot and almond roll 335

Sushi, continued
  bacon, lettuce and tomato roll 334
  blackened catfish 332
  California roll 316
  crab and edamame bean roll 320
  defined 310
  eel roll 319
  eggs McSushi roll 317
  English cucumber roll 316
  equipment 311
  etiquette 313-314
  ginger scallop roll 325
  goat cheese, corn and basil roll 325
  green roll 331
  grilled fig roll 334
  ingredients 312
  inside-out roll 312
  island shrimp roll 324
  Japanese eggplant 330
  Japanese phrases 313
  midtown roll (New York roll) 321
  Moroccan roll 327
  mussel shoals roll 326
  nectarine roll 335
  Northern Italian tuna roll 328
  Nutella roll 336
  peanut butter and jelly roll 336
  plantain and shrimp roll 322
  poached salmon 319
  portobello roll 318
  prosciutto and cantaloupe roll 329
  prosciutto and fig roll 327
  rice 314
  rolling method 311
  salmon 318
  Santa Monica roll 323
  scallop and avocado roll 329
  seared oyster roll 326
  shrimp and pineapple roll 322
  shrimp tempura roll 315
  skill 310
  smoked salmon and fig roll 327
  smoked salmon and mango roll 328
  spicy tuna roll 317
  spring roll 332
  steak roll 331
  sweet potato 323
  Tobiko roll 320
  tomato and cucumber roll 333
  trout amandine roll 333
  tuna fish roll 328
  a very "ducky" roll 330
  vegetable tempura roll 315
Sweet and sour
  dipping sauce 240
  meatball bruschetta 302
  meatballs 28
  pearl onions 110
  pupus 44
  sauce 52, 194
Sweet potato and carrot dip 61, 230
Sweet potato sushi 323
Swiss chard and and cheese packages, grilled 99

T

Taco snacks 45
Tangerine and mango salsa 272
Tangerine salsa 270
Tapas
  defined 78
  drinks accompanying 162
  pantry 79-83
  parties and menus 84-89
  preparing 78
Tapas menu
  for 6— 85, 86, 87
  for 8— 88
  for 8 to 10— 89
Tapenade (olive dip) 232
Taramasalata 55
Tartar sauce 193

Tarts
  basic tartlet pastry 161
  eggplant and tomato tartlets 109
  French quiche tartlets 54
  mushroom strudel 34
  smoked salmon and cucumber
    tartlets 133
  tuna and egg tartlets 137
Tempura
  184
  shrimp roll 315
  vegetable roll 315
Teriyaki
  chicken skewers 48
  chicken wings 12
  sauce 193
Tex-Mex dip 220
Toast; see also Bruschetta
  anchovy butter rounds 9
  cheesy crab 9
  fresh pear and anchovy 95
  hot goat cheese 97
  Oriental shrimp 50
Tomatillo apple salsa 257
Tomatillo, roasted, salsa 259
Tomato(es)
  almond sauce on monkfish 128
  and arugula bruschetta 288
  and avocado salsa 259
  and cheese pizza bruschetta 289
  cherry, bacon-stuffed 25
  chicken and rice-stuffed 142
  and cucumber roll 333
  -eggplant bruschetta 284
  and eggplant tartlets 109
  bacon and lettuce roll 334
  basil and cheese bruschetta 284
  bruschetta dijon-style 288
  bruschetta, Greek-style 287
  cheese bruschetta, Tuscan 283
  feta and mushroom bruschetta
    286
  fresh, bruschetta 283

  goat cheese and eggplant stuffed
    chicken breasts 141
  olive and basil bruschetta 285
  oven-dried (basic recipe) 119
  oven-dried, chicken and
    artichoke 138
  and portobello mushroom
    bruschetta 286
  and potato stuffing in peppers
    115
  sauce 149
  sauce, spicy 158
  stewed, bruschetta 282
  sun-dried, and anchovy sushi 324
  sun-dried and bean dip 229
  sun-dried, and mango salsa 271
  sun-dried, bruschetta 285
  and wine bruschetta 287
Tortilla, classic espanola 101
Tortillas, mini 102
Tropical salsa, spicy 270
Trout amandine roll 333
Trout, smoked, in endive leaves 136
Tuna
  baked la fondue hestere 200
  dip, creamy 245
  rarebit 211
  roll, spicy 317
Turkey
  baked fondue 201
  and eggplant bruschetta 299
  meatballs 28
  roll, smoked 11
Turnovers, crab 38

V

Vanilla fondue 214
Veal
  meatballs in almond sherry sauce
    150
  mixed grill fondue 182
  raisin and pine nut empanada 154

Vegetables
  antipasto giardineria 56
  artichoke salsa 254
  asparagus and ham rolls 107
  asparagus mayo dip 233
  asparagus mayonnaise 51
  avocado dip 224
  avocado-green onion
    bruschetta 296
  baba ghanoush 61
  bacon-stuffed cherry tomatoes 25
  baked asparagus fondue 203
  baked leek fondue 204
  baked spinach fondue 204
  caponata (eggplant antipasti) 46
  and chicken won tons, baked 64
  chutney-stuffed celery 63
  clams stuffed with spinach 125
  cream of celery rarebit 207
  creamy avocado veggie dip 67
  crisp potato slices 116
  cucumber mint coolers 24
  cucumbers with herbed cream
    cheese 25
  curry veggie dip 226
  dilled broccoli and carrots 62
  eggplant and tomato tartlets 109
  eggplant caviar 60
  eggplant-onion bruschetta with
    feta 294
  freezer salsa 254
  French caviar potatoes 47
  Grecian artichokes 55
  green roll 331
  grilled, bruschetta 295
  guacamole 68, 222
  horseradish salsa 255
  hot artichoke dip 237
  jicama salsa 262
  low-fat cucumber dip 63
  marinated 26
  marinated artichokes 106
  marinated broccoli 57

  marinated cauliflower 105
  mini-stuffed potatoes 116
  mixed grilled salad 120
  Moroccan roll 327
  oven-dried tomatoes (basic recipe)
    119
  oven-roasted baby potatoes with
    garlic 117
  peperonata 58
  peppers with tomato and potato
    stuffing 115
  pico de gallo 261
  pico de gallo with Mexican beer
    263
  rainbow peppers 114
  red onion foccacia 31
  roasted corn and red pepper salsa
    257
  roasted garlic salsa 260
  roasted garlic salsa bruschetta 297
  roasted pepper strips 114
  roasted red pepper dip 229
  roasted shallot salsa bruschetta 297
  roasted tomatillo salsa 259
  salad Russian-style 119
  salsa 62, 233
  salsa cruda 261
  salsa picante 262
  salsa verde 260
  Santa Monica roll 323
  sherry-glazed eggplant 110
  and shrimp-filled pasta shells 19
  spanakopitas 32
  spicy avocado and salsa
    bruschetta 295
  spicy baked potato wedges
    (papas bravas) 117
  spinach dip 232
  spinach and egg empanada 121
  spinach and walnut triangles 33
  spring roll 332
  stir-fry bruschetta 294
  sweet and sour pearl onions 110

Vegetables, continued,
    sweet onion salsa 258
    sweet potato and carrot dip 61,
     230
    sweet potato sushi 323
    tempura roll 315
    tequila salsa 263
    three pepper spread 71
    tomatillo apple salsa 257
    tomato and avocado salsa 259
    tomato and cucumber roll 333
    toppings for pizzettes 122
    veggie dip 225
    warm potato and leek salad 118
    zucchini salsa 256
Velvet chicken breast chunks 139

Watermelon and avocado salsa 264
Watermelon and papaya salsa 268
Welsh rarebit, quick 205
Western rarebit 208
Wine and garlic chicken nuggets
    142
Wine and tomato bruschetta 287
Won tons, baked vegetable and
    chicken 64

Z

Zucchini salsa 256